The Power of Human

The
Power
of
Human

How Our Shared Humanity
Can Help Us Create a Better World

Adam Waytz

W. W. NORTON & COMPANY

Independent Publishers Since 1923

NEW YORK LONDON

For M, A, and T

Contents

Introduction

DURING MY SOPHOMORE YEAR OF COLLEGE, A FRIEND AND I decided to reconnect after a busy semester. Despite spending virtually every day together along with three other friends the previous year, we had barely spoken this semester. Just before leaving for winter break, we grabbed dinner on Manhattan's Upper West Side and saw a Coen Brothers movie downtown. I recall chatting over nachos and margaritas, sitting in the back row of the theater, and discussing how much we enjoyed the movie on the train ride back uptown. Everything was back to normal. I flew home to Minneapolis the next day relieved that I had rejuvenated a relationship that was slipping away. That impression, I learned, my companion did not share.

Several months later, she told me that was the night when she realized we could no longer be friends. What I had considered to be a warm, easygoing evening of catching up, she described as being a cold and lonely disappointment. In particular, she described how I fidgeted during dinner, rarely looking her in the eye, and glanced around the restaurant instead. She told me she felt like she was invisible.

I immediately resonated with the experience of feeling invisible. Likely you have, too. To make another person feel invisible is to dehumanize that person, and chances are that you (like I) not only have felt dehumanized at times but also have played the role of the dehumanizer at other times. Although the most potent historical examples of dehumanization involve treating others as animals or objects, simply overlooking others' full humanity—like the mundane example of my dinner-and-movie companion—is far more common than we might expect and is becoming increasingly prevalent.

Although we might be experiencing a blip in history, I feel confident suggesting that dehumanization—that is, failing to consider another person as having a mind capable of complex feelings and rational thought—represents a contemporary concern. In the current moment, this disregard of others, including a willingness to call the humanity of entire social groups into question, is shockingly commonplace, consequential, and also curable. Merely eight years ago when deciding to base a book on this prescription, I felt this premise would require considerable convincing. Of course, this was before questions of whether certain lives mattered reentered the national discourse as major points of argument and protest. This was prior to the expansion of groups like ISIS and Boko Haram that treat helpless children as disposable in their ideological quests. And this was prior to a resurging fascism that gripped the United States and Western Europe, launching widespread hatred and discrimination toward refugees and immigrants.

The aftermath of the contentious 2016 US presidential election prompted many calls for warring political factions to find empathy and unity under a common human identity. Colby Itkowitz wrote for the *Washington Post* that "empathy for Trump voters" is what the election lacked.[1] In a *New York Times* op-ed titled "Stop Shaming Trump Supporters," Rabbi Michael Lerner wrote, "We need to reach out to Trump voters in a spirit of empathy and contrition."[2] Other media outlets posted do-it-yourself guides on how to converse at Thanksgiving dinner with your uncle of a different political persuasion.

In response to these pleas for civility, empathy, and unity, author

Chimamanda Ngozi Adichie wrote in *The New Yorker*, "The responsibility to forge unity belongs not to the denigrated but to the denigrators. The premise for empathy has to be equal humanity; it is an injustice to demand that the maligned identify with those who question their humanity."[3] Adichie's premise highlights why attempts to resolve conflict between different social groups often fail: appeals from historically advantaged groups focus on conciliation (toward finding a common humanity, in the future) whereas historically disadvantaged groups focus on contestation (of their humanity, in the past). Cycles of violence, misunderstanding, and conflict then persist because of this misalignment, rooted in a failure to recognize other individuals as having distinct opinions, desires, wants, and fears. Again, this failure is the essence of dehumanization, and it is perilous.

As dehumanization represents the failure to consider others as having minds capable of thinking and feeling, "seeing human," or the idea of humanization, represents the opposite: considering others as having minds capable of thinking and feeling (I expand on definitional issues in chapter 1). This book first describes the necessity for "seeing human" at this current point in time and then proceeds in two parts. In part one, I describe the *power of human*: how the perceived presence of humanity makes our lives and daily experiences feel significant, inspires moral care, and motivates and influences us toward taking effective action. In part two, I describe how to harness this power to improve work, more effectively partner with technology, reduce conflict, and improve our close relationships. Here I provide a road map of what is to come.

Humans Generate Meaning

One of J. D. Salinger's lesser-known literary masterpieces was a one-sentence note he wrote to his maid in 1989 requesting she complete her responsibilities before he went on vacation. This short instruction fetched $50,000 on an eBay auction, in part because of Salinger's known reclusiveness and his reputation for seeking injunctions against autograph dealers. Despite the commonness of celebrity auction sales like this, $50,000 for a piece of paper glossed with a few words makes no economic sense. These auctions reveal the substantial transformational value of human contact. Research in fact shows that celebrity auction items that have been physically touched by famous politicians and actresses generate higher bids.[4]

Celebrities are not the only ones who generate value through their touch, as research has also shown. A field experiment in a university bookstore showed that observing a desirable member of the opposite sex touch a garment made people more willing to pay for the garment.[5] Other work has shown that students described as highly intuitive performed better on creativity tests after touching a document previously handled by a notably creative student.[6] Of course, explanations for these effects are numerous, as I describe in chapter 2, yet they demonstrate the power of human contact to enhance the significance of everyday objects and experiences.

Humans Signal Moral Worth

Humans not only enhance significance but also instill morality. Evolutionary biologist Julian Huxley wrote of the Heikegani or "Samurai Crab," a crab species that populates the southern Inland Sea of Japan, as a product of artificial selection. The Samurai Crab is so named because its shell markings resemble faces of the Heike samurai warriors who, according to *The Tale of the Heike*, were vanquished at the Battle of Dan-no-Nura. Huxley and later astronomer Carl Sagan hypothesized that fishermen who caught the crabs, upon viewing the humanlike face on their shells, would throw them back to sea out of respect for the warriors. This practice would then increase the

Samurai Crabs' ability to reproduce and propagate.[7] Of course, this hypothesis primarily originates from a compelling story rather than hard science, yet it speaks to people's compassion toward anything slightly resembling a human being.

If being human grants the right to freedom from harm, following that premise, we can then reasonably expect that people will respond with moral concern to the slightest indication of humanity. A human-like name, face, or voice signals an underlying human mind, which grants moral status. For example, research shows that national park visitors will pay more for conservation efforts for animals that look more humanlike (e.g., the Iberian lynx) versus those that look less humanlike (e.g., the red-eared slider turtle). An animal's human-like appearance contributes to feelings of moral protection.[8] Other work has shown that, over the past several decades, dog names in the United Kingdom, the United States, and Australia have shifted from more dog-specific monikers like Fido and Rover to human names like Ben and Lucy, in parallel with the increasing moral standing of dogs in society.[9] Efforts toward protecting apes similarly center on apes' human likeness. Initiatives such as the Great Ape Project support extending legal rights to apes (to not be abused) on the basis that these animals share mental capacities with humans. Beyond animals, other work also shows that human likeness grants moral status to robots.[10] As an extreme example, Saudi Arabia recently granted citizenship rights to a humanoid robot named Sophia. When Sophia "addressed" the nation without the customary headscarf or in the presence of a male companion, many remarked that the robot has more rights than human women do in Saudi Arabia.[11]

Given that perceiving cues to human likeness enhances moral concern toward nonhumans, it is not surprising that the more we perceive other people's humanity—their underlying thoughts, feelings, and desires—the better we treat them. Chapter 3 examines the moral significance of humans.

Humans Influence

Because of humans' capacity to enhance meaning and moral value, humans also influence action to a degree that we underestimate. In political correspondent Edward-Isaac Dovere's autopsy of Hillary Clinton's 2016 presidential campaign and electoral loss, he described her overreliance on algorithmic targeting rather than human contact: "The Clinton campaign dismissed what political scientists call in-person 'persuasion'—no one was knocking on doors trying to drum up support for the Democratic nominee."[12] This remark echoed several political commentators who suggested that Clinton's staff neglected high-quality, face-to-face conversations with human beings to persuade voters toward the candidate. If this sounds overly simplistic, I assure you we consistently undervalue the power of humans to persuade. As I detail in chapter 4, humans have an immense capacity to influence action, a capacity that all of us, not just well-funded political operatives, tend to overlook.

Not only does human persuasion inspire action, but human action also inspires people to copy that action: people do as others do. That people conform based on "social proof" might seem obvious, but again, we greatly underestimate its power. In his book *Invisible Influence*, psychologist and marketing guru Jonah Berger describes his research showing people's blindness to the influence of other humans on their decisions. He found that although social influence often drives luxury purchases ("Are other people whom I like driving this very expensive car?"), BMW owners, for example, almost never viewed other people as affecting their purchasing decisions. Instead BMW drivers point to factors like price and gas mileage as influencing their decisions.[13] Research in chapter 4 shows that underestimating social proof is, in fact, an error; persuading people to act because "everyone is doing it" is far more effective than appealing to pragmatic reasons. Despite our blindness to social influence, chapter

4 demonstrates that other people's thoughts, and particularly other people's thoughts about us, are the greatest engines of our behavior.

Humans Motivate

Encountering an eight-foot, seven-hundred-pound polar bear in the wild would lead most of most of us to play dead or run away. Not Lydia Angyiou, a resident of a small northern Quebec village, someone a friend describes as "about five-foot nothing and ninety pounds on a wet day." One day, Angyiou fought an encroaching polar bear until it swatted her down, at which point she began bicycle kicking the bear from the ground. Her reasoning was simple: she felt her child's life was at stake when she first saw the bear sizing up her seven-year-old son and other children playing hockey nearby.[14] Angyiou's brave feat, often cited as an example of "hysterical strength," shows the lengths we go to for others, even in disregard of our own well-being.

Humans motivate us to expend effort in ways that we would not anticipate. The modern science of motivation suggests that people are not merely rational, cost-benefit calculators who work to maximize personal gain. Rather, humans often work harder on behalf of others than they do for themselves. Consider research by psychologists Ye Li and Margaret Lee that asked participants to complete rote tasks like typing letters and generating anagrams.[15] Participants learned that their performance on these tasks would either earn them money (e.g., every anagram generated would earn them twenty cents) or benefit another person in the study. Consistently, participants worked harder when compensation was tied to others versus themselves. Li described this phenomenon to me years ago when we attended graduate school together by calling it the "James Bond effect," referencing a classic spy film trope where a bound and captured Bond refuses to give secret information to his villainous captor even at the threat of torture. At that very moment, the villain produces Bond's girlfriend from behind a curtain, also bound and facing imminent torture if Bond does not disclose. Although Bond refuses to divulge secrets while facing his own torture, he is willing to reveal the secret to benefit his female companion. Of course, few of us will encounter the prospect of torture by a super villain or an errant polar bear attack, but we will do astounding things if we feel others will benefit. Chapter 5 details how other humans motivate us to do things we would never do for self-serving interests alone.

As part one of this book demonstrates the power of human, part two focuses on how to harness this power. Here I offer suggestions on how to rehumanize the workplace as well as our interactions with technology, considering how our lives have become increasingly dominated by things rather than by people. I then also offer humanization strategies for reducing conflict with our deepest enemies and for improving relationships with our closest friends and family members.

Humanizing Work

Legendary historian and broadcaster Studs Terkel's book *Working* masterfully examines working Americans' lives and experiences.[16] In one of Terkel's interviews, a steelworker ponders a machine taking his job, stating, "I'll be goddamned if a computer is gonna eat before I do! I want milk for my kids and beer for me. Machines can either liberate man or enslave 'im, because they're pretty neutral. It's man who has the bias to put the thing one place or another." Although the steelworker contemplates an automated future from 1974, his ambivalence perfectly captures today's automation concerns, which focus more on machines replacing humans than on liberating them. The actual emergence of artificial intelligence and machine learning algorithms at work as well as organizations' willingness to outsource human jobs to robots (what psychologist Michael Norton and I termed "botsourcing") have sparked worries about the increasingly dehumanized nature of work.[17]

One would think that recent workplace innovations from open offices to communal ping-pong tables and the obsession with organizational engagement would stave off work's dehumanizing nature, but employee engagement and job satisfaction have declined or remained stagnant over the past thirty years.[18] A second trend presents an even more insidious problem for attempts to humanize the workplace. Today, people identify with their jobs more than ever before. An advertisement for recruitment agency Juice Recruitment conveys a common sentiment, "A job isn't just a job; it's who you are."[19] Listlessness on the job combined with identification with one's work produces a dehumanizing workplace existence: one in which people feel like instrumental cogs in a machine with little sense of personal accomplishment.

The remedy for the dehumanized worker is twofold: instill humanity into work and detach personal identity from the job, tasks that require different approaches based on occupation and industry. Instilling humanity into work means providing work that capitalizes on distinctively human skills, making people feel that their capabilities have worth. What might these distinctively human skills be? I focus on two: sociability and variability. Sociability involves nudging workers to consider their colleagues' humanity and to recognize their work's impact on humans outside the organization. Variability involves freeing people from routine work and enabling them to use multiple skills.

Separating people's personal identities from their jobs is more vital and more challenging than instilling humanity into work because it requires abandoning the very American idea of the Protestant work ethic, that is, that work is inherently moral. An apocryphal story tells of an immigrant who upon adapting to American life came to believe the word "busy" meant "good," because people often responded "busy," when he asked, "How are you?" Part of humanizing work requires embracing idleness and rejecting the idea of busy-ness as virtuous. Completing these two steps of promoting distinctively human skills at work and de-identifying people with work is challenging because these efforts compete with each other. In chapter 6, I describe how to balance them.

Humanizing Technology

Not only has work become increasingly dehumanizing, but advances in automation have also literally eliminated humans from many lines of work. Managing this rise of the machines first requires accepting that we cannot stop the future, that technology innovation and adoption will not wane, and that botsourcing is irreversible. As one former Silicon Valley venture capitalist told me, we no longer decide whether we want new technology—Tim Cook and Mark Zuckerberg decide for us. And our response to this surrender has been mixed. A 2013 global survey of 12,000 young adults revealed that 86 percent stated that technological innovations made their lives simpler and 69 percent even stated these innovations improved their relationships; yet 61 percent said these innovations make us less human.[20] Even though people accept technology as dehumanizing, its positive effects persist.

My personal nihilism leads me to believe people will never overcome their addiction to technology's simplicity and efficiency. Therefore, the best solution to dehumanization-by-technology seems for humans and machines to form a simple, two-pronged peace treaty: (1) Humans shall develop technology that operates and appears humanlike without becoming repulsive or invasive. I will describe research (including my own) on how humanlike features of various technologies (e.g., androids, self-driving cars, or everyday gadgets), from facial design to voice, can promote positive engagement. (2) Humans shall form complementary partnerships with robots (machines capable of performing complex tasks) that divide labor effectively. Social theorist Karl Marx famously feared that the increasing use of machinery would serve to "deskill" workers, making them more like machines.[21] I describe in chapter 7 how to design human-machine partnerships that will instead optimize the strengths of both partners.

Humanizing Conflict

Humanization is necessary not only for navigating emerging relationships with automata but also for preserving our relationships with other people. The two extremes of our social world are our closest friends and most despised foes. The deepening chasm between those we consider "us" (e.g., members of our political party, our religious group, our nation, our ethnicity, our social class) and "them" (e.g., members of our out-groups) suggests the need to reduce this divide through humanizing the other side. Human conflict often goes hand in hand with dehumanization because perceiving an out-group as having "lesser" values, needs, and emotional capacities both enables and justifies violence.

Former US drone operators tasked with targeted assassinations in Iraq, Afghanistan, and Pakistan have illustrated how dehumanization feeds the war on terror. A major criticism of the drone program is that its imprecision kills innocent civilians including children. According to one veteran of the program, drone operators refer to these children as "fun-size terrorists" and compare these killings to "cutting the grass before it grows too long."[22] Enacting violence remotely (rather than through human-piloted aircraft) produces a psychological distance between drone operators and their targets that spurs dehumanization and perpetuates aggression. In less technologically sophisticated conflicts, the distance that occurs simply through viewing the other side as an out-group can produce similarly troubling outcomes.

So what can we do in an age of bitter ideological division? Conflict resolution strategists often suggest finding some common ground between warring factions. However, this suggestion neglects the fact that conflict inevitably occurs between groups with unequal power. Any attempt to reduce dehumanization in conflict must therefore account for this inequality. Doing so requires focusing on uncommon ground rather than on only common ground and on discrete interests rather than on just the parties' shared interests. This endeavor may sound daunting, but thankfully extensive social science research has provided a framework of how high-power and low-power groups differ in conflict settings. I describe this framework in chapter 8 and how to use it to find shared humanity with even our most despised foes.

Humanizing Intimacy

Whereas humanizing our enemies requires bringing them closer, humanizing our loved ones requires establishing greater separation. Although the sense of oneness we often feel with friends and family strengthens those relationships, this same oneness can inhibit us from seeing these individuals as distinct humans from the self, which has negative consequences. I learned this when my wife had our first son, Amartya. Becoming a first-time father was full of amazement and wonder. However, no experience was more magical than learning how to calm him to sleep using a now prominent method pioneered by Doctor Harvey Karp. I was skeptical of the mountain of self-help books we received before Amartya's arrival, but Karp's book came with a thirty-minute DVD, which seemed like a more efficient time investment.

Dr. Karp's method is exceedingly simple, but its magic, for me, was that it completely contradicted my assumption on how best to calm Amartya to sleep because my assumption was based on how I would want to be put to sleep. Karp's method suggests tightly swaddling the baby, placing him on his side, jostling him, and shushing in his ear as loudly as possible. I, on the other hand, sleep best by wearing loose clothes, lying on my back, and remaining totally still in complete silence. Karp's method works because it simulates the calming experience of being in the womb, whereas the assumption I held represents treating my child as a reflection of myself rather than as a distinct human with distinct preferences. Overcoming the tendency to treat loved ones as replicas of the self requires, as I describe in chapter 9, establishing critical distance to recognize these individuals as distinct human beings.

The Need to See Human

The time for a scientific guide to seeing human is now. As I detail further in the next chapter, the practice of seeing each other in our full humanity is on the decline. When I began writing this book, I expected that this claim would surprise. Steven Pinker's masterful tome, *The Better Angels of Our Nature*, described how violence with its concomitant dehumanization has declined to, at present, its lowest point in human history. In writing about ethnically targeted violence, Pinker writes, "Not only has official discrimination by governments been in decline, but so has the dehumanizing and demonizing mindset in individual people."[23] Undoubtedly, this is true, yet the more recent spike in hate crimes, terroristic acts, and inflammatory political rhetoric worldwide has raised questions of whether this decline will continue. Even Pinker notes in response to these questions, "As to whether violence might increase in the future: of course it might. My argument is not that an increase in violence in the future is impossible; it's that a decrease in violence has taken place in the past."[24] Aside from dehumanization as a corollary to violence, we see in the next chapter how society is shifting toward a subtler form of dehumanization, one in which we simply disengage from others' humanity rather than actively try to deny it.

Ironically, our unprecedented access to other human beings frees us from engaging with them. Technology enables us to immediately know a campaigning politician's views on gun control, immigration, and financial regulation; an avid traveler's knowledge of the best sushi restaurant in Melbourne; professional and amateur critics' opinions on *Blazing Saddles, The Fire Next Time,* and *Marquee Moon*; and the daily emotional fluctuations of our friends, who readily report their moment-to-moment feelings on social media. Furthermore, technology has given us considerable control, certainty, and predictability by enabling us to access facts, locations, and bank routing numbers that previously had to be gathered by talking to people.

In a recent interview, film writer and director Harmony Korine discussed his landmark 1995 film *Kids*, a film that critics praised for its humanizing portrait of urban youth.[25] Korine captured the more deterministic nature of today's world in stating, "You could never make [*Kids*] again, not because it's more difficult, but because there are more rules . . . You can't really get lost in America anymore, you can't make a road movie anymore because everyone has GPS . . . All the technology really made drama difficult in some ways, because in order to be accurate you have to address it." I asked filmmaker Joshua Safdie, whose films offer hyperreal, humanizing portraits of often dehumanized groups such as homeless people, drug addicts, and the developmentally disabled, about the challenge technology poses for dramatic storytelling. He reminded me that "even [in our film] *Heaven Knows What*, a film about homeless youngsters on the streets of NYC, they were on phones occasionally and using Apple Stores as free internet cafes, so even the homeless can avoid getting lost if they don't want to."[26]

Our inability to get lost frees us from relying on others for direction, connection, or any sort of interdependence that I will argue is critical to humanizing others. When technology fails, we reorient ourselves to rely on other people. Yet the frequency of people following GPS into danger (termed "death by GPS" by Death Valley park rangers) suggests we will go to great lengths to avoid asking another human being for directions.[27]

At present, despite technological advances that grant us certainty, control, and predictability, the rush of these advances creates a new uncertainty as well. Rapid change creates absurdity, and in the aftermath of absurdity, I take solace only in that it might make us better. Research I have coauthored has shown that people actively seek out humans and see humanness in the world when reminded of uncertainty and doubt.[28] In Fyodor Dostoyevsky's *The Idiot*, the titular character, Prince Lev Nikolayevich Myshkin, captures this sentiment, stating, "There is no reason to be troubled because we are absurd, is there? . . . To reach perfection there must first be much we do not understand. And if we understand too quickly we will probably not understand very well."[29]

I believe our present confusion will lead us to try to make sense of things through seeing human in the world and in others. It will also require a lot of time and effort. To walk us down this path, I provide evidence that seeing human is in decline, detail why seeing human is so important, and describe how to engage our uniquely human ability to treat others as, in fact, humans.

PART ONE

CHAPTER 1

The Dehumanizing Shift

AS I WRITE THIS, THE WORLD IS CURRENTLY EXPERIENCING several humanitarian crises. In Syria alone, over five million refugees have fled a civil war that has cost hundreds of thousands of lives. Meanwhile, European and American political referenda have rejected helping these refugees, over half of whom are children. Although Syria's civil war began in March 2011, the rest of the world largely began paying attention only when two emblematic images of children began to circulate. The first image was that of three-year-old Kobani-born Aylan Kurdi lying lifeless on the beach after drowning in the Mediterranean Sea, trying to reach Europe. The second was one of a child left behind in Aleppo: five-year-old Omran Daqneesh shell-shocked, coated in dust and blood and waiting for medical attention after being pulled from a building damaged by an airstrike. The images of Kurdi and Daqneesh highlighted the human toll of the Syrian refugee crisis, a crisis in desperate need of a human face. These images represent, I believe, the power of human—to create meaning and morality and to influence and motivate action.

Refugees, particularly in this context, are one of the groups people most commonly dehumanize. In 2015, American presidential candidate and secretary of Housing and Urban Development Ben Carson likened Syrian refugees to dogs, stating, "If there's a rabid dog running around in your neighborhood, you're probably not going to assume something good about that dog, and you're probably going to put your children out of the way."[1] During the influx of Syrian refugees to Europe, British Prime Minister David Cameron assured an interviewer that he would secure the French port of Calais (also referred to as the "jungle") despite a "swarm" of migrants trying to access Great Britain.[2]

In one of the stranger instances of refugee dehumanization during the 2016 US presidential election, Donald Trump Jr., the presidential candidate's son, tweeted an image of Skittles candy and wrote, "If I had a bowl of skittles and I told you just three would kill you, would you take a handful? That's our Syrian refugee problem." Many, including CNN host Chris Cuomo, immediately pointed out how dehumanizing the metaphor was. Others noted that the Skittles analogy stemmed from an anti-Semitic 1938 children's story, titled "Der Giftpilz" or "The Poisonous Mushroom," penned by Nazi propagandist Julius Streicher.[3] In this story, Streicher equates the Jews with the poisonous mushroom as Trump Jr. did with the poisonous candy.

Fearing that Syrians would import Islamic extremism to the United States, Texas Agriculture Commissioner Sid Miller posted on Facebook side-by-side images of rattlesnakes and refugees pouring into a truck. Next to the images, he wrote, "Can you tell me which of these rattlers won't bite you? Sure, some won't, but tell me which ones so we can bring them into the house."[4] Donald Trump Jr.'s Skittles analogy seems quaint compared to that of Miller's rattlesnakes. These statements explicitly represent Syrian refugees as dogs, snakes, and insects, deeming them subhuman. And Bosnian writer Aleksandr Hemon, writing in *Rolling Stone*, noted how these depictions are consistently reinforced by "syndicated images [that] show refugee hordes pushing against fences, overwhelming train stations, pouring out of ferries, resembling zombies, their individuality irrelevant and invisible."[5]

None of this surprises social science researchers. Research I have coauthored led by psychologists Nour Kteily and Emile Bruneau, for example, shows how Americans blatantly dehumanize Mexican immigrants and Muslims.[6] In these studies, we presented participants with the famous *Ascent of Man* image (also known as *The March of Progress*) depicting five figures showing humans evolving from *Dryopithecus* to *Ramapithecus* to Neanderthal to Cro-Magnon, and finally to modern man. We asked participants to indicate the image they felt best represented various ethnic and social groups. To our dismay (but not to our surprise), participants selected representations for Muslims and Mexican immigrants that were significantly less evolved than the representations they chose for the category Americans. Meanwhile, participants rated Japanese, European, French, Australian, Austrian, and Icelandic individuals to be no less evolved than Americans.

The genesis of this work comes from my graduate school training, when my doctoral advisor Nick Epley and I became dissatisfied with the existing measures of dehumanization. We had been relying on measures that involved asking people abstract questions but felt we needed something more visually powerful to illustrate dehumanization as a concrete phenomenon. Thus, we developed the *Ascent of Man* measure and, years later over coffee, Nour Kteily explained how he could put it to great use, taking it around the world to show how readily people dehumanize ethnic out-groups.

In follow-up work, Kteily and Bruneau demonstrated that people's dehumanization of Mexicans through depicting them as lower on the *Ascent of Man* scale predicted several negative consequences.[7] The more people blatantly dehumanized Mexicans this way, the more they endorsed statements like "Illegal aliens apprehended crossing the border must be detained until they are sent home, no more catch-and-release," and the more willingly they signed an anti-immigration petition. Blatant dehumanization of Muslims on the *Ascent of Man* measure also statistically predicted anti-Muslim attitudes (e.g., endorsing statements like "Muslims are a potential cancer to this country") and willingness to sign a petition urging Congress to support a ban on visas to Muslims. Most troublingly, follow-up studies by Kteily and Bruneau with Latino and Muslim participants revealed that these groups sensed this dehumanization, perceiving that Republicans, in particular, viewed their groups as subhuman. This sense of being dehumanized led these groups to support more violent collective action and to avoid assisting counterterrorism efforts. Thus, this work shows how dehumanization perpetuates distrust and conflict across intergroup boundaries.

When people feel dehumanized, they respond by asserting their agency and, hence, their humanity through self-defense. For example, when in 2012 Israel carried out eight days of strikes on Gaza Strip, Palestinian engineering student Ahmed Al Sabany stated, "We want them to know that when they attack us mercilessly, when they treat us like animals, we will fight back."[8] This cycle of dehumanization and violent response explains why conflicts like that between Israel and Palestine are often intractable (although we examine ways to quell these conflicts in chapter 8).

Other research conducted in Canada shows that both refugees and immigrants, especially Muslims, face vicious dehumanization north of the American border as well. Studies by University of Western Ontario psychologist Victoria Esses and colleagues conducted surveys showing that many Canadians endorsed statements that depicted refugees as barbaric and rejected statements like "Refugees raise their children to be humane."[9] In work examining how subtle media depictions perpetuate dehumanization, Esses and colleagues asked participants to read a short newspaper article that included an unrelated editorial cartoon depicting an immigrant carrying suitcases arriving at a Canadian immigration booth.[10] For some of the participants, the suitcases were labeled with diseases (AIDS, SARS); for others, the suitcases did not include labels. When prompted, participants barely recalled seeing the cartoon. However, when they later completed surveys evaluating immigrants, those exposed to the dehumanizing cartoon reported that immigrants lacked core human values and were barbaric.

Research by psychologists Gordon Hodson and Kimberly Costello at Brock University (also in Ontario) examined links between "contamination" concerns and the dehumanization of immigrants.[11] This research showed that dehumanization of Muslim immigrants—measured by participants' unwillingness to attribute traits considered uniquely human (e.g., openness and conscientiousness) to immigrants—stemmed from feelings of interpersonal disgust. Hodson and Costello asked participants how disgusted various scenarios made them feel (e.g., "You sit down on a public bus, and feel that the seat is still warm from the last person who sat there"). The more disgusted they reported feeling toward scenarios like this, the more they dehumanized immigrants. These findings suggest a link between fears of being contaminated by disease and dehumanization.

Author Andrea Pitzer has written an extensive history of concentration camps, describing how a newfound focus on disease and public health in the late nineteenth century set the stage for the invention of concentration camps. She notes that "the germ theory of disease revealed the nature of contagion and how illnesses spread . . . But the same Enlightenment rationality and efficiency could be mixed in a stew of irrational fears and ignorance to assault those seen as inferior." She also describes how in the early twentieth century, European institutions ranging from the British press to the German film industry used the "language of degeneracy, dishonor, and disease to frame the risk posed by immigrants, particularly Jewish ones" and to blame Jews for "filth and disease."[12] Today this disease-laden rhetoric toward outsiders persists. Donald Trump has warned that immigrants will "infest" the United States.[13] And Polish right-wing political leader Jaroslaw Kaczynski has warned against refugees by stating, "There are already signs of emergence of diseases that are highly dangerous and have not been seen in Europe for a long time: cholera on the Greek islands, dysentery in Vienna."[14] This link between contamination fears and dehumanization of immigrants and refugees is particularly worrisome as it implies a need to eradicate them.

Research has also examined how the media perpetuates these dehumanizing representations of immigrants and refugees. For his dissertation, political scientist Stephen Utych analyzed *New York Times* articles during April and May 2010 surrounding Arizona's passage of restrictive immigration law HB 2162 on April 23, 2010. Utych found that approximately one-third of articles on immigration contained dehumanizing language, referring to immigrants as animals, vermin, natural disasters, or viruses.[15]

As the research makes clear, blatant dehumanization of immigrants and refugees is insidious. In the wake of the Syrian refugee crisis, several right-wing European political campaigns including the campaign for Brexit (the United Kingdom's decision to leave the European Union), France's National Front Party, and Hungary's Ordesz Party have capitalized on these depictions of foreigners as subhuman and animalistic who are harbingers of disease and barbarism. In response, more socially liberal groups have argued for welcoming immigrants and refugees in the United States and Europe.

Socially liberal narratives surrounding foreigners have intended to counter overt dehumanization, yet these narratives often provide a different, subtler, and unintended dehumanizing message. They treat immigrants and refugees as commodities instead of humans who deserve dignity and freedom, regardless of their benefit to society. The politically liberal website *The Huffington Post*, for example, has published numerous stories on the positive economic impact of refugees and immigrants with headlines like "Immigration Is Good for Economic Growth. If Europe Gets It Right, Refugees Can Be Too," "What Europe Needs Most Is What It Fears Most: Migrants," "Resettling Syrian Refugees Won't Destroy the US Economy," and

"The Economic Case for Admitting Refugees Is (Again) Strengthened." Many of these articles reference a January 2016 study conducted by the International Monetary Fund (IMF) focusing on the recent wave of refugees into the European Union. The study reports that "the expected initial effects on aggregate EU GDP are positive but small, with a more significant impact on the countries where the refugee inflows are concentrated."[16] The main destination countries for refugees including Austria, Germany, and Sweden stand to reap the greatest benefit, largely because of increased fiscal spending on asylum seekers and an increased labor supply. According to the IMF report, the economic benefit of refugees is modest and is more likely to emerge over the long term; nonetheless, refugee and immigration proponents have used economic growth as a major talking point.

The impetus behind this message is to alleviate people's anxiety that "outsiders" will "steal" jobs or drain economic resources through relying on social benefits. This message also serves to elevate the image of refugees and immigrants as contributors to society. Parallel arguments praise the children of refugees and immigrants for serving in the American military. However, these messages treat such individuals only as instrumental to American prosperity. In doing so, they too become dehumanizing in presenting refugees and immigrants only in terms of their economic worth.

Another egregious example of this messaging around economic impact is a meme noting that the father of Apple founder Steve Jobs was a Syrian refugee. One version of this meme (that spawned numerous variations) posted by a liberal Facebook group called "Occupy Democrats" and shared nearly 90,000 times states, "Steve Jobs was the son of a Syrian Refugee . . . Remember this when Republicans say we shouldn't take any." *The Nation* writer John Nichols tweeted similarly, "Those who propose sweeping bans on refugees might want to consider this: Steve Jobs was the son of a Syrian migrant."[17] Even famed street artist Banksy adopted this reasoning, painting an image of Steve Jobs on a wall in the Calais refugee camp. Banksy depicted Jobs in his trademark black turtleneck and blue jeans, slinging a sack over his shoulder and holding a Macintosh computer in his other hand. In a public statement, Banksy wrote, "We're often led to believe migration is a drain on the country's resources, but Steve Jobs was the son of a Syrian migrant. Apple is the world's most profitable company, it pays over $7bn (£4.6bn) a year in taxes—and it only exists because they allowed in a young man from Homs."[18]

Aside from implying that Jobs's father was a refugee (in fact, he was an immigrant), Banksy's statement also strikes me as wrong-headed and dehumanizing. The rationale behind Banksy's painting and the Jobs meme more generally is—like the economic arguments for immigration and refugee resettlement—that refugees and immigrants have financial worth aside from worth in terms of human dignity. Today's Syrian migrant might birth the next great entrepreneur, suggests the artist. The idea for the next iPhone might originate on a boat leaving the port of Lakatia. Banksy produces great fodder for dorm room walls and freshman-year philosophizing, but his argument's logical end suggests that foreigners who do not generate financial capital are less worthy of their rights than the ones who do. Such arguments are a far cry from philosopher Immanuel Kant's guiding principle (described further in chapter 3) that we should treat human beings as ends in themselves rather than means to something else.

Late restaurateur and TV host Anthony Bourdain expressed a similar sentiment in response to Donald Trump's inflammatory campaigning around deporting immigrants at record levels. In response to Trump's plan targeting Mexican immigrants, Bourdain stated that in his thirty years of restaurant industry experience he noticed, "The person who had been there the longest, who took the time to show me how it was done, was always Mexican or Central American. The backbone of the industry . . . not once, did . . . any American-born kid walk into my restaurant and say I'd like a job as a night porter or a dishwasher." Bourdain added that if Trump deported eleven million immigrants, "Every restaurant in America would shut down . . . they'd be up the creek . . . It is really, really getting hard to find people to do the jobs."[19] Bourdain's statement champions those not born into American good fortune and who are thus willing to do the literal dirty work that enables the restaurant industry to run. Yet again, such a statement prioritizes immigrants' economic worth rather than their intrinsic value as human beings.

Economic arguments like those of Banksy and Bourdain treat human beings as stores of potential capital waiting to be tapped. Of course, people often use such arguments to sway detractors of immigration and refugee resettlement, but in doing so they fail to acknowledge the central importance of just being a human. These economic arguments that frame migrants in terms of costs and benefits make no moral case for their freedom. And this tendency to cast moral issues in market-based terms, known as *marketization*, has increasingly dominated societies across the globe over the past four decades. It represents one of four pillars suggesting a rise in mundane dehumanization. This claim requires unpacking, and I will do so. But, first, we must delve more deeply into defining dehumanization. Then I will present empirical evidence of this four-decade dehumanizing shift, pointing to marketization as well as the three other pillars of this shift: stratification, polarization, and mechanization. These arguments provide the basis for the claims to follow: that this dehumanizing shift is a trend worth reversing and that there are scientifically proven strategies to do so.

Defining Dehumanization

Defining dehumanization requires defining *human*, which, for the linguistic sticklers out there, is a term that philosophers, dictionaries, and laypeople largely use interchangeably with the term *person*. What defines a human is the possession of a mind, and philosophers' consensus on this conceptualization is strong.[20] In the sixth century, the philosopher Boethius defined *person* as "an individual substance of a rational nature"; modern definitions reflect the centrality of mind as well.[21] In a 1972 essay discussing abortion and the right to life, philosopher Michael Tooley notes that a person "possesses the concept of a self as a continuing subject of experiences and other mental states, and believes that it is itself such a continuing entity."[22] In a 1980 article on abortion, philosopher Joe Feinberg states, "Persons are those beings who are conscious, have a concept and awareness of themselves, are capable of experiencing emotions, can reason and acquire understanding, can plan ahead, can act on their plans, and can feel pleasure and pain."[23] In philosopher H. Tristram Engelhardt's 1986 treatise on bioethics, he notes, "What distinguishes persons is their capacity to be self-conscious, rational, and concerned with worthiness of blame or praise."[24] The common theme of these definitions is *mind* and two dimensions of mind in particular, *experience* and *agency*. Experience refers to feelings, emotions, and desires and agency refers to intentionality, goals, thoughts, and reason.

Critically, philosophers are concerned with what actually constitutes a human whereas we psychologists focus more on how people perceive what constitutes a human. For example, in one study with my graduate student Shane Schweitzer, we asked hundreds of people to write about what distinguishes humans from animals and what distinguishes humans from technology. When we coded their essays for the types of words they used, we found that words related to agency and experience such as "feel," "perceive," and "perspective" prominently featured to a statistically significant degree.[25]

A 2007 study provides the most definitive empirical evidence that everyday people use the same agency-experience conceptualization of mind as philosophers do.[26] This study, led by psychologists

Heather Gray, Kurt Gray, and Daniel Wegner (the latter two have written the definitive book on perceiving other minds, *The Mind Club*), asked people to evaluate various entities—from robots to dead people to frogs to children to God to adult humans—on several mental characteristics. Gray and colleagues found that people's evaluations mapped onto two categories—an experience dimension and an agency dimension. In their survey, people perceived targets to have varying amounts of agency and experience, stating, for example, that frogs had low agency and high experience and that robots had high agency but low experience. The only case where people afforded full agency and full experience was their evaluations of adult humans. So, we know that perceiving agency and experience in others represents the essence of humanization. Denying these capacities or overlooking them in others, conversely, represents dehumanization.

Trying to come up with a definition for *human* on your own is a daunting task. What comes to mind is likely an image of a stick figure or a human face. However, putting this image into words is far more difficult, and people vary considerably when trying to categorize whether marginal cases count as humans. Is a fetus human? What about a stem cell or a person in a persistent vegetative state? I'm not sure I could say with certainty. Despite this variability, if we again turn to the research on this question of defining *human*, once more a consistent pattern emerges.

Beyond Gray, Gray, and Wegner's work, other studies also show that many people equate *human* with *mind*. A vast research program led by Australian psychologist Nick Haslam has shown that people conceptualize humanness in terms of two dimensions akin to agency and experience: human uniqueness, or what they believe distinguishes humans from other animals (such as vermin) including capacities such as self-control, intelligence, and rationality, and human nature, or what they believe are qualities essential to humanity (and distinct from automata) including interpersonal warmth and emotion.[27] Again, these two dimensions focus on mind, and denying these characteristics to a person would represent denying that person experience and agency.

A separate research program developed by Belgian psychologist Jacque-Philippe Leyens also demonstrates that mind is central to people's conceptions of what is human. Leyens's work shows that, on one hand, people believe that humans alone can experience emotions like nostalgia, optimism, and humiliation.[28] Notably, these emotions require some mental capacity such as memory, prospection, or self-reflection. On the other hand, people believe emotions like panic, surprise, and fright are not uniquely human and are shared by lower animals—again, these judgments reflect only people's beliefs, not any hard evidence on whether these emotions extend across species. The source of these beliefs is unclear, but I suspect it involves how much the emotion represents a response to the external environment versus a response to oneself. Panic, fright, and surprise represent emotions triggered by external events and manifest in behavioral reactions (e.g., shaking) whereas nostalgia, optimism, and humiliation involve self-reflection. Dehumanization, in Leyens's view, results when people deny distinctively human emotions—namely, those that require mental engagement—to other people.

What people say constitutes a human being may not map onto what actually happens when the concept of human comes to mind. Luckily, neuroscience research provides evidence beyond self-reporting. This research shows that the brain regions that respond specifically when people observe images of humans or think about humans are those regions involved in processing others' mental states. Two decades' worth of neuroimaging studies now show that a proscribed set of regions termed the *mentalizing network* activates whenever people think about the minds of others—their preferences, beliefs, and desires. These regions include the medial prefrontal cortex, the precuneus/posterior cingulate cortex, and the temporoparietal junction.

The typical neuroimaging study used to identify this network involves participants lying in a brain scanner machine while observing stimuli (e.g., shapes, words, objects, faces) that momentarily appear on a computer screen across hundreds of trials. Study after study has shown that whenever people are asked to reason about persons compared to reasoning about objects (e.g., tools, musical instruments), regions in the mentalizing network are involved.[29] And, as might be expected, when people are asked to evaluate an entity's mental characteristics (e.g., whether an entity is "curious") versus its physical characteristics (e.g., whether an entity has arteries), regions in the mentalizing network again become active.[30] One study even demonstrated that this network activates more readily when people play a computerized rocks-paper-scissors game against a human compared to when they play against a machine.[31]

The moral of the story told by two decades of sophisticated brain research is that when people reason about humans, they are reasoning about minds. Neuroimaging research by psychologists Lasana Harris and Susan Fiske has also shown that when people think about commonly dehumanized social groups (e.g., homeless people or drug addicts), the mentalizing network is less active than when people think about groups like Olympic athletes or middle-class Americans.[32] And work that I have led shows that when people think about technology that behaves in a humanlike fashion, the mentalizing network becomes more active than when people think about non-humanlike technology.[33] In this work, we presented people in the brain scanner with descriptions of various gadgets that people reliably see as humanlike (e.g., an alarm clock with "eyes" that rolls around on wheels and controls its own movement) or gadgets that people see as simply machinelike (e.g., a user-controlled air purifier). When participants viewed the humanlike technology compared with the more mechanistic technology, the same brain regions became active as when people think about other humans' minds.

This brain research further indicates that perceiving someone or something to have a mind is the essence of humanization. By extension, this work indicates that neglecting another person's mind is the essence of dehumanization. Next, we explore evidence suggesting that humanization has declined over the past five decades while dehumanization has gradually, and disturbingly, ascended.

Evidence for the Dehumanizing Shift

You have probably already heard that people are growing apart. Perhaps even you have lamented how young people don't call their parents like they used to or write letters to each other anymore. Perhaps you have wondered what happened to the neighborhood pharmacy or watering hole? Maybe you have asked how we could ever solve Israeli-Palestinian tensions when we can't even look up from our smartphones to glance kindly at the barista taking our coffee order. We can feel dehumanization around us, and we have felt it pulling us apart over time. Yet feelings aren't enough to tell whether we are truly fracturing, or whether this Norman Rockwell–like image of an idealized communal past is simply something every generation wishes for when they reach a certain age. Instead, we must look at the evidence.

Actually demonstrating a dehumanizing shift over recent decades requires digging into diverse data sources that examine assorted variables "standing in" for people's tendency to humanize. Because no research has explicitly measured humanization over time, we must instead turn to variables that closely approximate this construct. Empathy is the closest such proxy variable because it involves engaging with others' minds. Although social scientists bicker over how to define empathy precisely, psychologists Jamil Zaki and Kevin Ochsner's tripartite definition, in my view, captures the construct best.[34] In their view, empathy involves mentalizing (i.e., considering another person's perspective), experience sharing (i.e., vicariously sharing another person's emotions), and displaying prosocial concern (i.e., expressing the desire to improve another person's well-being). Each of these three processes presupposes that one has considered another's mind, the core process underlying humanization.

The research on empathy supports evidence for rising dehuman-ization. Psychologist Sara Konrath, for example, has led a now famous study showing a decline of self-reported empathy among college stu-dents between 1979 and 2009.[35] This study analyzed seventy-two samples of American college students (13,737 in total) who completed a well-validated questionnaire that asks students to indicate how well various statements describe them. These statements tap explicitly into empathic concern (a construct akin to both prosocial concern and experience sharing, e.g., "I often have tender, concerned feelings for people less fortunate than me") and perspective-taking (a construct akin to mentalizing, e.g., "I sometimes try to understand my friends better by imagining how things look from their perspective").[36] Kon-rath's analysis found that empathic concern and perspective-taking have dropped considerably over time, suggesting a marked decline in students' willingness and tendency to get into the minds of others.

Related work that supports the dehumanizing shift comes from psychologist Jean Twenge. Twenge has painstakingly examined sur-vey data on Americans from the 1970s through the 2000s that show people becoming more individualistic. Individualism represents a con-stellation of traits including narcissism, mistrust in others, cynicism, entitlement, and materialism, and these traits produce an overall sense of disengagement from others. In Twenge's book, *Generation Me*, she describes this phenomenon stating, "Generation Me believes, with a conviction that approaches boredom because it is so undisputed, that the individual comes first."[37] This individualism frees people from the need to connect with others or to rely on others. Although scholars have debated the strength of these patterns,[38] with some suggesting a decline in narcissism in particular, the data trend toward showing a generation less socially engaged and potentially more dehumanizing than in the 1980s.[39]

Both Konrath and Twenge's studies suggest an emerging younger generation less inclined to engage deeply with others, reflecting a broader retreat from communal life. Perhaps no scholar has more famously documented this decline than sociologist Robert Putnam, whose 2000 masterpiece *Bowling Alone* described the American decline in social capital between 1950 and the late 1990s. Social capital, in this context, means participation in civic groups like religious organizations, Boy Scouts, and labor unions. These broader community trends correspond to declines in basic communal activities such as having friends over, playing cards, and having family dinners. Putnam argues that these declines, in turn, contribute to people becoming more isolated. Putnam offers several potential causes of these trends including women entering the workforce, which limits a person's time to participate in, for example, the PTA or League of Women Voters. He also points to increased mobility, demographic shifts like increased divorce and fewer children, and the "transformation of leisure" by technology whereby television and other gadgets have made downtime more individualizing and less communal.[40]

Revisiting these trends in 2010, Putnam qualified his original findings by noting that young people became more civic-minded following the September 11 attacks on the United States.[41] However, only upper-middle-class young people have become more engaged in their communities, producing a troubling engagement gap between this group and their less affluent contemporaries. Adult Americans, Putnam reports, have become no more civically engaged, suggesting a persistence of the phenomenon he described in 2000.

A concomitant trend to the decline in social capital is the decrease in general trust of others, which has persisted in recent years. The General Social Survey, a nationally representative survey of Americans, has long included a question asking, "Generally speaking, would you say that most people can be trusted or that you can't be too careful in life?" Putnam has observed that people's responses to this question were about split in the early 1970s and had declined considerably by 1998. In 2012, just over 30 percent of people responded that they felt people could be trusted.[42] Although scholars have proposed several reasons for this decrease in trust, one of the most robust causes appears to be the rise of income inequality,[43] which I discuss further below.

At this point, two qualifications are necessary. The first is to reiterate that none of the research I have cited here measures dehumanization per se. Reduced empathy constitutes dehumanization insofar as it involves disengaging from others' thoughts, feelings, and emotions. The rising individualism and declining social capital that Twenge and Putnam describe, respectively, represent a surge in independence, which I see as dehumanization's root cause. Independence is simply the opposite of interdependence—that is, a state in which one's goals depend on another person. In my earliest work with my graduate school mentors Nick Epley and John Cacioppo, we demonstrated that people are most likely to humanize others when they're in an interdependent state. This means that when we seek connection with others or seek to understand others' behavior, we spend more time considering other people's mental states and treating them as fully human.[44] The trends that Twenge and Putnam describe represent a departure from people seeking to connect with and understand others and a clear shift toward independence.

The second qualification is that independence does not equal loneliness, although studies generally point to a steady rise in loneliness over recent decades as well.[45] Loneliness (subjective social isolation from others) and independence (freedom from others) are not perfectly correlated, but overall research on social isolation generally suggests that people are less socially engaged with others than they were four decades ago.[46]

The next natural question is whether increasing fragmentation is primarily an American phenomenon. Although the bulk of the data presented so far comes from the United States, evidence also suggests individualism has increased worldwide in recent decades. The World Values Survey, a global survey of people's values, opinions, and beliefs administered in 100 countries since 1981, demonstrates the rise of what political scientist Christian Welzel refers to as "emancipative values." These values, which are central to individualism, include preferences for individual choice, freedom, and autonomy. Welzel's book, *Freedom Rising,* documents the rise of emancipative values in the past three decades in virtually every country for which data exist.[47] The World Values Survey measures these values by asking people's opinions on issues such as freedom of speech, women's equality, and tolerance for practices like divorce and abortion. In other words, emancipative values capture how much people care about the rights of individuals to make autonomous choices, independent of others' views and reactions.

Research led by psychologist Henri Santos has also confirmed this shift toward individualism by looking at World Values Survey data as well as census data from 1960 up to 2011. Santos and colleagues found that individualist values (e.g., feeling that it is important to teach independence to children) and practices (e.g., living alone) have risen over this period by 12 percent across fifty-three countries. And this pattern toward individualism emerges even for traditionally collectivistic countries in Latin America and Asia that are typically thought to prioritize group values over individual ones.[48]

Critically, emancipative values and individualistic values as measured in this research do not correspond to selfishness or egotism and don't simply equate to animosity toward others. I personally characterize individualism as a "live and let live" philosophy in which people value all individuals equally but feel little obligation to engage deeply or meaningfully with these individuals. When I think of individualism, I think of my Northside Chicago neighborhood, whose lawn signs, communal Facebook posts, and coffee shop exchanges champion equality for all and proudly display support for immigrants, the LGBT community, and the homeless. However, when faced with a referendum on granting a nearby apartment complex a permit to transform into a sober living facility for folks struggling with drug and alcohol abuse, most voted to oppose the permit. One online commenter wrote, "Just seems to allow its residents to congregate en masse on street corners. We do not need another facility like that." Another sarcastically noted, "Potential buyers LOVE halfway houses next door. Recovering addicts hanging out with my kids—SIGN ME UP! It is GREAT for property values." In other words, individualism represents a sort of tolerance that says, "We tolerate everyone; we just don't necessarily want to live next to them."

Having provided some preliminary evidence for a rise in independence and social disengagement over the past five or more decades, let's next turn to four pillars of the subtle dehumanization that emerges from these trends. These pillars represent both causes and consequences of the dehumanizing shift.

Marketization

The first pillar, as noted earlier in this chapter, is the global trend toward marketization, a corollary to the global rise of free market economies. By free market economies, I simply mean economic systems whereby open competition and consumers' willingness to pay determine the prices of goods and services. Despite the economic efficiency of these systems, there is a potentially troubling implication for human relationships. As political philosopher Michael Sandel documents in his treatise *What Money Can't Buy*, the rise of what he calls "market triumphalism" over the past three decades has corrupted people's relationships with one another. Sandel describes how relationships that typically operate on moral and social norms—sense of community, fairness, and reciprocity—are now based on market exchange (i.e., buying and selling). Sandel states, "Putting a price on the good things in life can corrupt them. That's because markets don't only allocate goods; they also express and promote certain attitudes toward the goods being exchanged."[49] Treating our social relationships—the "goods being exchanged" in this context—in transactional, buyer-seller terms fundamentally transforms them in a dehumanizing way.

In fact, a clever study by Lasana Harris created a labor market where participants could "purchase" individuals to complete a time estimation task.[50] Participants received an endowment of twenty-five dollars to spend on five individuals (about whom they received minimal information) and learned they would earn additional money based on how well their "purchased players" performed. Consistent with the idea that participants now saw these players as commodities, when participants later viewed these players' faces in a brain scanner, their brain scans revealed deactivation in the mentalizing network, suggesting dehumanization.

Understanding how this process works requires understanding the seminal work of anthropologist Alan Fiske. Fiske conducted extensive cross-cultural research to demonstrate that across the globe, all social relationships can be captured by one of four templates: Communal Sharing (people care for all others equally as in kin groups), Authority Ranking (people operate in terms of a hierarchy such as the student's interaction with his teacher), Equality Matching (people attempt to reciprocate favors and exchanges as in the case of work colleagues assigned to complete a report together), and Market Pricing (people's relationships are based around the utility they receive in an often monetary-based transaction as in the case of buyer and seller).[51] The first three of these are governed by social norms of group unity (Communal Sharing), respect for authority (Authority Ranking), and egalitarianism (Equality Matching). Only the Market Pricing template operates based on market norms.

Fiske has traditionally suggested that dehumanization occurs when people fail to form relationships with others at all. However, I would argue that Market Pricing is just as dehumanizing. Market Pricing considers people in terms of their financial and instrumental value instead of their sheer value as human beings.

I have already described how the characterizations of refugees by Banksy and Bourdain capture Market Pricing well, but let's look at two additional examples that more explicitly illustrate how marketization dehumanizes. The first comes from Disney World. For many years, the popular theme park held a policy that allowed individuals with disabilities to get priority access to rides by using an auxiliary entrance at each attraction. According to a *New York Post* article, wealthy Manhattan mothers participated in a practice of hiring "black market" tour guides with disabilities for just over a thousand dollars for an eight-hour day.[52] This practice objectifies these individuals and, even with their consent, treats them as luxury goods for those who can afford them.

The second example of dehumanization via marketization occurred at popular music, film, and technology festival, South by Southwest, in Austin, Texas. During the 2012 festival, marketing firm Bartle Bogle Hegarty equipped homeless people (some of whom had been displaced by Hurricane Katrina) with wireless router devices that allowed them to function as mobile Wi-Fi hotspots. The homeless individuals fitted with these devices wore T-shirts that read:

I'M [FIRST NAME],
A 4G HOTSPOT
SMS HH [FIRST NAME]
TO 25827 FOR ACCESS
www.homelesshotspots.org

Festivalgoers were asked to pay two dollars for fifteen minutes of wireless internet access with the homeless individual receiving the money. One could charitably interpret this endeavor as providing money to the homeless and visibility to their cause. Most observers, however, criticized the effort as exploitation. These two examples demonstrate how marketization transforms our interactions with two of society's most vulnerable groups, the disabled and the homeless, to stores of value. And yet they are extreme examples. The more mundane plight of workers, from the Uber driver who must sleep in her car to the automotive factory worker exposed to phosphoric acid, is the experience of being treated as a commodity. This is the essence of marketization.

Polarization

The second pillar of the dehumanizing shift is political polarization, which has reached an apex in the United States, with the gulf between liberals and conservatives continuing to widen. Congress has reached record levels of polarization.[53] Presidential approval ratings at one time showed George W. Bush and Barack Obama to be the most polarizing presidents ever.[54] Following their administrations, the presidency of Donald Trump surpassed both Bush and Obama in terms of polarization.[55] Partisan media bias in the political press has also approached record levels.[56] A 2016 Pew Research Center study showed political polarization among the general population to be at its highest in twenty-five years.[57] The survey revealed that both Democrats and Republicans describe the other party as immoral, close-minded, dishonest, and lazy. Research has also found that social media can exacerbate this polarization, with Twitter users clustering into liberal or conservative echo chambers when discussing issues ranging from the presidential election to the Newtown school shootings of 2012.[58]

This polarization represents a widening social distance between political tribes that degrades people's capacity and desire to consider the other side's thoughts, feelings, and motivations. In research with psychologists Liane Young and Jeremy Ginges, we found that Democrats and Republicans dehumanize each other in a very specific way—both sides believe that the other side is driven by hate and is relatively less capable of love.[59] We call this phenomenon the motive attribution asymmetry.

Other research goes further to demonstrate that people neglect to consider that their political opposites exhibit basic human sensation. Research by psychologists Ed O'Brien and Phoebe Ellsworth showed that Democrats and Republicans assume people who possess opposing political views from them would not be cold while standing outside during winter or would not be thirsty after eating salty snacks, despite the ostensible universality of these experiences. Participants in these studies literally fail to recognize that ideologically dissimilar others experience the same degree of cold or thirst.[60] Other studies have demonstrated that Democrats and Republicans judge opposing party members as less evolved and less likely to have minds at all.[61]

Of course, dehumanizing rhetoric in politics ramped up during the 2016 presidential election and in its aftermath. Rather than focusing on policy differences, politicians on both sides described the other side as relatively mindless. Democrats, for example, painted Trump voters as bigoted, misinformed, and blind to the truth with Hillary Clinton encapsulating this rhetoric by calling them a "basket of deplorables."[62] Republicans, on the other hand, painted Hillary Clinton's supporters as uncaring, unethical, and unaware of real Americans' struggles. Even more bluntly, Trump called Clinton supporters "animals" when accusing them of firebombing North Carolina's Republican headquarters.[63] The widening gap between the two sides of the political spectrum continues to grow, representing both a consequence and a cause of a broader societal dehumanizing shift.

Stratification

Stratification, a third pillar of the dehumanizing shift, refers to the global rise in income inequality that has increased the social distance between the haves and have-nots. Economist Thomas Piketty most definitively documented these trends in his book, *Capital in the Twenty-First Century*.[64] Piketty showed evidence that in the United States the upper decile's share of national income has steadily increased since the mid-1940s. More recent analyses have shown these trends continuing as well. Pick your favorite statistic—average income, household share of net worth, or wealth (property and financial assets minus debt)—and each one reveals an increasingly widening gap over the past five decades between society's richest and those at the bottom.[65] Notably, economic recovery efforts following the Great Recession of 2008 have done little to reduce the divide between the super-wealthy and everybody else.

Although statistics on rising stratification are plentiful, they insufficiently illustrate the social divide between lower-class and upper-class individuals and the inherent dehumanization that results. Aside from mere income, low socioeconomic status (SES) individuals and high SES individuals differ on several dimensions—for example, preferences for classical music versus heavy metal music, consumption of organic versus processed foods, prevalence of smoking, and various moral beliefs—that make relating to one another more difficult. The expansion of suburban sprawl and gentrification within cities means that poverty is more concentrated within the United States and the poor and rich are more geographically separate from each other now than in the past couple of decades.[66] The physical and psychological isolation of the poor from the rich (and, really, from everyone else) helps explain why studies find poor people to be one of the most commonly dehumanized social groups.[67]

One widespread form of dehumanization in this context is the critique of low-wage workers as mentally inferior. Hardee's CEO (chief executive officer) Andrew Puzder once criticized efforts to increase the minimum wage by asking, "How do you pay someone $15 to scoop ice cream?"[68] Others resist political efforts to increase low-wage workers' minimum wage by suggesting such a raise will just lead companies to automate workers' jobs instead.

Another common dehumanizing narrative is to disparage individuals who use social welfare programs. An op-ed in *The Tennessean*, titled "Feeding Animals Makes Them Dependent," criticized these programs by stating, "It's like animals at the zoo—they are totally taken care of—food, shelter, medical help, etc."[69] Rejecting basic human services for people who most need them is an unfortunately common tendency.

It is not only the rich who dehumanize the poor, but the opposite is true as well. The rich have faced the wrath of the masses in the aftermath of the 2008 financial crisis and the rise of the Occupy Wall Street movement. Research led by psychologist Susan Fiske and her colleagues reveals that most people view the rich as lacking warmth and compassion, a perception only strengthened by the growing economic divide.[70]

Automation

Automation, the fourth pillar of dehumanization, is the most complicated. The exponential advances in technology and technology's intrusion into every aspect of our lives are obvious, yet the contribution of automation to the dehumanizing shift is not uniform. Technology is dehumanizing in several ways. It has eliminated the fundamentally human elements such as vocal tone and facial expressions, gesture, and interruption (cues that even emojis cannot replicate) from conversation. It has generated content from video games to pornography that displaces the time we might spend with others. And most critically, technology reduces our dependence on others through taking over tasks once performed by humans. Each of these factors increases indifference toward the minds and the humanity of others.

Let us not forget that technology also has the potential to humanize us, as it connects us and makes our world smaller. Recent research on digital screen use and general well-being demonstrates that although excessive technology use diminishes well-being, so does the absence of technology use.[71] Moderate technology use can benefit happiness, and a review of scientific literature that Kurt Gray and I conducted shows the same to be true for empathy and, hence, humanization.[72] We learn more about the relationship between technology and humanity in chapter 7, where I show how to optimize our interactions with and through technology to rehumanize rather than dehumanize each other.

* * * *

NOW THAT we've established evidence for a dehumanizing shift, I want to turn to why reversing this trend is beneficial. In the next chapter, we begin to understand why seeing human is important.

CHAPTER 2

Humans as Meaning Makers

FABLES THROUGHOUT HISTORY HAVE DEPICTED HUMANS with magical powers of touch. The Greek myth of King Midas describes a king who could turn to gold any object—food, drink, rivers, roses—by touching it. The Greeks depicted Apollo's son Asclepius, god of medicine, as able to cure ailing people by touching them. The Bible's New Testament depicted Jesus Christ as also capable of healing the sick through mere contact with them. One notable passage describes Jesus' healing powers, stating that by touching the "hem of his garment," an ailing woman was "made whole" within the hour. Several Christian saints as well as English and French monarchs from the late Middle Ages through the nineteenth century similarly believed their touch possessed healing powers. As a result, they practiced "royal touch," a ceremony of touching their subjects with intent to cure them of illnesses such as tuberculosis or rheumatism.

Modern behavioral science has shown that the magic of touch is not only reserved for mythical Greek heroes, European monarchs, saints, or Jesus Christ. Consider Andre Roberson, a small forward for the Oklahoma City Thunder professional basketball team and a self-professed hugger. "I give hugs around the building when they're needed," Roberson has stated. "Somebody's feeling down, I go over there and cheer them up."[1] When reporters once observed Roberson emotionally hugging his coaches after a film session, rumors spread that the Thunder had traded Roberson and he was saying his good-byes. No, it turned it out Roberson just likes hugging, and this penchant for touch turns out to improve on-court performance as well.

Research by psychologists Michael Kraus and Dacher Keltner showed that National Basketball Association (NBA) teams that touch each other more frequently earlier in the season—for example, hugging, back-patting, butt-slapping, and high-fiving—perform better later in the season. Kraus and Keltner carefully watched games by all NBA teams during the first two months of the 2008–9 season and coded the teams for how often they touch each other. They then used these "touch scores" to predict team performance and cooperation, which they quantified by combining these cooperative on-court behaviors: passing the ball to a teammate who was less closely guarded by an opposing player, setting screens, or pointing and gesturing to a teammate.

Kraus and Keltner's analyses showed that teams that touched more often earlier in the season exhibited more cooperation, which in turn predicted later season team performance. In other words, touch signaled an intention to cooperate, and cooperation spurred team success. These same effects of human contact on cooperation appear in studies that show just lightly touching another person increases that person's willingness to sign a petition.[2] Touching a person lightly also encourages that person to return a dime that someone left in a phone booth (remember those?).[3] A brief touch by a waitress can even cause customers to tip more.[4]

Human touch also can also soothe another's pain. Take a fascinatingly unpleasant study by psychologist James Coan and colleagues, who administered electric shocks to sixteen married women while scanning their brains.[5] Unsurprisingly, these shocks activated brain regions such as the anterior cingulate cortex that commonly respond to threat, pain, and negative affect. These women also reported how painful the shocks were and, sure enough, they rated them to be reasonably unpleasant. The more interesting findings resulted from an experimental manipulation introduced at various points during the study. Throughout the brain scan, participants received the shock while (a) holding the hand of their husband, (b) holding the hand of a male stranger, or (c) not holding anyone's hand. Touching another person's hand reduced brain activity in the threat-sensitive brain regions and reduced reports of unpleasantness. The shock levels were the same, but participants perceived them differently. Remarkably, even a stranger's touch had this calming effect, but husbands' hands provided the greatest analgesic; this was particularly true when participants' self-reported marital satisfaction was high.

In more recent work, psychologist Sarah Master and colleagues showed that holding a romantic partner's hand reduced the experience of pain from exposure to extreme heat and that this effect was greater than holding a stranger's hand.[6] It also turns out that some partners are more effective than others. Follow-up work demonstrated that holding a male partner's hand is particularly effective at reducing pain when that partner reports himself to be highly empathic.[7] These findings demonstrate that a loving hand is a powerful analgesic and that human touch can alleviate physical pain.

The research described in this chapter so far demonstrates that human touch has seemingly magical powers because it signals social support and cooperative intent. Yet human touch can do more than establish social bonds. Human touch, and in some cases, mere human presence can enhance the value of material things, experiences, and products. Humans generate meaning because they signal effort, intentionality, and authenticity through association.

The Value in Human Effort

During graduate school, my weekly Sunday routine involved visiting a neighborhood staple, Valois, where the motto is "See Your Food." Valois was one of the few venues that brought the Hyde Park neighborhood together, with churchgoers, students, families, and even President Barack Obama every so often congregating to the counter-service cafeteria. At Valois, customers queue efficiently, ordering whatever they like—in my case, eggs, French toast, bacon, breakfast potatoes, coffee, and lemonade (a meal intended to last until evening)—while observing the cooks prepare each item. Customers slide down the line in perfect single file and meet the cashier at the end, along with their food. Although the food itself is excellent comfort fare, the procedure is what makes the experience so enjoyable.

A field experiment conducted by operations professor Ryan Buell and colleagues sheds light on the Valois experience.[8] Buell recruited customers at a university dining hall to participate in an experiment in exchange for a free sandwich. Buell randomly assigned some customers to order a sandwich for the following day and observe workers preparing their sandwiches that following day before paying. He assigned other customers simply to order a sandwich and then pick it up the following day without observing workers preparing their sandwiches. When customers observed the sandwich-making process, they reported enjoying their food more because they could see the effort the human workers put into preparing it. Even though participants who watched the workers had to wait longer for their food (sometimes four times as long as others), they preferred their experience. Precisely because of this waiting period, they appreciated the human work behind the sandwich and enjoyed their food more as a result.

Our tendency to value food based on human effort that produced it reflects a broader tendency referred to as the effort heuristic. The effort heuristic is a rule of thumb whereby people consciously or subconsciously judge the value of something based on the perceived effort put into it. The first studies examining this effect, led by psychologist Justin Kruger (of Dunning-Kruger Effect fame), demonstrated that people valued poems, paintings, and medieval armor more highly when they believed these artifacts required more human effort to produce.[9] For example, when participants learned that an artist named Deborah Kleven (a name invented for the experiment) spent four hours painting one work of art and twenty-six hours painting another work of art, they reported that the more effortful work was of higher quality and would sell for more money. Indeed, art historians suggest that one reason why experts so value the *Mona Lisa* is because of Leonardo da Vinci's painstaking use of *sfumato*, an effortful painting technique that gradually melds colors rather than using clear lines to separate them. People find value in this effort.

So predominant is this tendency to equate human effort with value that two of history's most famous social theorists anticipated it, despite agreeing on little else. Both Adam Smith and Karl Marx, preeminent architects of capitalism and socialism, respectively, endorsed a version of what is known as "the labor theory of value." Smith noted that "labor, therefore, is the real measure of the exchangeable value of all commodities," suggesting that a capitalistic society enables humans to attain wealth through their own efforts rather than through predetermined natural resources or treasure bestowed to one group or another.[10] Marx viewed this equating of value with labor to be precisely the problem with capitalism. He noted that "the worker not only replaces what he consumes but gives to the accumulated labor a greater value than it previously possessed."[11] Marx suggested that capitalists exploit workers by essentially taking this value (and therefore wealth) from the people who expended the labor in the first place. Although scholars debate how consistently and strongly both Smith and Marx held this view that labor produces value, both captured how people infer significance from the human effort spent on producing a commodity.

Intention Signals Purpose

Not only does human effort produce value, but so can mere human intention as well. Psychologist Ellen Winner and colleagues demonstrated the importance of intention for value in examining an issue that plagues modern art: whether people distinguish between art made by humans compared to art made by animals such as elephants and chimpanzees.[12] Although the results of these studies might seem obvious given this book's thesis regarding the importance of human beings, collectors have shown surprising interest in artwork by nonhumans, suggesting that animal artwork has its own unique value. In 2005 at London's Bonhams auction house, an Andy Warhol painting and a Renoir sculpture attracted so little attention that they were withdrawn from auction while a relatively lesser known artist, Congo, sold three paintings for £14,400. In fact, Congo was a chimpanzee who died in 1964 of tuberculosis at ten years of age. Congo rose to such fame during his brief life that Picasso, Miró, and Dalí all purchased work from him, with Dalí remarking, "The hand of the chimpanzee is quasihuman; the hand of Jackson Pollock is totally animal!"[13]

In Winner's studies, she and her colleagues examined whether Congo is an anomaly or whether people more broadly appreciate animal art. They presented participants including both art students and non–art students with pairs of artworks—one created by a professional adult artist and one created by a nonhuman animal or child. Participants had to indicate which work in the pair they preferred and then judge their quality. Sometimes the works were unlabeled, sometimes the works were labeled correctly (with animal art labeled as being generated by an animal and human art labeled as being generated by a human), and sometimes the works were labeled incorrectly (the human and animal labels were reversed).

Impressively, both art students and non–art students consistently preferred works done by professional artists even when choosing works erroneously labeled as generated by a child, chimpanzee, or elephant. Most critically, when participants explained why they preferred works by professional adults, they did so by appealing to the artists' intentions. Participants perceived a mind behind the artworks generated by adults, and the presence of mind enhanced people's evaluations. In follow-up work by Winner and colleagues, participants had to identify which of a set of artworks was produced by a human professional artist, child, or animal and found that even nonexperts could identify human-made artworks with better-than-chance accuracy. Again, participants discriminated between human and nonhuman works by identifying greater intentionality (the degree of intention) in the artworks by adult humans. Intentionality signaled the presence of a human, which in turn created value.

Human intention not only enhances the significance of objects but also the significance of experiences. Research led by Kurt Gray, for example, has demonstrated that awareness of the human intention behind an experience makes it more pleasurable.[14] In one of his studies, participants received candy and were told that either another human intentionally chose the candy for them or that the candy was selected at random. Participants consumed the candy and then evaluated how much they liked it. People who learned of the benevolent human intention behind the candy selection process rated the candy as better tasting than those who learned the candy was chosen randomly. Gray conducted another experiment showing that people experienced more pleasure from an electric massage administered by a human versus a computer because knowing a human's benevolent intentions enhanced the experience.

I often think of this research when I interact with anyone on LinkedIn. Often, the social network suggests I congratulate one of my contacts on starting a new job. When I click to offer my congratulations, it automatically composes a message ("Congrats on the new job!") that I can post without having to think of some celebratory sentiment on my own. Similarly, when someone sends me a congratulatory message on LinkedIn, the system automatically composes reply options for me to send including "Thanks," "Thank you," and a thumbs-up emoji. Out of laziness I often use the automated options, but I imagine my contacts would experience them less meaningfully if they knew these messages were generated by a machine rather than through my benevolent intentions.

In examining intentionality, Gray also demonstrated in a follow-up study that not just positive intentions but negative intentions as well can amplify the meaning of an experience. In this study, all participants received electric shocks from another person, their study partner. Participants either believed their partner was shocking them with good intentions (to win them a large prize) or bad intentions (out of simple malevolence). Participants reported how much pain they felt from each shock, and results revealed that positive intentions made the shock feel more pleasant and negative intentions made the shock feel more painful (compared to when participants received no information about human intentions). Beyond mere positivity, human intentions convey significance. Compliments that we receive by accident feel less meaningful than compliments we receive on purpose, and the same is true of insults.

The significance we ascribe to intentions also explains why people value human-made objects more than machine-manufactured ones. The work of psychologist Robert Kreuzbauer and colleagues shows that the confluence of two factors drives this tendency: (1) how symbolic the particular object is—that is, how much the object is meant to communicate something, and (2) how much intentional control the creator has over the particular object.[15] In Kreuzbauer's studies he described to participants several objects in terms of either their symbolic properties (i.e., aesthetics) or their functional properties (i.e., utility). One study, for example, described a wine glass by highlighting its shape as a symbolic property or its durability as a functional property. In addition, some participants read that the wine glass company has developed a special glassblowing technique that reflects each glassblower's unique agency over the process, whereas other participants read that the glassblowing technique removes the agency of any particular glassblower so that the wine glasses are identical. People reported valuing the wine glass more when they read about the glass in terms of its symbolic property and learning that each one varied according to the glassblower's work. In other words, when an object is intended to convey a symbolic expression and a human being has agency in crafting that expression, people view the object as meaningful and, therefore, valuable.

In other studies, Kreuzbauer and colleagues show that the joint presence of symbolic expression and human agency explains why people prefer handmade entities. The combination of these two factors highlights the role of the creator's intention in generating value in a particular product, object, or work of art. Fashion designer Christian Louboutin captures this preference for human-generated objects in stating, "I hate the idea of natural. For example, I prefer gardens to wild nature. I like to see the human touch. High heels are a complete invention—an extravagance. They're far from natural, but it's the impracticality that I adore. I prefer the useless to the useful."[16] Louboutin, known for his ostentatious designs and signature red-bottomed high heels, conveys how people come to value human-produced objects. Humans can communicate something expressive beyond mere function, and this expression coupled with intentionality can give an object enhanced meaning.

Marketing scholar Stijn van Osselaer and colleagues have conducted research showing that this preference for human-crafted entities extends toward less symbolic objects as well.[17] In their studies, participants evaluated various consumer goods (e.g., stationery, scarves, and soaps) learning that these goods were either handmade or made by machine. Participants who learned the goods were handmade expressed more willingness to buy them, purchase them as a gift, and pay more for them.

A recent lawsuit against Maker's Mark Whisky illustrates the premium that consumers place on human touch. Californians Safora Nowrouzi and Travis Williams claim they were defrauded by Maker's Mark labeling their bourbon as handmade. Their lawsuit noted that despite this claim, a video of the company's factory shows the use of machines to mix ingredients, break up grains, ferment, and distill. The plaintiffs argued that "they overpaid for the bourbon based on the claim and wouldn't have bought it—or would have paid less—if they'd known otherwise."[18] Although their lawsuit was dismissed, it nonetheless highlights the value that the human-made designation confers.

Van Osselaer's studies provide critical insight as to why people prefer handmade to machine-made products: love. Participants reported believing that handmade products contained more love and were made with more love than machine-made products. In an increasingly technologically advanced age, the demand for handmade goods has never been higher. Websites like Etsy have helped independent craftspeople who specialize in handmade products sell their goods to a broad market. And Amazon.com has similarly launched "Amazon Handmade," a marketplace specifically for handmade products. As automation enables quick mass production of various products, the unique love perceived within handmade goods takes on enhanced value.

Similar to van Osselaer's work, psychologist Veronika Job and colleagues showed in their research that the mere trace of a human creator enhanced people's assessments of an object's value.[19] Learning that a mug was "made by people in Small Factory in Nebraska" led people to value these products more compared to learning they were "made by a Small Factory in Nebraska" (with no mention of people). As with van Osselaer's studies, Job's participants believed that the human touch imbued objects with social qualities such as warmth, friendliness, and sincerity.

Still other research shows that human intentions convey aesthetic value. Neuroscientist Ulrich Kirk and colleagues demonstrated this belief in scanning participants' brains while asking them to evaluate artworks.[20] Sometimes Kirk labeled the artworks as computer generated, and at other times he labeled them as coming from a real-life art gallery, even though the actual works were the same. Ostensibly human-generated artwork (relative to ostensibly computer-generated artwork) produced greater activation in the medial orbitofrontal cortex, a key region involved in representing value and pleasure. People also rated human-made works as more appealing. This research fits with Winner's work on human versus animal art and suggests people intuitively infer that humans have intentional minds, and these minds create value.

Positive Social Contagion and Authenticity

Independent of effort or intentionality, mere human contact can enhance an object's significance. This is because many people subscribe to what social scientists call the "law of magical contagion." This law represents the belief that a person can transfer his or her essence to that object simply by touching it. Anthropologist James G. Frazer in 1980 was the first to document this tendency as prevalent in "savage and barbarous" society, yet we still succumb to this belief in the modern age.[21] I personally disavow magical thinking, but when pondering what items I would save from my house if it were burning down, I find myself indulging in contagion beliefs. I turn to two objects: a wristband worn in-game by NBA legend Kevin Garnett emblazoned with his initials and number "KG 21" and a vial of my cousin's ashes. I consider both objects to be priceless despite their finite value in an open market—a few hundred dollars in the case of the wristband (per eBay) and likely nothing at all in the case of the vial. For me, the objects derive their value from the essence of those people contained within them and from these people's significance to me.

Contagion effects in fact go beyond personal attachments. In one notable demonstration, psychologists Carol Nemeroff and Paul Rozin demonstrated that people refused to wear a sweater that Adolf Hitler had previously worn.[22] Consistent with the idea of contagion, Nemeroff and Rozin also found they could nudge people to wear the sweater by telling them that Mother Teresa had also worn it. Good people can imbue goodness into whatever they touch.

Psychologists George Newman and Paul Bloom have also demonstrated social contagion in showing that celebrity contact with objects enhances their value. In one set of studies (alluded to in the introduction) Newman and Bloom examined the estate auctions of John F. Kennedy, Jacqueline Onassis, and Marilyn Monroe.[23] The researchers coded each item in the auction—antiques, art, decorations, furniture, literature, tableware, clothing, and jewelry—in terms of how much physical contact the former owners had with it. They found this measure of perceived physical contact predicted larger final bids on these items, even when accounting for preauction estimates of the items. To fully capture the contagion phenomenon, Newman and Bloom also examined how perceived physical contact affected disgraced businessman Bernie Madoff's estate auction and found that perceived physical contact predicted reduced final bids for his items (think back to people's unwillingness to wear a sweater worn by Hitler). These findings again demonstrate that humans transmit their essence into objects through contact, significantly altering their significance and value.

What is it specifically about contagion that creates significance? The likely mechanism is through establishing authenticity, which people value greatly. Research shows that people trust and cooperate more with others who flash an authentic smile versus a fake smile.[24] People also view themselves more positively when they feel authentic versus inauthentic.[25] Consumers prefer to buy authentic goods ranging from travel souvenirs to athletic shoes and value products more when they were manufactured in the company's original factory than manufactured elsewhere.[26]

Other work by Newman and Bloom showed that contagion explains why people value original art over perfect duplicates.[27] People valued original artwork more because of contact with the original human creator, which signals authenticity. In the real-world art market, authenticity can mean the difference between millions of dollars and worthlessness. Famed art forger Wolfgang Beltracchi received a six-year jail term for creating and passing off perfect duplicates of works by Max Ernst, Georges Braque, and Fernand Leger. He fooled collectors and expert art historians into multimillion-dollar sales until his 2016 arrest, when those artworks completely lost their worth. Franziska Beltracchi, daughter of Wolfgang and his wife/accomplice Helene, remarked, "I think they didn't really hurt anybody. They took money for pictures that people wanted. Maybe now they're not worth anything, but they still got the picture."[28] The younger Beltracchi's remark suggests that the link between human contact, contagion, authenticity, and value may not necessarily be intuitive or obvious.

One other domain where authenticity rules is in the experience of dining out, with research suggesting that a hint of human presence can convey a restaurant's authenticity, thereby boosting its appeal. Organizational behavior scholar Balázs Kovács and colleagues demonstrated this phenomenon by examining over one million Yelp restaurant reviews.[29] They found that restaurants that garnered reviews containing more authenticity-related words (e.g., "authentic," "real," "genuine") received higher ratings. Also, this relationship was strongest for family-owned restaurants, which people perceived as particularly authentic, compared with restaurant chains. A follow-up study showed that the presence of humans, conveyed by family ownership rather than some ostensibly faceless corporate ownership, made people like the restaurant more through establishing authenticity.

To summarize the research on this point, we've learned that human presence, human touch, and human creation give objects value through instilling them with authenticity. This transfer process is most effective when the human who has touched the object is perceived positively. The effects of positive social contagion, combined with the value-enhancing effects of human effort and human intentionality, make humans a vast source of meaning, capable of boosting the significance of artifacts and experiences with their presence.

*   *   *   *

AS WE see in further detail in chapter 7, the significance we attach to humans may become problematic in an increasingly automated world. In certain cases, nonhuman agents may perhaps serve us better than humans, as some research is beginning to illustrate.

As a mundane example, if faced with a choice of hearing a funny joke selected by a human or selected by an algorithm, most choose a human. Yet selecting a joke turns out to be something that algorithms do better than humans. Behavioral economist Mike Yeomans and colleagues discovered this by implementing algorithmic joke recommender systems and comparing them to human joke recommenders.[30] Across several studies, algorithmic recommenders consistently selected jokes that people rated as funnier than jokes selected by human recommenders. However, when people predicted which one would recommend a funnier joke, they predicted a human recommender more frequently than an algorithmic recommender. In one study, 69 percent of people guessed a person rather than an algorithm would better predict what jokes people would prefer, and 74 percent of people preferred to receive joke recommendations from a human compared to an algorithm. In other words, people predicted that human-selected jokes would be funnier, but in practice they found machine-selected jokes to be superior. The significance we ascribe to humans can mislead us.

Psychologist Berkeley Dietvorst and colleagues captured a similar phenomenon (that they termed *algorithm aversion*) in the domain of forecasting. They showed that people consistently placed greater bets on human predictors versus algorithmic predictors for forecasting things like the success of applicants to an MBA program or which US states would generate the most airline passengers.[31] In fact, Dietvorst's participants placed greater confidence in human forecasters than algorithmic forecasters even when the algorithms outperformed the humans.

Of course, people prefer humans to algorithms for several reasons, and Yeomans's and Dietvorst's studies suggest at least two: (1) people (falsely) believe that humans are more capable at improving than algorithms and (2) people dislike the opaqueness of algorithms (although they seem comfortable with the opaqueness of humans). Separately, the simple significance granted by human touch leads people to overvalue humans and to undervalue algorithms. Given the increasing need for humans to trust algorithms in tasks ranging from cancer diagnosis to flying a plane, imbuing algorithmic systems with some humanness is essential to demonstrating their worth to users. Again, I expand on how to humanize these systems in chapter 7. In the next chapter, we continue to see how humans' mere presence gives our worlds not only a sense of meaning but a sense of morality as well.

CHAPTER 3

The Morality of Humanity

BEYOND THE CAPACITY OF HUMAN PRESENCE TO ENHANCE the value of objects and experiences, humans also possess an inherent, intrinsic value. As I mentioned in the introduction, this is because humans are moral entities. This recognition that humans therefore deserve care and freedom from harm represents a universally held law, present in philosophical traditions ranging from that of Immanuel Kant to the Chinese philosophies of Confucianism, Mohism, and Taoism.[1] Kant called this law "the second formulation of the categorical imperative," which he described by stating, "Act in such a way that you treat humanity, whether in your own person or in the person of any other, never merely as a means to an end, but always at the same time as an end."[2] In other words, owning, objectifying, or mistreating a human being is morally unacceptable.

The Confucian philosopher Mencius described the inherent value of humans in stating, "To feed a scholar and not love him is to treat him as a pig. To love him and not respect him is to keep him as a domestic animal."[3] In this view, humans are unique from other animals in that they require respect and care.

Even in the throes of war, humans see moral worth in their sworn enemies and struggle with having to harm them. Dave Grossman, a retired United States army lieutenant colonel and expert on the psychology of violence, details this in his book, *On Killing*. Grossman suggests that during the American Civil War, the kill rate was as low as two per minute among groups of two hundred soldiers standing only thirty yards apart, and only 5 percent of Civil War soldiers were responsible for all killing.[4] Combat historian and Brigadier General S. L. A. Marshall similarly writes in his book, *Men Against Fire*, that at most 20 percent of individual riflemen during World War II fired their weapon at enemy soldiers.[5] Although Grossman's and Marshall's findings have become the subject of some debate by historians, they point to the uncontroversial actuality that humans resist harming each other even when explicitly tasked with doing so.

Other research from the social sciences conveys just how unwilling people are to harm others. One study by neuroscientist Molly Crockett and colleagues offered people money to receive a painful electric shock or administer a painful shock to another person. She found that people required more money to harm another human than to receive harm themselves and that people will sacrifice money to avoid harming another person.[6] Work by psychologist Lukas Volz and colleagues show that although people avoid harming themselves to benefit others, they will indeed sacrifice money to prevent another person from receiving electric shocks.[7]

Even simulating harm to another human evokes significant distress, as demonstrated by psychologist Fiery Cushman and colleagues.[8] Cushman's studies asked participants to commit faux-harms toward a male member of the research staff while ensuring participants he would not actually experience pain. For example, participants shot a fake handgun (with no actual ammunition) at a staff member's face or smashed his shin with a hammer while the victim wore a metal pipe underneath his pants to soften the blow. Another task involved participants smacking a realistic baby doll against a table. The researchers asked participants to report their moods following performing each action, always emphasizing that no actual harm would occur to any human present in the study. They also measured participants' blood pressure response both before and after these actions. Participants reported feeling worse following these actions (even just witnessing these simulated actions made participants feel bad). They also exhibited greater vasoconstriction—constriction of blood vessels, which typically increases blood pressure—before performing these acts. Thus, these studies demonstrate that our unwillingness to harm humans is so powerful that even pretend moral violations toward another human evoke distress. Such findings help explain why violent TV shows and movies evoke a similarly distressing reaction even when we know the violence isn't real.

Other research shows the flexible nature of the humanity/morality link—whereas humanizing an entity increases care toward that entity, dehumanizing an entity increases aggression toward that entity. Famed psychologist Albert Bandura illustrated this process by studying people's behavior toward others who were actively humanized, actively dehumanized, or observed neutrally.[9] In one of Bandura's initial studies, participants operated a device that administered electric shocks at varying levels of intensity. Participants learned they were taking part in a study examining how punishment affects decision-making and that they would play the role of supervisors. They learned that other participants, located in obscured cubicles, were playing the role of decision-makers. Decision-makers' task was to complete a twenty-five-trial problem-solving exercise. These "supervisors" received instructions that on each trial, if a decision-maker's solution was adequate, an amber light would flash on the display panel of the shocking device. If it was inadequate, a red light would flash on the display panel, indicating that the supervisor participant had to administer a shock.

Critically, Bandura ensured that all participants "accidentally overheard" a conversation among the research staff about the decision-makers—this conversation served as the experimental manipulation. In a humanized condition, participants overheard the experimenter describe the group as "perceptive" and "understanding" (i.e., mentally capable). In a dehumanized condition, participants overheard the experimenter describe the group as "an animalistic, rotten bunch." In a neutral condition, participants heard no relevant discussion evaluating the group's characteristics. The critical test was how these descriptions affected the intensity of the electric shocks that participants administered over ten "red light" trials.

Perhaps unsurprisingly, participants administered the highest-intensity shocks when the decision-makers had been described in dehumanized terms. Supervisor participants willingly electrocuted people stripped of humanity compared to the neutral and humanized conditions. In fact, questionnaires completed after the experiment revealed that the dehumanizing description made participants feel the shocks were justified. More interestingly, however, supervisor participants gave more lenient shocks in the humanized condition than in the neutral condition. The researchers replicated these results in a follow-up study as well, producing the simple conclusion: highlighting an individual's humanity increases kindness toward that individual whereas denigrating an individual's humanity fosters aggression.

Other work by Bandura in collaboration with Philip Zimbardo (of Stanford Prison Experiment fame) and Michael J. Osofsky showed that people also use dehumanization to justify harm in the criminal execution process.[10] The researchers surveyed 246 prison employees from three southern US maximum-security penitentiaries, including support team members who counseled the inmates, prison guards largely uninvolved in the execution, and the executioners themselves. Participants all completed a survey on moral disengagement, including some items measuring dehumanization (e.g., asking whether participants agreed that "murderers who receive the death penalty have forfeited the right to be considered full human beings"). Executioners endorsed these dehumanizing statements significantly more than prison guards or support team members, suggesting that their relatively more direct role in the execution contributed to them dehumanizing inmates. Dehumanization enabled them to view the inmates as worthy of harm, thereby morally justifying execution.

Small Cues Guide Morality

The studies described here suggest that people do not always automatically see humans as humans. Small cues to humanness, such as a face or humanlike body movement, are often necessary to trigger people to see something or someone as human. When these cues prompt people to see human, people behave more morally as well.

One domain that illustrates this phenomenon is critical care, with work showing that photographs of patients can improve engagement and treatment. For example, a survey of nurses and anesthetists in a Swedish intensive care unit (ICU) revealed the benefits of personal photographs placed by the beds of unconscious patients.[11] These medical professionals reported that these photos helped them see patients as human—"more an individual rather than a parcel," one reported—and that helped them relate to and care for them. A similar study at two ICUs in Toronto found that a majority of critical care nurses reported patient photographs help them relate better to patients and help them visualize their goals for nursing care. As with the Swedish study, nurses noted how photographs helped humanize these patients. "I feel that having pictures of patients with their children and/or extended family makes us realize that they are 'human'," one noted, "not just as an 'edematous, jaundiced, septic' patient."[12]

Another medical domain where humanness cues engender moral concern is that of abortion decisions. Recent legislation in certain US states has required women considering abortion to view their fetal ultrasound, listen to the fetal heartbeat, or agree to bury the fetus after the abortion. These methods all intend to dissuade women from electing abortion through reminding them of the fetus's humanity, but do they work? The only two studies that have comprehensively examined this question have found the answer to be: somewhat.

The first study examining this question was published in 2014, examining over 15,000 women seeking abortion care at Planned Parenthood Los Angeles.[13] A major caveat to this study is that it could not randomly assign women to view the ultrasound or not. That is, because ultrasound viewing was voluntary, researchers could not experimentally manipulate whether women chose to view the ultrasound. Random assignment in experiments is typically important to ensure that the primary variable of interest (in this case, ultrasound viewing) explains the findings and not some other factor that might differ between those who chose to view and those who did not. For example, in this study women who chose to view the ultrasound were younger, more likely to be African American, and more likely to have higher levels of poverty (although the researchers accounted for these variables in their analysis).

Despite the lack of random assignment, the study was illuminating. Patients chose to view 42.5 percent of the time and abortion decisions were compared between those who viewed versus those who did not. Importantly, this study also measured women's decision certainty (low, medium, or high) about proceeding to abortion. Among those with high certainty, viewing the ultrasound made no difference—97.5 percent who viewed and 98 percent who did not view proceeded to abortion. Among those women who were wavering on their decision, however, viewing the ultrasound had a significant effect, with 95.2 percent who viewed the ultrasound proceeding to abortion compared to 98.7 percent who chose not to view. Of course, this effect is small, and we should interpret it cautiously, yet a 3.5 percent reduction is significant particularly among women specifically seeking abortion care.

A second study assessed medical charts at a Wisconsin abortion clinic one year before and one year after a 2013 law took effect requiring abortion providers to show preabortion ultrasound images to patients.[14] Again, this study does not involve random assignment and cannot account for factors that might have differed between the different time periods. Nonetheless, in looking at 5,342 cases, this research showed a clear increase in women electing to continue their pregnancy after the law went into effect (11.2 percent) than before (8.7 percent). This study also statistically showed that viewing the ultrasound, in particular, accounted for this finding and the law similarly affected women of high and low certainty about their decision. Taken together, the two studies on ultrasound viewing provide additional evidence that small cues to humanness can evoke moral concern.

In recent years, antiabortion activists have also capitalized on progress in medical science that can identify a fetus's capacity for agency, experiencing pain, and living outside of the womb earlier in development than previously thought (certainly earlier than when abortion was decriminalized in 1973). These findings result partially from advances in ultrasound technology, which now reveal more vivid and, hence, more humanlike images of fetuses. Pro-life activist Ashley McGuire notes, "When you're seeing a baby sucking its thumb at 18 weeks, smiling, clapping," it becomes "harder to square the idea that that 20-week-old, that unborn baby or fetus, is discardable." Journalist Emma Green in *The Atlantic* described how McGuire and the pro-life movement have rallied around scientific and technological advances, stating, "New technology makes it easier to apprehend the humanity of a growing child and imagine a fetus as a creature with moral status."[15] Abortion politics aside, these small cues to a fetus's humanity can engender a sense of ethical care.

Well outside of the medical domain, Honda Motorcycles has also capitalized on the moralizing power of humanness cues. In efforts to increase safety, Honda's researchers designed motorcycle fronts to resemble a human face with eyebrows that operate as blinkers. Visibility tests demonstrated that the facelike design nearly doubled drivers' ability to recognize the motorcycle compared to a traditional motorcycle design.[16] Researchers also scanned people's brains while they viewed various motorcycle fronts and found that the facelike front evoked the same activity in the fusiform gyrus brain region as did viewing a human face. Honda's design builds on considerable psychological research showing that faces—as reminders of human beings—capture our attention like very few other stimuli do. In this context, this attention grab makes the bike more visible and, as a result, makes people more cautious.[17] The face appears angry, which might also encourage safer on-road behavior through communicating harsh judgment. Regardless of how it works, Honda's design again shows how small cues to humanness can increase moral sensitivity.

The Power of Being Identifiable

Small cues to humanness not only alter moral behavior toward single entities but toward groups as well. Let me explain. When we think about any social group (e.g., nurses, Latin Americans, left-handers), several things might come to mind—the name of that collective group, the number of group members, or the image of a prototypical single group member. Considerable research shows people behave more compassionately toward a group when that group is represented as a single individual rather than as a collective or as a number. In these cases, single individuals serve as cues to the group's humanity, evoking greater moral concern and echoing the famous quote, erroneously attributed to Josef Stalin, that "the death of a single Russian soldier is a tragedy; a million deaths is a statistic." In other words, people typically care more about the value of a single life than the value of multiple lives.

Economist Thomas Schelling was the first to describe this phenomenon in 1968, writing, "Let a 6-year-old girl with brown hair need thousands of dollars for an operation that will prolong her life until Christmas and the post office will be swamped with nickels and dimes to save her. But let it be reported that without a sales tax the hospital facilities of Massachusetts will deteriorate and cause a barely perceptible increase in preventable deaths—not many will drop a tear or reach for their checkbooks." Schelling's parables suggest a single human being's suffering inspires moral action whereas the mass suffering is imperceptible and, therefore, evokes little sympathy. Schelling proceeds, "To evaluate an individual death requires special attention to feelings . . . a marginal change in mortality statistics is unlikely to evoke these sentiments . . . The avoidance of a particular death—the death of a named individual—cannot be treated straightforwardly as a consumer choice. It involves anxiety and sentiment, guilt and awe."[18] Here, Schelling notes that identifiable human lives (and deaths) evoke moral emotions, foreshadowing a vast program of research that would empirically illustrate this phenomenon.

Schelling's idea became known as "the identifiable victim effect," and in the late 1990s researchers began documenting it. One paradigmatic experiment led by psychologist Deborah Small gave participants information about famine in Africa and offered them the opportunity to donate money to Save the Children, an organization that helps those affected. In one condition, participants read a passage highlighting statistical information about the famine stating, "Food shortages in Malawi are affecting more than three million children . . . Four million Angolans—one third of the population—have been forced to flee their homes. More than 11 million people in Ethiopia need immediate food assistance." In another condition, participants viewed a young girl's photograph and read a passage about her stating, "Any money that you donate will go to Rokia, a 7-year-old girl from Mali, Africa. Rokia is desperately poor, and faces a threat of severe hunger or even starvation. Her life will be changed for the better as a result of your financial gift."[19] Comparing donations revealed that participants gave more than twice as much in the identified condition than when they read statistical information even though the latter condition emphasized that more people were affected.

Outside the laboratory, psychologist Paul Slovic and colleagues found that charitable donations to refugee causes skyrocketed in the week after the death of Aylan Kurdi (the drowned Syrian child mentioned in chapter 1) and the circulation of his photograph.[20] During this week, the number of donations to a Swedish Red Cross fund designated specifically to help Syrian refugees increased by a hundredfold and the amount of donations increased by a factor of 55. Slovic notes, "The photograph of a single identified individual captured the attention of people and moved them to take interest and provide aid in ways that were not motivated by statistics of hundreds of thousands of deaths."

Other research led by psychologist Jeff Galak demonstrated identifiability's power in micro-finance lending. By studying Kiva, an online platform where people can lend money to low-income entrepreneurs across the globe including farmers, retailers, and educators, Galak found that lenders favor individual borrowers more than group borrowers. On the Kiva website, one can select from various borrower profiles. Some are individuals like Mery Yolanda, an Ecuadorian woman asking for a loan of $1,500 to buy local potatoes, cooking oil, and sausages. Others are collectives like the Mujeres Emprendedoras Group, a Peruvian bank asking for a loan of $1,525 to buy milk, rice, and sugar. Galak's work showed lenders were more likely to fund individuals like Yolanda than groups like Mujeres Emprendedoras, and as the size of the borrower group increased, lending decreased.

What can account for the power of an individual human to drive compassion and charity? Recent neuroimaging work by neuroscientist Alex Genevsky sheds some light on the process. In Genevsky's study, when people viewed a photograph depicting a single child in need, brain regions involved in emotional processing became more active compared to when people viewed faceless, silhouette depictions of children.[21] Genevsky found that activity in these regions, particularly regions associated with positive emotion, then predicted greater donations to the children depicted identifiably (versus facelessly). These findings suggest that identifiable individuals generate emotion, which in turn guides giving.

These neuroimaging findings only partially explain identifiable victim effects—humans evoke emotions and these emotions promote moral behavior—as the question remains, why do identifiable individuals evoke emotion in the first place? Decision scientist Cynthia Cryder and psychologist George Loewenstein offered a unifying theory that proposes helping an identified victim feels tangible, and this tangibility has two positive side effects: (1) tangibility makes the helper feel his or her help has impact, which increases a helper's own positive emotions, and (2) tangibility amplifies the moral emotions people feel toward another person.[22]

A more recent program of research complicates things slightly by suggesting an opposing explanation of identifiability effects.[23] Psychologists Daryl Cameron and Keith Payne suggest that the suffering of the masses (rather than an individual) overwhelms us emotionally, forcing us to suppress these emotions and turn toward the single victim instead.

Without digging into the minutiae of the empirical support for either side, my sense is that these two camps have asked different questions in different circumstances. Personally, I think both views demonstrate how humans are psychologically special in evoking moral concern. One view centers on the depth of a single human's suffering, whereas the other view focuses on the breadth of suffering across multiple humans. In endorsing the latter view, Cameron and Payne still acknowledge the moral power of single victim identifiability, simply suggesting that the reason that identifiability prompts compassion relative to group suffering is because group suffering overwhelms us emotionally. Their view echoes Mother Teresa's famous sentiment, "If I look at the mass I will never act. If I look at the one, I will."[24]

Overall, the literature described here shows people behave more morally toward individuals than groups unless groups resemble individuals (i.e., when humanness cues are salient). Yet another major factor that prompts this resemblance is a group's cohesiveness—that is, how similar its members are to each other, how closely knit they are, and how much they share a common fate. For example, in my work with Liane Young we showed that people perceive groups like "the New York Yankees" to be highly cohesive but "all Facebook users" to be low on cohesion.[25] A definitive 1996 theoretical article by psychologists David Hamilton and Steven Sherman demonstrated that people process cohesive groups in the same way they do individuals.[26] Subsequent work has shown how cohesiveness can prompt moral behavior.

In research on cohesiveness and charitable giving, marketing scholar Robert W. Smith and colleagues presented British participants with a group of six African children who needed financial assistance for education. In a high-cohesion condition, the researchers presented the six African children as siblings, and in another no-cohesion condition, they did not mention the relationship between the children. Presenting the children as siblings increased donations to the children, on average by 2.88 GBP (about $3.75), more than double the condition that presented no family information.[27] Other work with Swedish participants showed people were more willing to help a group of eight children when they learned the children were related versus when they believed the children were unrelated.[28] Cohesiveness makes groups appear more like a single identifiable human, eliciting more compassion and moral concern as a result.

Although it may seem obvious that highlighting humanness cues engenders moral care whereas obscuring these cues licenses harm, other work demonstrates that these cues are largely invisible to people making moral decisions. Studies led by psychologist Lisa Shu support this idea, showing first that people express greater concern when a named (and, thus, identifiable) individual experiences harm versus when an unnamed (and, thus, unidentifiable) individual experiences the same harm.[29]

In one of Shu's studies, half of the participants read a vignette about a shady real estate agent exploiting "Sam" and half read about a shady real estate agent exploiting "a person" (unnamed). When participants evaluated the agent's actions, they judged them to be significantly more unethical when given the victim's name. The mere humanness that a name confers increases moral concern for the buyer's financial well-being.

A follow-up study by Shu indicated that people only notice the moralizing power of identifiability when reading about the same victim presented in two ways—named and unnamed—side by side. In this study, which involved three experimental conditions, two involved participants read either about a named individual or about an unnamed individual receiving a faulty treatment from a physician. In the third condition, participants read both "named" and "unnamed" versions of the same scenario side by side. People judged the ethics of the treatment, and results showed these judgments were far more aligned when people read about the named victim and same unnamed victim side by side than when people read separately about the named victim or the unnamed victim. These studies show that cues to humanness, no matter how small, imbue an entity with moral status, yet the power of these cues largely goes undetected.

Anthropomorphism and Ethics

The best evidence that cues to humanness induce moral concern comes from research on humanizing clearly nonhuman entities. In 2007, Nick Epley, John Cacioppo, and I published the first psychological theory of why people anthropomorphize (i.e., perceive non-humans as humanlike) and began empirically testing that theory. At the time, I hoped our work would legitimize anthropomorphism as a scientific topic. However, it attracted less attention from academics than from assorted folks beyond the academy. We received constant media requests from journalists writing articles about why people put sweaters on their pets or why people name their cars. Others wanted to know about the psychology of Furries (people who routinely dress up in costumes as animal characters) or why people create Twitter accounts for animals like the Bronx Zoo cobra snake. Although these inquiries were each fascinating in their own right, they also concerned me. I began worrying whether I was studying a fringe topic rather than a consequential phenomenon.

Critically, then, we felt the need to examine whether anthropomorphism has moral consequences to show that humanizing a nonhuman could mean the difference between harming it and helping it. We developed a scale called the Individual Differences in Anthropomorphism Questionnaire (IDAQ) that asked people questions like "To what extent does a television set experience emotions?" and "To what extent does the average reptile have consciousness?"[30] The accuracy of the answers to these questions is irrelevant, and perhaps unknowable, yet people's responses turned out to significantly predict their moral beliefs. In one study, we found that people who score high on the IDAQ (meaning they anthropomorphized more) were more likely to state that harming a computer, a motorcycle, and even a bed of flowers is immoral. In another study, we found that higher scores on the IDAQ predicted people's concern for the natural environment and how much they valued protecting plants, trees, and forests. In other words, people prone to humanizing nonhumans expressed more moral concern. This was our first step to demonstrating that anthropomorphism is not merely cute or quirky, but it is in fact consequential.

One of the more bizarre examples of how humanization can engender moral care comes from a study of cows and their milk production.[31] In this work, researchers Catherine Bertenshaw and Peter Rowlinson surveyed 516 British farm stock managers about attitudes toward human-animal relationships on their dairy farms. Approximately 46 percent of these farmers reported naming their cows and calling their cows by name. On the farms where naming occurred, milk yield was 258 liters higher than on farms where cows were not called by name. Bertenshaw and Rowlinson explain this finding by suggesting humanizing the cow increases attentiveness to the cow. They also suggest that naming the cows goes hand in hand with treating the cow with care, thereby reducing stress and consequent production of cortisol, a hormone that interferes with milk production. Of course, other factors might explain this finding and the causal relationship in this study could run in the reverse direction as well. That is, better-performing cows might elicit more favorable evaluations from farmers, who therefore name them. Nonetheless, this provocative study suggests a relationship between humanizing animals and treating them humanely.

Other work has examined how the humanization of cows affects preferences for or against eating meat. Psychologists Brock Bastian and Stephen Loughnan have explored in depth what they call the meat paradox, "the apparent psychological conflict between people's dietary preference for meat and their moral response to animal suffering."[32] Given that Bastian and Loughnan are both Australian, this question might have particular relevance given their local cuisine offerings. They have demonstrated across several studies that the extent to which people consider cows and other animals to be humanlike reduces their willingness to eat these animals. In one emblematic study, they found that the more people judged animals to possess humanlike mental capacities such as emotions, self-control, and memory, the less willing they were to eat these animals.[33]

This humanization-care link also applies to companion animals such as cats and dogs. Animal ethics scholar James Serpell suggests that people have bred pets over multiple generations in ways that exaggerate their humanlike features, making them easier to anthropomorphize, which in turn increases humans' desire to care for them.[34]

A *Fortune* magazine article titled "Pets Are Basically People" described how Americans' spending per pet increased 25 percent from 2010 to 2016, mirroring humanlike perceptions of these animals. The article found that nearly 80 percent of Americans considered pets beloved family members compared to less than a fifth of people who stated their "pets are well cared for but still considered animals."[35] This humanizing tendency motivates spending on premium pet food, pet day care, and enhanced veterinary care, all intended to better nurture these animals.

Experimental research also demonstrates how humanization increases compassion toward pets. One study led by psychologist Max Butterfield found that asking people to consider a dog's capacity for humanlike traits (i.e., a sense of humor, being a good listener) increased their willingness to adopt a dog compared to asking people to consider a dog's capacity for mere doglike traits (i.e., obeying commands or having a good sense of smell).[36] Slight shifts toward an anthropomorphizing mind-set can produce greater concern toward animal welfare.

Wayne Hsiung, cofounder of Direct Action Everywhere, an international animal rights organization, described to me how recognizing animals' humanlike qualities helped spark his interest in animal advocacy.[37] Although Hsiung does not overstate animals' mental similarities to humans, he described to me how several personal experiences highlighted to him how animals' "capacity for suffering is similar to ours." One was a childhood trip to a restaurant in China where patrons could order animals to be killed and cooked on the spot. Seeing dogs dragged to the kitchen that he says were "clearly scared, trapped, and alone" immediately compelled him to save them. Hsiung also described his first encounter with a bull, accidentally spooking it after grabbing its neck. Hsiung says the bull "shriveled up, he reared up, and stepped back, I could just see in his eyes . . . There are all these things that happen to us [humans] when we're scared." When I asked Hsiung about parallels between human rights and animal rights, he said, "I see them as the same movement," noting that both movements oppose "otherization" and the idea that "different is inferior." Hsiung told me that his first organizing experiences around racial injustice enabled him to see the parallel struggles between animals and marginalized humans, motivating his work in fighting for the humane treatment of animals.

I also spoke with Glenn Greenwald, who is known for his Pulitzer Prize–winning reporting of Edward Snowden's global surveillance disclosures.[38] Greenwald has devoted most of his career to championing civil rights and civil liberties, and in recent years he has also become a staunch animal rights advocate, opening a stray animal shelter in Rio de Janeiro staffed by homeless people. Similar to Hsiung, he described how his interest in human rights informed his animal rights advocacy, identifying the common thread between the two causes as "suffering combined with voicelessness and powerlessness." Greenwald added that to promote the cause of animal rights, "Strategically, being able to humanize animals and getting people to empathize with their suffering and the way they experience the world is important," noting "dogs are a gateway drug into animal rights" because of their human likeness. Again, Greenwald speaks to the importance of humanizing animals to promote moral concern.

The organization People for the Ethical Treatment of Animals (PETA) makes extreme arguments for animals' human likeness in dissuading people from eating meat or wearing fur. In a 2010 demonstration, PETA members wrapped themselves in cellophane, doused themselves in fake blood, and placed themselves in human-sized supermarket packaging. They explained this stunt on their website by stating, "All meat comes from somebody. And when you show human bodies in those neatly plastic-wrapped supermarket packages, the point hits home . . . every piece of meat comes from an individual who suffered miserably and died violently."[39] This analogy, heavy-handed as it might be, nonetheless underscores how equating animal suffering with human suffering can generate moral concern. That most cultures use different words for the same animal when it is cooked (e.g., beef, pork) versus when it is alive (e.g., cow, pig) likely helps people rationalize eating meat without considering the animal's former sentience.

Early research on this topic by psychologist Scott Plous corroborates how humanness confers moral status to animals. Plous presented participants with six animals, a Gorilla, Black Rhinoceros, Hooded Crane, Hierro Giant Lizard, Giant Catfish, and Tooth Cave Ground Beetle and asked them to assess (a) how similar to humans each animal was and (b) how important it was to save each animal from extinction. People's preference for saving the animal corresponded tightly with perceptions of its human likeness, with people rating the gorilla the most humanlike and most worthy of protection, and people rating the beetle the least humanlike and least worthy.[40]

Other research shows how anthropomorphism can promote wildlife conservation, suggesting that people prioritize saving endangered species that look the most humanlike.[41] Scientific historian Gregg Mitman notes that various anthropomorphic media depictions of elephants in particular have furthered public sympathy for their protection. For example, in a review of conservationist Cynthia Moss's *Elephant Memories*, which chronicles Moss's thirteen-year study of an extended elephant family in Kenya, Mitman states that the book "did much to promote pachyderm personalities and instill in the public a belief in their moral rights."[42] In *Elephant Memories*, Moss describes elephants burying their dead and tending to a wounded family member that had been shot. A *New York Times* review of the book read,

"One is soon swept away by this 'Babar' for adults . . . One wants to curse human civilization and cry out, 'Now God stand up for the elephants!'"[43]

Wildlife advocates have also used human likeness to promote the conservation of whales, orangutans (animals that conservationists describe as "among our cousins," and "one of our closest living relatives"[44]) and, of course, chimpanzees. As noted in this book's introduction, the Great Ape Project, an organization established to confer legal rights to chimpanzees, argues for these rights based on their humanlike capacities.[45]

Many cultures that anthropomorphize animals also treat them more protectively. The Nayaka people of South India, for example, anthropomorphize animals such as elephants (deeming them capable of humanlike wisdom) and treat them with empathy as a result.[46] Anthropologists Danny Naveh and Nurit Bird-David write of how the Nayaka people forgave an elephant that killed two Nayaka brothers because of how deeply they understood its personal history. Relatives of the two slain brothers called this animal "the elephant who walks alone" because it used to wander the forest alongside another elephant that the Forest Department had since captured. They attributed the elephant's aggression to its grief and loneliness resulting from losing a companion.[47] This extreme anthropomorphism of attributing complex humanlike emotions and motives to the elephant enabled the Nayaka people to empathize with the elephant and forgive it.

Beyond animals, anthropomorphism can enhance moral concern toward nature generally. A recent example of this comes from the Indian state of Uttarakhand where in 2017 the high court declared the Ganga and Yamuna rivers to be "living entities." This edict means that harming the river through pollution is legally equivalent to harming a human being.[48] Similarly, in 2017, the Maori people in New Zealand fought for their river, the Whanganui, to be recognized as an ancestor and won their case. This victory means the law no longer distinguishes between harming the Maori tribe and harming the river. Human status grants the river human rights.

* * * *

IN THE years following the 2007 publication of our psychological theory of anthropomorphism, it has become a more serious topic of scientific inquiry in psychology and beyond. Examples of the link between anthropomorphism and moral care are now plentiful. One study showed how anthropomorphizing a car or personal computer reduces willingness to replace these objects.[49] Another study showed that children's anthropomorphism of a robot reduced their willingness to put the robot in a closet (out of concern for the robot's welfare and a desire not to hurt its feelings).[50]

One experiment took anthropomorphism to the extreme, demonstrating the ease with which people humanize and consequently empathize with vegetables. This study, led by psychologist Jeroen Vaes, presented participants with images of vegetables like eggplants and zucchinis being swabbed with a Q-tip (a neutral action) or pricked by a needle (a "painful" action). Vaes measured participants' brain responses to both types of images using electroencephalography. Sometimes, participants learned that each vegetable had a human name like "Laura" and "Carlo" and other times the vegetables went unnamed. When, during the experimental task, participants viewed human-named vegetables pierced by a needle, their brains responded with greater activity consistent with an empathic reaction. When participants viewed unnamed vegetables pierced by a needle their response was similar to viewing it being swabbed by a Q-tip.[51]

All these studies start to make us seem a bit odd or at least suggest that adults are indistinguishable from children crying over a prized teddy bear's arm getting ripped apart. Yet they speak to humans' extraordinary capacity for social thought, showing that we are so capable of viewing the world in social terms that we extend social attributes toward entities like zucchini that are incapable of social interaction. These studies also demonstrate the fundamental power and flexibility of seeing human. Once triggered to see the slightest bit of humanness in another entity, whether animal, vegetable, or mineral, we consider it to be worthy of moral rights, including freedom from harm and basic dignity. The importance that we place on humans means that we do incredible things on humans' behalf. The next two chapters describe this phenomenon to illustrate just how capable other humans are of influencing and motivating us to act.

CHAPTER 4

Human Influence as the Engine of Action

OUTSIDE OF WRITING AS AN ACADEMIC PSYCHOLOGIST, I have also dabbled in cultural criticism. I wrote music and concert reviews for the *Columbia Spectator*, our daily college newspaper, and later wrote about music under a pseudonym, Sam Ada, for *Fader* magazine. I grew up revering people who wrote about art, film, music, and books and can better recall several Roger Ebert film reviews and Minya Oh *Source* magazine music reviews than the works they were reviewing. My respect for the cultural critic's profession, however, began waning around the turn of the twenty-first century, as I felt that reviews became highly homogenous. That is, I started seeing outsized consensus in reviews of various cultural products. Films like *Lost in Translation* or music like the Libertines' *Up the Bracket* album received universal acclaim whereas works like Liz Phair's 2003 self-titled album and Adam Sandler's film *Mr. Deeds* received universal scorn.

Perhaps art had simply gotten less complex and easier to sort into good and bad buckets. Yet I also noticed that this tendency for consensus—particularly among music critics—coincided with two technological developments: the rise of social media websites like Friendster, Facebook, and MySpace and the rise of file-sharing services like Napster and Limewire. As I have written elsewhere, the combination of these two forces seems to have produced a decline in music criticism with reviews reflecting the crowd's opinions rather than an individual's evaluation of the artistic product.[1]

Let me explain: Prior to file-sharing services and torrent websites, music albums landed exclusively in the hands of music critics before their release. These critics would listen to them well before the general public could and preview them for the rest of the world in their reviews. Once the internet made music easily accessible and allowed even advanced releases to leak through online social networks, availability of new music became democratized, which meant critics no longer had unique access. That is, critics and laypeople alike could obtain new music simultaneously. Social media services also enabled people to publicize their views on new songs, list their new favorite bands in their MySpace bios, and argue over new music endlessly on message boards. The result was that critics now could access the opinions of the masses on a particular album before writing their reviews. Thus, instead of music reviews guiding popular opinion toward art (as they did in preinternet times), music reviews began to reflect—consciously or subconsciously—public opinion. Given that public opinion tends to crystallize into a generally positive or generally negative view of a particular object, cultural criticism then began to reproduce this polarization. Whereas music reviews initially reflected the views of independent minds, the internet age changed that. The newly unavoidable exposure to other humans meant that cultural criticism has come to reflect popular opinion.

A few years ago, I finally encountered empirical research that supported my pet theory on cultural criticism's decline. This research, led by sociologist Matthew Salganik, generated an online music market in which over 14,000 participants listened to songs from musicians that at the time were unknown.[2] In one experimental treatment, the "independent" condition, participants learned only the name of the song and the band and could rate the songs from one to five stars and download the song if they wanted it. In eight other treatments that comprised the "social influence" condition, participants learned the same song and band names as well as an additional critical bit of information—namely, other participants' downloads and star ratings of each song. In other words, these treatments simulated the circumstances of the modern internet where we are subjected to others' opinions constantly. Compared with listeners in the independent condition in which opinions were private, listeners in the social influence worlds sorted songs readily into "good" and "bad" piles, with some songs receiving many downloads and other songs receiving only a few. In the independent world, no such consensus on good or bad songs emerged as there was no observable opinion to sway the success or failure of a particular song.

What Salganik's study shows, ultimately, is that absent exposure to other people's opinions, the success or failure of cultural products is relatively arbitrary. In the real world, our preferences for music, food, sneakers, or hand soap largely result from encounters with other people's preferences. Given the psychological significance we ascribe to human beings, it is unsurprising that their opinions influence our tastes and actions so profoundly.

The most impressive empirical demonstration of human influence, in my view, comes from one of psychology's most famous studies: Stanley Milgram's 1963 demonstration of obedience to authority.[3] Twenty years ago, if you were to tell a fellow airplane passenger that you were a professional psychologist, this would evoke images of Sigmund Freud or Dr. Phil; today, Milgram's rising celebrity has helped people understand that there is another group of psychologists that exists, one that performs research.

Milgram's study of obedience has become such a known cultural reference it is almost not even worth describing here. Most people know a version of the study in which a Yale experimenter in a white lab coat asks participants to administer increasingly severe electric shocks to another individual who eventually writhes in pain. When the experimenter asked one group of participants (the "predictor group") to predict how many individuals would inflict the maximum level of shock (450 volts), they estimated on average that only 1 percent would proceed. In fact, 65 percent of those who participated in the focal study (the "study" group) administered the maximum voltage. Despite humans' aversion to harm, the commands of a powerful authority figure to administer electric shocks led participants to obey.

Less commonly known is that Milgram conducted multiple versions of this study to determine how to turn up or turn off obedience to authority.[4] In these studies, Milgram found the factor that most affected obedience rates was the presence of another human. In a version of the study where subjects participated alongside two peers who refused to administer the electric shocks, only 10 percent of subjects obeyed. In a version where a peer administered the shocks, 93 percent obeyed. Milgram's studies demonstrate the power of another human being to sway our gravest actions.

That other people influence us to do things is unsurprising. Every McDonald's sign we see proclaiming "Billions and Billions Served" reminds us that the behavior of others still serves as a powerful marketing tool. Research on the power of social influence pervades popular culture thanks to best-selling books like Robert Cialdini's *Influence*, Malcolm Gladwell's *The Tipping Point*, and more recently, Jonah Berger's *Contagious*. These masterworks recognize other humans as the most powerful force behind changing people's minds, generating collective action, and transmitting viral information. These books have helped spread the gospel that, even in the age of individualism, what fundamentally drives behavior is what other people do.

Despite the rise of thought leadership on this topic, we will discover that, in fact, people underestimate the breadth and depth of other humans' influence to change behavior. First, people underestimate the ability of human influence to change societally and politically important behaviors, not simply trivial ones like buying hamburgers or listening to pop songs. Second, people underestimate the depth of just how much humans change our minds and therefore alter our behavior. Let's look at some examples of humans' capacity to change what I consider consequential behaviors and then we'll discover evidence that we underestimate the degree to which other humans change our minds.

The Breadth of Human Influence

One case of humans' capacity to change a consequential behavior comes from a Facebook experiment during the 2010 midterm congressional elections.[5] The experiment involved nearly 61 million Facebook users and aimed to increase voter turnout by exposing people to information about others' voting behavior. Researchers randomly assigned some Facebook users to a control condition that received no information. In a separate, purely informational condition, a message atop users' newsfeed encouraged voting, provided information about local polling places, and contained a clickable "I Voted" button alongside a counter of how many other Facebook users had clicked the button to indicate that they had voted. In a third "social" condition, users received the exact same information atop their newsfeed alongside faces of six of the users' randomly selected friends who had also clicked the "I Voted" button.

Researchers tracked participants' self-reported voting (via clicks on the "I Voted" button) and frequency of participants clicking to find their local polling place. The researchers also validated participants' self-reported vote through accessing publicly available voting records. Critically, users in the social condition (who saw friends' faces coupled with peer voting information) voted more than users in the other two conditions and clicked more to find their polling place. Furthermore, the purely informational and control conditions did not differ in getting people to vote. In other words, seeing the faces of one's friends—human beings—alongside information about voting drove behavior, whereas seeing information alone did not. The social message that included people's faces, when amplified across 61 million people, accounted for a 340,000-person increase in voting in 2010 (according to the researchers' estimates), a 0.6 percent uptick from the previous midterm election.

Other work has used social norms to change another important behavior: adolescent bullying. Two separate studies led by psychologist Betsy Levy Paluck demonstrated how changing specific individuals' behavior in the high school social ecosystem can reduce bullying across an entire school.[6] As many of us recall from high school, certain students are bestowed the status of being "popular" and Levy Paluck showed how to leverage this popularity for impressive ends. In her first bullying study, she and sociologist Hana Shepherd identified highly connected clique leaders (i.e., the popular kids) in a Connecticut public high school and randomly assigned some of them to a participate in an intervention program to promote anti-peer-harassment norms.

The program involved leading a schoolwide assembly called "Names Can Really Hurt Us" where students discussed verbal and physical abuse. Students who led the assembly also later conducted publicity campaigns to remind others about the assembly's themes. The researchers surveyed students immediately after the assembly and at the school year's end about their social networks, their perceptions of collective norms (i.e., what people think is acceptable behavior), and their experiences of harassment. The researchers found that students with more social ties to the popular kids who had undergone the anti-peer-harassment intervention dramatically shifted their attitudes and perceptions of norms around bullying. Exposure to the intervention group led people to describe harassment as more undesirable and abnormal.

In a later experiment, Levy Paluck and colleagues studied a similar conflict intervention in fifty-six New Jersey middle schools. The researchers randomly assigned groups of twenty to thirty-two students in half of the schools to attend a program encouraging publicly opposing bullying, ostracism, and spreading mean rumors. The other schools did not have students attend such a program and served as control group schools.

In schools that received the intervention, teacher reports of disciplinary events dropped by 30 percent over the course of the year. Students in the intervention schools (compared to the control schools) also reported talking with friends more about reducing bullying and wearing wristbands to promote an anticonflict message. Furthermore, as in Levy Paluck's prior study, within the intervention schools, the popular kids had the greatest effect on reducing conflict. When just one-fifth of the students assigned to the conflict reduction intervention were popular (assessed through reports that these students were highly socially connected), the effect on reducing disciplinary reports was twice as strong as the average.

Additional survey data showed that these students affected change by communicating social norms around conflict. Average students who became "exposed" to these popular students expressed greater disapproval of conflict. Overall, this work demonstrates that altering the behavior of a few key human beings can substantially reduce conflict and aggression within a broader community.

Just as Levy Paluck's work demonstrates how humans can change minds about nonfatal violence in middle schools and high schools, an organization called Cure Violence has employed a similar logic to stop fatal gun violence in high-risk neighborhoods. Founded in 2000 by epidemiologist Gary Slutkin, who had previously worked on treating infectious diseases like AIDS and tuberculosis in Africa, Cure Violence models the spread of violence like the spread of these diseases. Cure Violence began by working to curb gun violence in Chicago's most dangerous neighborhoods and has since expanded globally, helping stop violence in South Africa, Syria, Honduras, and beyond. Treating violence as an infectious disease involves identifying and treating the highest-risk individuals most prone to violence and therefore most likely to "spread" violence to others. The Cure Violence approach also involves changing norms around violence to mitigate violence contagion, just as promoting norms around vaccination or condom use can prevent the contagion of diseases.

Cure Violence's primary method involves targeting high-risk individuals and changing social norms by deploying "violence interrupters" who respond to specific shootings and identify people who might retaliate. These interrupters "cool off" potential retaliators by removing them from the conflict and follow up with them over time to deescalate the situation. Interrupters monitor violent neighborhoods and stay "on call" to respond immediately when shootings occur. The interrupters' effectiveness comes from their credibility—many of them are former gang members, residents of the neighborhoods they monitor, and many have experience as both victims and former perpetrators of violence. Community members trust them and willingly build relationships with the interrupters to avoid violent situations.

The Cure Violence method is verifiably successful, with independent scientific evaluations of Baltimore and Chicago indicating that shootings and killings drop by between 41 percent and 73 percent in neighborhoods that Cure Violence monitors.[7] Only recently, however, has evidence emerged to explain why the method sees positive results—namely, interrupters change minds and change norms. In an evaluation of the Baltimore Cure Violence program from 2007 to 2009, young male residents from dangerous neighborhoods that had implemented the program and neighborhoods that had not were questioned.[8] Survey participants in Cure Violence neighborhoods reported greater opposition to using guns to settle disputes, and this opposition persisted over a year after the program began. This finding suggests that exposure to the violence interrupters robustly changed minds about violence.

More recently, an evaluation of New York City's Cure Violence program between 2014 and 2016 surveyed young males in intervention neighborhoods and comparison neighborhoods, showing a similar pattern.[9] A year or more after neighborhoods implemented the Cure Violence program, survey respondents reported more opposition to using violence in conflict situations. Although many anti-gun-violence efforts often focus on increasing policing and jail time or simply reducing access to guns, Cure Violence's efforts suggest that contact with the right human beings carrying the right message might be more powerful.

The power of other humans to change minds and guide behavior extends to reducing prejudice as well. One striking study demonstrated how a brief conversation with another person dramatically reduced prejudice against transgender individuals.[10] Political scientists David Broockman and Joshua Kalla conducted an experiment that sent canvassers door-to-door to talk to registered voters in Miami, Florida. In one experimental condition designed to persuade, canvassers told voters about an upcoming vote to repeal a law protecting transgender people and then asked them to think about a time that others had evaluated them negatively for "being different." The conversation typically lasted around ten minutes. In a control condition, canvassers focused their conversation on recycling instead. Prior to the canvassing, and at intervals of three days, three weeks, six weeks, and three months after canvassing, these voters answered survey questions assessing attitudes toward transgender people.

At every time point after canvassing, attitudes toward transgender people improved for participants exposed to the persuasion intervention. These participants reported more positivity and tolerance toward transgender people and showed greater support for antidiscrimination laws. Broockman and Kalla stated that this single ten-minute con-versation reduced transphobia to a greater extent than Americans' average reduction in homophobia between 1998 and 2012. Of course, exposure to another human on its own did not reduce prejudice, but rather the nature of the conversation was what changed attitudes so significantly. By asking people to consider their own experiences of stigma, the canvassers implicitly urged participants to take the per-spective of a transgender person—to occupy the minds of people fac-ing prejudice for nonconformity. In fact, Broockman suggests that a similar canvassing experiment of his failed to persuade people around abortion because of difficulty in engaging people in perspective-taking on that issue.[11] The exercise of considering others' desires, feelings, thoughts, and beliefs during this experience proves to be a formidable way to change minds.

The Power of Daughters

Broockman and Kalla's work provides evidence of a simple, broader phenomenon: considering the full humanity and plight of someone who one might not naturally consider can promote positivity toward that person's entire social group. This is why having a daughter seems to be the most effective intervention for improving men's attitudes toward women more broadly.

Sportswriter Bill Simmons illustrated this phenomenon when reflecting on his career prior to having a daughter. In a *Hollywood Reporter* interview, Simmons recalled ridiculing the professional women's basketball league (the WNBA) stating, "I was definitely a chauvinist with men's and women's sports before. I'd always make WNBA jokes and stuff like that. And now I'm like a feminist, and it's all because of her."[12] Simmons faced considerable scrutiny for his comments, with many remarking it unfortunate that it took having a daughter for Simmons to confront his chauvinism. More recently, public figures from Matt Damon to Mitch McConnell to Geraldo Rivera have all used some variant of the phrase "as the father of daughters" to preface their public disapproval of sexual misconduct.[13] Like Simmons, they too faced mockery, yet scientific evidence suggests their experience is real: daughters reduce sexism by heightening attention to the plight of women more generally.

In one example of the power of daughters, finance scholars Henrik Cronqvist and Frank Yu studied what happens to firms when the CEO has a daughter versus when the CEO does not.[14] They assessed S&P 500 firms' investment in corporate social responsibility (CSR) efforts from 1992 to 2012 and found that when a firm's CEO has a daughter, it spends 10.4 percent more on CSR. The effect was strongest for investments in diversity policies that promote gender equity. Although Cronqvist and Yu's study cannot establish the causal effect of daughters, it supports the possibility that having a daughter might prompt CEOs to adopt pro-female attitudes that trickle down to a firm's behavior.

Research by economists Paul Gompers and Sophie Wang shows a similar effect for venture capital partners with daughters.[15] They found that among 1,403 investors in start-ups backed by venture capitalists from 1990 to 2016, male partners with more daughters than sons were 24 percent more likely to hire a woman. This increased gender diversity also enhanced profitability. These findings suggest daughters expose fathers to women's inner lives (their wants, capabilities, and aspirations), and this consideration improves behavior toward women more broadly.

The effect of daughters extends to the legal realm too, as political scientists Adam Glynn and Maya Sen have shown that judges with daughters tend to vote in a more pro-female fashion.[16] Glynn and Sen examined 224 United States Court of Appeals judges who voted on cases related to gender discrimination between 1996 and 2002. They found that having at least one daughter translates into a 9 percent increase in a judge ruling in a pro-female fashion. Although the explanation for these effects is not completely clear, Glynn and Sen consider several interpretations and ultimately suggest the pro-female shift in judgment results from simple learning (especially given that their sample is primarily male). Having a daughter acquaints fathers with issues related to reproductive rights and discrimination based on pregnancy that they otherwise might not encounter firsthand. Exposure to these issues then tangibly affects judges' decisions.

The Surprising Depth of Human Influence

Up to this point, we have seen that the presence of other humans influences several consequential behaviors from voting to bullying, gun violence to prejudice, and corporate social responsibility to legal rulings. I shared these examples to illustrate the breadth of humans' capacity to influence, recognizing that for many readers humans' capacity to change minds might seem obvious. We are constantly being sold things as a result of targeted marketing. We have heeded parental advice that just because our friends jump off a cliff doesn't mean we should, too. We have become increasingly aware of the power of social media and cable news to influence our political views and we are hypervigilant toward any potential propaganda. Yet, repeatedly, when surveys ask people to guess the ability of other humans to change minds, they underestimate just how powerful human influence is.

A classic illustration of underestimating human influence comes from a study led by psychologist Jessica Nolan on energy consumption.[17] Nolan analyzed phone interviews with 810 California residents that asked how influential four different factors were in guiding residents to conserve energy: saving money, protecting the environment, benefiting future generations, and following social norms (i.e., the degree to which other humans are also conserving energy). This survey revealed people indicated social norms to be the least influential factor of the four. In phase two of the study, the researchers actually visited 981 households in San Marcos, California, to place various signs on the doors of homes urging people to conserve energy, later surveying these households and measuring their energy usage.

Critically, the researchers created four different door-hanger signs that either argued for energy conservation in terms of saving money, protecting the environment, benefiting society, or offering social proof (this message indicated that "a majority of your neighbors are turning off their lights to conserve energy"). When Nolan measured household energy use one month after the initial placement of door-hanger signs, she found that contrary to what people reported in phone interviews, the social proof messaging reduced household energy consumption to the greatest degree. Interviews with these households also confirmed that those who received the social norm information were least likely to report being consciously influenced by the argument on the door-hanger.

Everyday people are not the only ones who underestimate the power of social norms to change conservation-related behavior. In another study, Nolan and colleagues asked energy experts from the United States and Dubai to evaluate different energy conservation appeals.[18] The researchers called up energy companies, surveyed an energy conservation listserv, and attended an energy conservation conference to find these experts. They then asked them to evaluate the effectiveness of the same energy conservation messages used in their California household study—messages that emphasized environmental protection, saving money, societal benefit, a neutral message, and social norms (saving energy because one's neighbors are saving energy). Just like the California residents, these experts rated the social norms message as less motivating than a message to save money and indicated that, of all the messages, they would be least likely to use the social norms message to promote energy conservation. When Nolan presented the energy experts with evidence of social norms' effectiveness, they embraced this appeal, but they required hard data to do so. In other words, even experts underestimated the power of other people to change minds and drive action.

In related work, psychologist Markus Barth and colleagues interviewed German electric vehicle experts and nonexperts about people's willingness to adopt these vehicles.[19] Both sets of interviewees most often said cost-related factors like purchasing price were most likely to drive adoption, with nobody mentioning the potential influence of social norms on electric car use. In a follow-up study, Barth asked 601 people about various factors (including issues related to cost and social norms) that might predict their acceptance of electric vehicles. As with Nolan's research, Barth's study showed that social norms—whether other people approve of and express interest in driving electric vehicles—significantly predicted people's personal willingness to use an electric vehicle. Again, this research demonstrates that people underestimate human beings' capacity to change minds. Social norms indeed drove willingness to adopt electric vehicles despite none of the initial interviewees anticipating their influence.

Underestimating Our Own Influence

The research we have seen in this chapter so far suggests that other people powerfully influence our behavior, and we underestimate their ability to do so. Yet another line of research suggests that we also underestimate our own ability—as humans—to get other people to alter their behavior. A recent legal decision surrounding the suicide of eighteen-year-old Conrad Roy illustrated the deadly effects of underestimating one's influence. Roy, who had long suffered from depression and social anxiety, eventually killed himself by inhaling carbon monoxide while parked in his truck at a Kmart. Just before the incident, Roy stepped out of his truck and expressed doubts about suicide on a call to his girlfriend Michelle Carter. Carter then urged him to "fucking get back in."[20] In days just prior to Roy's death, Carter also texted Roy several times to encourage his suicide, writing, "Just go somewhere in your truck and no one is really out there right now because it's an awkward time. If you don't do it now you're never gonna do it, and you can say you'll do it tomorrow, but you probably won't."[21] As a jury convicted Carter of involuntary manslaughter, experts suggested that the case may set a new legal precedent for criminalizing speech. A day after Roy's death, Carter posted on Roy's Facebook wall, "I'm sorry I couldn't save you, I'm sorry I let you do this." Her apology, albeit perhaps self-serving, suggests that she never understood the power of her words to drive Roy to death.

Extensive research led by psychologists Vanessa Bohns and Francis Flynn demonstrates that even in an age where anyone can be an "influencer," people consistently underestimate their influence on others. The general methodological design documenting this tendency—what Bohns and Flynn call "the underestimation of compliance effect"—tends to be similar across studies.[22] In the first phase, they ask participants to predict how many people they would have to ask to get a certain number of them to do something (e.g., "How many people would you have to ask to get five to agree to fill out a short survey?"). In the second phase, the researchers send people out into the world to actually ask around. Bohns and Flynn then compare people's estimates with the actual number of people it takes to get compliance.

Their work finds that college students underestimate, by as much as 50 percent, the number of people they would have to ask to get people to fill out a survey, lend them a cell phone to make a call, escort them to the campus gym, or contribute money to a cancer charity.[23] And people not only underestimate their influence over others to comply with requests for help, but they also underestimate how easily they can get others to behave unethically—for example, telling a white lie (i.e., sign a form stating the participant gave them an introduction to a college course) and defacing a library book by writing "pickle" inside of it.[24] For good or for ill, we consistently fail to recognize how much power we have, as humans, over others' behaviors. This also means that the few of us who do recognize our influence can wield it adeptly.

One recent study by management scholar Mahdi Roghanizad and Bohns provides a critical caveat to the underestimation of compliance effect.[25] This study again compared help requests over email versus face-to-face requests. As in previous studies, people underestimated their capacity to get others to comply with a face-to-face request to complete a questionnaire. However, people overestimated—by a factor of more than twenty-six—their capacity to get others to comply with an email request to complete a questionnaire. Roghanizad and Bohns found that this overestimation occurs because recipients of email requests are particularly suspicious of such emails and hesitate to comply. On the other hand, face-to-face requests—because they involve interacting with a real, live, present human being—are far more influential, a fact that study participants consistently underestimated.

Rather than present the totality of evidence on humans changing minds, my goal is to convince you how little we appreciate this phenomenon. What we have seen here is that people change their minds on major societal and political issues, they do so far more effectively than pragmatic appeals, and they change minds to a degree we do not anticipate. To explain why human influence holds such sway, social scientists have offered two broad reasons. First, humans represent a useful source of information—it makes sense to do what we believe other people are doing. Second, fitting in with others, by doing what they do, feels good. One study of brain activation during instances of conformity—for example, male participants agreeing with others' judgments of women's attractiveness—showed that changing one's mind to conform to others' opinions recruits brain regions associated with intrinsic reward.[26] This study provides an important corrective to the idea that people resist conformity to avoid feeling like "sheep" and contradicts author Rita Mae Brown's claim that "The reward for conformity [is] that everyone likes you but yourself."[27] Instead, it seems aligning ourselves with other humans makes us feel pretty good.

CHAPTER 5

Human-Centered Motivation

BECAUSE OF THE VALUE WE ASSOCIATE WITH OTHER HUMANS, they have a vast capacity to change our minds, and in this chapter we also see how humans motivate us. The psychological significance of humans leads us to work harder when we know our work can benefit others. This tendency to expend effort to have social impact is what psychologists call prosocial motivation, and it often drives people to work harder for others than for personal benefit alone.[1] Anyone with children has experienced this—for example, doing something for them (perhaps waking up early) that you would rarely do just for yourself. Many of us also work long hours at mind-numbing jobs primarily to feed our families, and the motivating effects of other people extend beyond our loved ones as well.

Take my friend John, whom I have known since high school. Outside of his day job, John runs a college access program for first-generation, low-income high school students. He describes his work by stating, "I'm always doing stuff that either I never have done for myself or would drag my feet doing . . . for them I would do it in a heartbeat." He told me, "I hate professional networking, but I will make that call or email or meeting for them and actually enjoy it." Another example is navigating financial aid packages. He said he often makes cold calls to financial aid offices and told me, "Asking and advocating for someone other than yourself is so much easier for me, not to mention rewarding."

John's experience is not uncommon, as experimental research shows. Psychologist Adam Grant and colleagues conducted a now famous study on prosocial motivation at a University of Michigan call center where fund-raisers called Michigan alumni to ask for donations.[2] Call center work, it turns out, tends to be monotonous and dreary. Even though most of the money these workers raise supports useful causes like scholarships for students, workers rarely interact with the scholarship recipients and therefore rarely see their impact on other humans. Grant and his team decided to test whether better highlighting this impact affects motivation.

In one condition of their experiment, they brought into the call center a University of Michigan scholarship student to share a testimonial with some employees. The student spent ten minutes telling the employees how their work made his scholarship possible and how it had benefited him. Employees in this group were the "human contact" group, encountering a real live human who praised their work for improving his well-being. Grant assigned other employees to two comparison groups. One served as the "pure control group" that had no contact with a scholarship student, and the other was a "letter control group" that read a letter by (but never met) the scholarship student expressing thanks and explaining how the scholarship donation money improved his life.

Grant then tracked each group's work performance. He assessed the minutes each caller group spent on the phone per week and donation money raised, both two weeks prior to and one month after the intervention. He found that exposure to a human being in person, even for just ten minutes, dramatically increased minutes spent making calls. These employees spent on average 108 minutes prior to the exposure to 261 minutes after the exposure, significantly outperforming employees in the letter-only or no-contact groups. In addition, the employees who met with the scholarship student went on to raise almost twice as much money as those in the comparison groups.

This initial study involved fund-raising from people who might not typically donate to the university. However, in a follow-up study, Grant demonstrated that contact with a scholarship student motivated callers to contact repeat donors, generating a fivefold increase in revenue.[3] Grant and colleagues also replicated the effect of personal contact in another experiment that asked participants to help edit a student's job application cover letter. When participants merely saw the student or briefly chatted with him, they spent considerably more time editing the letter because they believed their effort would have more impact.[4] This research demonstrates that knowing one's impact, through firsthand contact with a human beneficiary, can inspire and motivate.

Grant's studies also speak to why corporate philanthropy programs, in which companies donate money to social causes, can increase motivation and performance. Although Grant's studies demonstrate the power of personal contact—there is nothing as motivating as a real live human—simply knowing that one's work improves other humans' welfare is highly motivating as well.

Large-scale analyses have demonstrated a positive link between corporate philanthropy and firm financial performance, but only recently has work examined how corporate philanthropy might boost individual performance and motivation.[5] For example, research by strategy scholar Vanessa Burbano shows that people will work for less money and perform beyond their pay-based duties after learning their employer invests in helping others.[6]

For one experiment, Burbano posed in an online marketplace as a "firm" recruiting workers for a very rote task. The task involved judging whether images of bodily cells were benign or malignant (based on various visual features). She randomly assigned participants to receive no additional information about the firm or to four conditions that informed participants in different ways about the firm's philanthropic efforts. These messages either stated that the firm donates 1 percent of its profits to charities like Red Cross or that the firm will donate a small amount to charity if the participant completes the task. She then asked them how much pay they would accept to perform the image interpretation task. She also provided optional nonrequired questions that constituted "extra work." Participants who learned of the firm's philanthropy accepted 11 percent lower wages to perform the task and did more of the extra work for no additional pay. These findings suggest that opportunities to help others, through the firm's charitable contributions, enhanced performance.

In a follow-up study, Burbano again posed as a fictional company in a different online marketplace where participants can "bid" for various jobs. She advertised a data entry task for a start-up company, informing some participants about the company's social responsibility goals (e.g., the company desires to have a "positive impact on the broader community") and providing others with no social responsibility information. Participants who received social responsibility information bid 44 percent lower for the job compared to those who did not, indicating they would take less money to work for a company that helps other humans.

Other work by economists Mirco Tonin and Michael Vlassopolous also demonstrates that these prosocial incentives make people work harder.[7] They recruited students for an online experiment that involved performing, as in Burbano's studies, an exceedingly dull task involving entering bibliographic records into an online repository (social scientists like measuring motivation using tasks that are inherently demotivating). In a condition involving purely financial incentives, participants received pay for their performance. In a separate condition, participants received pay for their performance and learned that the research team would donate money on participants' behalf to a charity of their choice (including charities that promoted human rights and helped the elderly). Exposure to this prosocial incentive increased productivity on the bibliographic entry task by 13 percent and boosted performance in particular for workers with the lowest productivity.

The research mimics what my MBA students often tell me about being willing to work harder when they have opportunities to do something good and about forgoing higher-paying jobs for work that has more social impact. Perhaps, I get a self-selecting group of students given that I often teach an ethics class (that happens to be an elective), but I do not think they are outliers—testimonials like these are seemingly everywhere. Take Jim Ziolowski, who founded BuildOn, a nonprofit that provides youth services in underserved neighborhoods to try to break the cycle of poverty. Ziolowski describes entering General Electric's financial management program that ensured him a high-paying career but quitting after fifteen months to found BuildOn, a more human-focused organization.[8] Take Scott Harrison, who describes living a "selfish life as a nightclub promoter in New York City" before deciding to develop charity:water, a nonprofit dedicated to bringing clean water to people around the world. Or take Yvonne Carter, who describes leaving a high-paying career in finance to become an asset manager for a nonprofit that helps revive struggling neighborhoods.[9] Of course, when relying on anecdotes like these, we are more likely to hear the stories of those who gave up financial stability for social good than those who took the reverse career path. Nonetheless, I find these stories increasingly common as I encounter young people entering the workforce who seek to have an impact on others.

Research using real companies empirically backs these stories. Management and strategy scholars Christiane Bode and Jasjit Singh surveyed 665 employees at a consulting firm and found that 87 percent of them would take a pay cut to work on a social impact initiative.[10] This initiative offered discounted services to nongovernmental organizations such as female micro-entrepreneurs in rural communities (rather than to corporate clients). Interviews with the company's employees revealed that employees' desire to tangibly improve others' lives drove actual participation in the initiative. Other work by Bode, Singh, and strategy scholar Michelle Rogan showed that consulting employees participating in such a social initiative (that involved taking a pay cut) were more likely to stay with their firm.[11] This positive effect on retention again suggests that, even in a corporate, profit-driven setting, employees remain motivated to help other humans at the expense of their own earnings.

This work also indicates that people benefit most from corporate philanthropy efforts when directly participating in them. IBM has capitalized on this idea with a program that "loans out" tech-savvy employees to do pro bono work for social good initiatives. Employees take a leave from IBM to partner with organizations that promote health, education, and nonprofit entrepreneurship. So far, the program seems to have energized participants. Tom Eggebraaten, an eighteen-year IBM veteran and software engineer developer, worked on a project to deliver chemotherapy and cancer drugs in sub-Saharan Africa. He described how the experience rejuvenated him, stating, "I was . . . really able see my work in a different perspective. [That] renewed my passion for my day-to-day work. And I found a way to get my motivation back."[12]

A former student of mine, Ted, described the energizing effects of a single volunteering day as part of a corporate philanthropy initiative at Discover Financial Services. Ted and other Discover employees helped repaint buildings and build a playground in a city park. He told me, "The experience had a positive benefit back at the office because it gave everyone a low stakes place to work together and make connections outside their own department." And in terms of affecting employee motivation, he said the experience "made people feel more connected and committed to the company." Again, although this is one individual story, Ted's experience demonstrates that people can and do feel better about their work when they feel it is tied to helping others.

For Love or for Money

So far, I have shared evidence—both anecdotal and research based—that people are motivated on behalf of helping others. However, those who believe that humans are rational, self-interested, cost-benefit maximizers might question whether prosocial incentives can compete with self-serving ones. The research we've seen so far only minimally addresses this issue, suggesting that people will do things on behalf of others, even sacrificing some of their own earnings to help other humans. Yet this does not tell us whether people are motivated to a greater degree to do something that benefits other humans than they are to do something that serves their own self-interests. The work by Ye Li and Margaret Lee that we learned about in the introduction suggests that people will indeed work harder on behalf of others. The totality of research on this topic, however, offers a slightly messier and nuanced picture, which we sort out below.

One question regarding prosocial motivation concerns the issue of stakes. Sure, people will work hard if it means that others get a few extra bucks, but what happens when this prosocial payoff is pitted against the possibility for a big personal payoff? The most direct test of this question comes from behavioral economist Alex Imas.[13] He designed a simple experiment to measure participants' effort on a task that required physical strength: how hard they could squeeze a hand dynamometer for sixty seconds. Participants learned either that they were performing the task for themselves (increased effort would earn them more money) or that they were performing the task for others (increased effort would trigger donations sent to the Make-a-Wish Foundation). Imas also varied the amount of money that participants could earn for themselves or for the charity.

Imas found that when the stakes were relatively low (at five cents per degree of effort), people expended more effort on behalf of the Make-a-Wish children than for themselves. However, when the stakes were relatively higher (at two dollars per degree of effort), effort did not differ between people working for themselves and people working for others. Thus, human-centered motivation appears more powerful than self-centered motivation in this study, but the effect weakens when the stakes are raised.

Other research comparing personal versus prosocial incentives using a hand-grip task found that people become more selfish as reward and effort increase.[14] Psychologist Patricia Lockwood and colleagues asked participants over several trials to decide between two options: squeezing a hand-grip with essentially no effort (the baseline option) or squeezing the hand-grip at varying higher effort levels to earn varying higher amounts of money (the alternate option). In addition, some participants learned that the money earned would go to them, whereas other participants learned that the money earned would go to others. When the effort required to earn money was low, participants expended this minimal effort to benefit both themselves and others. However, when the effort required to earn money was high, people expended greater effort to help themselves than to help others. When the stakes were higher, personal incentives outperformed prosocial ones.

Additional complexity to this issue of prosocial versus personal incentives is illustrated in a study of a very different "motivational" context. Behavioral economist Ayelet Gneezy and colleagues studied people's willingness to purchase a souvenir photograph at Disneyland.[15] Over 113,000 individuals rode a rollercoaster and afterward learned they could purchase a photo of them taken during the ride. Gneezy and colleagues established four separate pricing conditions to manipulate personal and prosocial incentives. In one condition, riders could purchase the photo for $12.95. In another, the price was $12.95 and riders learned that half of that money would be donated to charity (a patient support foundation). In a third condition, the price was "pay what you want" (PWYW)—riders could pay as little or as much as they wanted for the photo. And a fourth condition combined PWYW with charity—participants could pay whatever they wanted and learned that half of their payment would be donated to the patient support charity.

Several interesting findings emerged. First, few riders purchased the photographs in the two $12.95 conditions, suggesting simply people hesitate to spend money for a souvenir. However, purchase rates sky-rocketed in the two PWYW conditions, with riders' willingness to purchase in the "pure" PWYW condition almost doubling their willingness to pay in the PWYW-plus-charity condition. This finding could suggest that people were more motivated by selfishness than the opportunity to benefit others, yet this is only part of the story. Examining how much participants who purchased the photograph (in the two PWYW conditions) actually paid revealed that riders in the PWYW-plus-charity condition paid over five times as much as riders in the PWYW with no charitable opportunity: $5.33 per photo on average compared to $0.92. Thus, the PWYW-plus-charity condition produced the most profit for the theme park (even with lower overall sales).

This study demonstrates how personal and prosocial incentives interact. Comparing the opportunity to purchase a souvenir for free (if you want) with no questions asked versus an opportunity to purchase with a charitable contribution attached reveals that people clearly prefer no questions asked. However, the opportunity to buy a souvenir with a charitable component activates our social emotions—a little bit of empathy and perhaps some guilt as well—and these emotions motivate us to spend more to benefit others.

To this point, we have examined tasks like squeezing a hand-grip and buying a souvenir photo that are relatively divorced from job performance. However, other recent work examines how prosocial versus personal incentives affect a highly consequential workplace behavior: getting airline captains to increase their fuel efficiency on flights. Given that large-scale companies produce over one-fifth of carbon emissions in the United States, boosting fuel efficiency could dramatically affect the planet. Economist Greer Gosnell and colleagues thus explored incentivizing Virgin Atlantic captains to save fuel using three novel schemes.[16] Their experiment randomly assigned captains to three treatment groups and one control group that received no meaningful incentive. One treatment group of captains simply received feedback on their fuel efficiency performance from February to October 2014—this group's only "incentive" (if you could call it that) was feedback. Another group of captains received this feedback and set personalized targets to improve their fuel efficiency. If captains met their targets, the research team told them, "Well done!" Thus, this second condition produced two small personal rewards: (1) goal completion and (2) recognition. A third condition used prosocial incentives to motivate captains. Captains set personal targets, received feedback, and learned that, for each target they met in a given month, the research team would donate 10 GBP (about 13 USD) to charity.

So, which group performed the best? The prosocial incentives group outperformed the control group in improving efficiency but performed no better than the group that set personal targets. In fact, all incentive treatments improved performance compared to the control group. The prosocial incentive group did improve considerably compared to other groups on one critical metric, however: job satisfaction. Captains in the prosocial incentives group reported being 6.5 percent more satisfied with their job than captains in the control group, an increase on par with the difference between an employee in poor health and an employee in good health. Furthermore, job satisfaction was positively associated with job performance. Thus, prosocial incentives and personal incentives affected fuel efficiency equally, but prosocial incentives boosted job satisfaction, which may affect performance more durably.

In a very different workplace context, Adam Grant and organizational behavior scholar David Hofmann directly compared prosocial motivation versus personal motivation in getting doctors and nurses to wash their hands while on the job.[17] Hand washing is nontrivial, with research estimating that if health workers washed their hands more often, they could prevent 70 percent of patient hospital infections.[18] Yet only about 40 percent of health care professionals comply with hand-washing guidelines.[19] Grant and Hofmann experimented with personal and prosocial incentives by placing various signs on hand-washing stations in a hospital. Some signs emphasized the personal benefit of hand washing by stating, "Hand hygiene prevents you from catching diseases." Some emphasized the benefits to patients by stating, "Hand hygiene prevents patients from catching diseases." A control-condition sign simply stated "gel in, wash out."

The researchers measured the weight of soap dispensers below these signs two weeks prior to putting them up and then two weeks after. Although no meaningful changes occurred at the stations with the personal benefits signs or the control condition signs, soap use increased by 45 percent at stations with the sign promoting benefits for patients, suggesting that hand washing increased at the stations emphasizing benefits for others. Again, these results suggest that people will go beyond the bare minimum for their jobs to benefit others compared to benefiting only themselves.

Other work has compared prosocial incentives to personal incentives in collaborative contexts.[20] In one study, psychologist Lalin Anik distributed bonuses of two types to recreational dodgeball teams. Some teams received a "personal bonus" of twenty dollars for each player to spend on himself or herself. Other teams received a "prosocial bonus" of twenty dollars for each player to spend on a teammate. Two weeks later, dodgeball teams in the prosocial bonus condition performed better, almost doubling their win percentage compared with teams in the personal bonus condition.

Anik and colleagues showed similar effects for sales teams at a Belgian pharmaceutical company. Similar to the dodgeball study, they randomly assigned some sales teams to receive personal bonuses and others to receive prosocial bonuses. The researchers measured sales performance just prior to the bonus distribution and one month after the distribution. As we might expect by now, prosocial bonuses increased sales performance whereas personal bonuses had no measurable effect. Prosocial bonuses made employees aware they were working on behalf of their teammates, which improved team performance. These studies demonstrate that not only does effort increase when people are incentivized to do things for others but collaboration increases as well.

PollEverywhere, a company that provides online polling platforms for lectures and classrooms, implemented a peer bonus program (I will say more on these programs in the next chapter) that lets employees send gift cards to each other to recognize great work. Not only did employees enjoy the initiative, but the company also found that two-thirds of the peer bonuses were sent by employees working remotely, enabling them to feel more integrated in the organization.[21] Again, the opportunity to benefit others seemed to spark better collaboration than an opportunity to benefit themselves.

So, what distinguishes cases when prosocial incentives clearly beat personal incentives from cases when the winner is less clear? In situations that involve squeezing a hand-grip, deciding whether to purchase a rollercoaster souvenir, and saving fuel on an airline flight, personal incentives sometimes outperform prosocial ones or at least motivate people as much as prosocial incentives. In the dodgeball team, sales team, and hand-washing scenarios, prosocial incentives clearly outperform personal ones. The difference, as far as I can tell, is that the latter situations are ones that are clearly more collaborative, more social, and more naturally human centered—people depend on each other in these situations. Prosocial incentives seem particularly effective in contexts where humans are already top of mind. Still, even in less social situations, personal incentives rarely outperform opportunities to benefit others.

* * * *

HAVING DESCRIBED in chapters 2 and 3 the power of humans to imbue meals, massages, objects, and artwork with meaning, value, and morality, I hope chapters 4 and 5 have shown the very real consequences of humans' psychological impact. That is, other humans influence us to do things in ways that we underestimate and fail to anticipate, and they also motivate us to work harder and perform tasks we might not otherwise perform.

What does this mean if our tendency to see other humans declines? If other humans are a primary source of influence, would people benefit from simply thinking autonomously instead of following others? And in cases where humans are a primary source of motivation, would people just become motivated by other incentives? The answer to each of these questions is a firm maybe, yet I think that the loss of humans as a source of influence and motivation has several downsides.

Without humans as the predominant source of influence, social norms—namely, the customs, practices, and rules we follow simply because others are following them—would evaporate. Given that these norms form the basis of our ability to cooperate in large groups, the loss of social norms would represent a larger erosion of our communities. The central thesis of historian Yuval Noah Harari's book *Sapiens* is that our ability to thrive as a species results from our capacity for cooperation. Our capacity for cooperation, in turn, stems from our willingness to follow the rules of what we believe everyone else believes in, what Harari calls the "mythical glue" that binds us.

Harari writes of history's great societies, "All these cooperation networks—from the cities of ancient Mesopotamia to the Qin and Roman empires—were 'imagined orders.' The social norms that sustained them were based neither on ingrained instincts nor on personal acquaintances, but rather on belief in shared myths."[22] Such myths include not just religions but also laws, national borders, and even money—things with no inherent objective reality but that govern our lives and thereby sustain large-scale cooperation simply because we agree on them.

The benefit of humans as sources of influence is that they produce a necessary conformity. Although conformity is a dirty word to many in the United States, it turns out that Americans are outliers relative to the rest of the world in disparaging it. Our drive for individualism neglects the critical importance of having guidelines for social interaction that everybody follows simply because, well, everybody else follows them.

Similarly, the dehumanizing shift I describe in chapter 1 could diminish the role of prosocial motivation, impairing our ability to function collectively. Prosocial incentives only work insofar as people consider and care about other people's needs, desires, and feelings— a shift away from considering others could be bad for business. Of course, people are also motivated by personal gain (as we have seen in this chapter), but this type of motivation often directly erodes their motivation to work for communal benefit. For example, incentivizing salespeople through paying them a commission for every sale leads them not to create the most value possible for their company or even to provide the customer with the best product—commissions often just motivate people to sell. Furthermore, incentivizing people through personal benefits, such as increasing people's commission bonuses, base salaries, or stock options, is far more expensive and less enduring than incentivizing people to work on behalf of others. Not to mention, some research suggests that prosocial motivation is a special motivation that specifically improves worker morale when self-oriented intrinsic motivation is lacking.[23]

We humans are not only powerful sources of influence and motivation, but also our power to guide and inspire action enables collectives of people to function, sustaining the basis of civilization. Neglecting other humans, as our lives become more dependent on technology and as our work depends more on systems, platforms, and machines, is likely to reduce cooperation, performance, and purpose. In the following two chapters, we learn how to rehumanize areas of life that have come to be dominated by things rather than people and how to stave off this dehumanizing shift, to improve our productivity, social connection, and happiness.

PART TWO

CHAPTER 6

Humanizing Work in the Automation Age

THE RISE OF AUTOMATION AND MOBILE TECHNOLOGY HAS ushered in a golden age of technology criticism. A 2008 *Atlantic* cover story asked, "Is Google Making Us Stupid?" while a 2017 *Atlantic* article wonders, "Have Smartphones Destroyed a Generation?" In the *New York Times*, *The New Yorker*, the *Washington Post*, and other prominent outlets, accusations pop up weekly claiming technology has caused society's demise. These critiques are, of course, nothing new, and they are not confined to the digital age.

One overlooked pioneer of such technology criticism was civil rights leader Martin Luther King Jr., who stated, "We must rapidly begin the shift from a 'thing-oriented' society to a 'person-oriented' society. When machines and computers, profit motives and property rights are considered more important than people, the giant triplets of racism, materialism, and militarism are incapable of being conquered."[1] Although the technology of King's day was far less advanced, he acknowledges it as a dehumanizing force, conflating technology with profit and property to demonstrate how society has come to value "things" as much as, if not more than, human beings.

"Things," although a nebulous term, are inherently inanimate and nonsentient entities that have one important commonality. Whether tangible things like technology that we use for work, intangible things like markets and data that dictate governmental and corporate decision-making, or quasi-tangible things like property that has both symbolic and real value, things share one particular quality: they separate people from each other. Time spent engaging with things displaces time spent engaging with other humans, and it is these things that mediate our interactions with each other—they stand between us. As I noted in chapter 1, the increasing tendency for people to communicate through technology (versus meeting face-to-face) can impede understanding others' thoughts, feelings, and desires. Outside the realm of technology but fully in the realm of things, we also know that increased marketization determines people's value in terms of their contribution to their employers' profits or in terms of the property they own. Again, these tendencies neglect people's inherent worth as humans irrespective of their contributions or property ownership. King's proclamation that the focus on machines, profits, and property is transforming society to become more oriented to things impeccably predicts the data presented in chapter 1.

King's distinction between persons and things is also useful because it maps on perfectly to psychological theories of human cognition. These theories suggest two processes that psychologist Simon Baron-Cohen calls systematizing and empathizing, which characterize much of human thought. Baron-Cohen and colleagues described these processes in a landmark article by stating, "Empathizing is the capacity to predict and to respond to the behavior of agents (usually people) by inferring their mental states and responding to these with an appropriate emotion. Systemizing is the capacity to predict and to respond to the behavior of nonagentive deterministic systems by analyzing input-operation-output relations and inferring the rules that govern such systems."[2] In other words, empathizing involves making sense of humans, and systematizing involves making sense of things. In Baron-Cohen's theory, these tendencies can be in balance, or one can dominate the other with systematizing outperforming empathizing, as is characteristic of many cases of autism. Although this theory suggests a perhaps overly simplistic dichotomy, measures of empathizing and systematizing reliably map on to activation in brain region networks associated with social thinking and nonsocial thinking, respectively.[3] What is more, these brain networks often show a negative correlation such that more activity in one network inhibits activity in the other.[4]

The sum of these findings again suggests that the relationship between cognition directed toward things and cognition directed toward humans is largely zero-sum—our focus on things suppresses our focus on other people. In this chapter and the following chapter, we examine the twin engines of the thing-oriented society: work and technology, both of which promote systematizing at the expense of empathizing. I argue, however, that neither work nor technology need be dehumanizing and that both can be used to promote person-oriented thinking.

When the Robots Will Come—And Who They're Coming For

The joint dehumanizing effects of work and technology are most evident in the shift toward automation, in which machines have replaced tasks and processes traditionally performed by humans. The specter of automation has already begun to have considerable economic effects; thus, several interested parties have begun attempting to predict how long it will take before machines dominate the workforce.

Hard empirical research on the question is scant, with the most highly cited study on this topic coming from scholars Carl Benedikt Frey and Michael Osborne. In 2013 Frey and Osborne predicted the susceptibility of 702 different occupations to becoming fully automated within the next twenty years.[5] They drew on a US data set describing dozens of characteristics for each occupation (based on workers' self-reports). They labeled a set of seventy of these occupations (in their opinion) as able to be automated or not able to be automated. Then they taught a machine learning algorithm to classify any job's likelihood of automation based on this starter set of seventy occupations, each occupation's characteristics, and the researchers' labeling. From this analysis, Frey and Osborne identified that 47 percent of jobs were at risk, with jobs such as telemarketers and accountants facing over a 90 percent probability of automation and jobs such as dentists and recreational therapists facing virtually 0 percent probability of automation.

Some have criticized Frey and Osborne's analysis for failing to account for how heterogeneous occupations are (i.e., jobs often involve multiple tasks) and how capable they are to adapt to digitization. For example, one analysis by economist Melanie Arntz and colleagues shows that when accounting for these factors only 9 percent of US workers face a considerable risk of their jobs being replaced by machines.[6]

The next best forecasting attempt comes from a 2015 survey that asked 1,634 of the world's leading artificial intelligence (AI) experts to estimate the rate at which machines would outperform humans on various jobs.[7] Just over one-fifth of experts responded, estimating a 45 percent chance that AI will outperform human beings on all jobs in forty-five years and that full automation will occur in 120 years. The survey also assessed specific occupations with respondents estimating that AI will be able to outperform humans on, say, truck driving by 2027 and performing surgery by 2053.

Whereas these analyses are largely based on sophisticated speculation from limited sampling, other work has examined historical data to study how automation affects employment. Economists Daron Acemoglu and Pascual Restrepo examined how industrial robot use between 1990 and 2007 affected the United States labor markets to find that introducing robots has a uniformly negative effect on employment.[8] Unsurprisingly, they find the strongest negative effects for the manufacturing domain and for occupations related to assembly and routine manual labor.

I find these reports largely unhelpful because of the responses they inspire, and we will grapple with why. Commentators dispense endless advice about the types of skills that are less able to be automated because computers and robots cannot accomplish them. The implication is that to avoid being replaced in your job, you might have to change who you are. You must acquire more education and training even if you cannot afford it, and you must master new skills even if you consider those skills to be undesirable or uninteresting. Several industries threatened by automation have begun to invest in "reskilling" programs, training employees whose skills are easily automated (e.g., driving a truck, mining for coal) to ones that appear more distinctively human.

And what exactly are those skills that people consider distinctively human? One broad set of skills involves attributes related to social and emotional intelligence. In my research on botsourcing with Michael Norton (described in this book's introduction), we found that people stereotype robots as proficient at thinking (i.e., being capable of cognition, analysis, and deliberation) but relatively unskilled at feeling (i.e., being capable of experiencing emotion, pain, and pleasure).[9] We found that these stereotypes lead people to oppose robots replacing humans in jobs like a social worker or preschool teacher that ostensibly require sociability, social understanding, and emotional responsiveness. People also oppose robots taking their jobs when we first ask participants to reflect on how their jobs require emotion versus how their jobs require cognition—thinking about the role of emotion in your job makes you less likely to believe a robot could do it.

Our findings resonate with expert advice that suggests honing your socioemotional skills to avoid losing your job to automation. For example, economist David Deming analyzed job growth between 1980 and

2012 and found jobs that require social skills grew by 24 percent, whereas math-intensive jobs grew by only 11 percent.[10] In a *Harvard Business Review* interview, Deming stated that "the days of being able to plug away in isolation on a quantitative problem and be paid well for it are increasingly over," adding that now many jobs require both quantitative skills and social skills.[11] Ryan Feit, CEO and founder of crowdfunding platform SeedInvest, similarly stated in *Forbes*, "Robots are still horrible communicators and problem solvers . . . schools should evolve to emphasize critical thinking and social skills."[12] Feit added, "It is also highly unlikely that during the next couple decades robots will learn how to design and manage themselves, so schools should stress creativity and management skills." These suggestions again emphasize humans' superiority to robots in social and emotional skills including communicating with and managing other humans.

After suggestions to develop one's sociability to avoid becoming automated, the second most commonly mentioned skill is variability. Commentators tell us that humans' capacity for unpredictability, creativity, and nonrandomness can counter machines' capacity to do rote work. Given that much of what variability amounts to is "going off script," I decided to ask an expert in improvisation, Matt Besser, about this issue. Besser is an actor, director, and comedian best known for cofounding the legendary comedy improv troupe Upright Citizens Brigade at the Improv Olympic theater in Chicago. Besser invited me on his podcast, Improv 4 Humans, to chat. When I asked him if he thought a robot could ever master improv comedy, he was skeptical.[13] "Two robots could not be funny, but I think you could have one robot be a straight man and have a funny scene [with a human]," he told me. Besser's cohosts added the robot could be taught to learn comedic patterns such as the "rule of threes" but would have to use its "robot-ness" to generate laughs. In other words, robots could master the basic rules of comedy but would struggle with true improvisation.

Business experts often agree that humans outperform machines in variability. For example, John Hagel, a management consultant and former strategic planning vice president at Atari, stated, "If you have tightly scripted jobs that are highly standardized where there's no room for individual initiative or creativity, machines by and large can do those kinds of activities much better than human beings. They're much more predictable. They're much more reliable." Hagel added that the tightly scripted nature of jobs has made them replaceable, stating that "the real reason that we have such an issue in terms of unemployment and job loss through automation is that we've crafted these jobs exactly so that they would be vulnerable to automation."[14] Making work less routine, in Hagel's view, is therefore key to buffering against the threat of automation.

Another *Forbes* article titled "If You Want to Avoid Being Replaced by a Robot, Here's What You Need to Know" similarly recommends avoiding routine work. In the article, physician Lynda Chin describes leading a project to automate cancer diagnosis and treatment using IBM's Watson computing system, stating, "While most doctors work on routine cases, there was a great need for expert advice when something rare came up."[15] Chin suggests that her project (which ultimately folded) revealed that the automated system could evaluate more standardized cancer cases but that human doctors were necessary for more atypical ones.

I discussed this issue with Sharmila Mulligan, founder and CEO of ClearStory Data, a business analytics company that provides insights to industries ranging from manufacturing to retail to media to financial services.[16] She has built several technology companies, serves on the board of many others, and is at the forefront of thinking about how humans can partner with machines. Mulligan described to me advances in autonomous work including manufacturing and autonomous flying, explaining "autonomous flying is already further along than autonomous driving" in part because planes have "fewer events they encounter" and therefore experience fewer "outlier" events. In describing what the role of humans will be in human-machine partnerships, she notes that "humans are essential for handling outliers." In other words, humans are necessary to address anomalous rather than routine behavior.

What do the data say about jobs that lack variability? A recent paper called "Disappearing Routine Jobs" by economist Guido Cortes and colleagues examined labor market data to show that the share of Americans working jobs that, in Cortes's terms, have "well-defined instructions" and lack "flexibility, creativity, problem-solving, or human interaction" has dropped dramatically.[17] Employment in these jobs has dropped from 40.5 percent to 31.2 percent from 1979 to 2014, again suggesting the need for individuals to build skills around work that is less rote and manual. Related work by economist David Autor finds a similar pattern, as Autor states one of the "key contributors to job polarization [is] the automation of routine work."[18]

One way companies are responding to these trends is to train people to improve at learning.[19] Learning is relatively nonessential when work is routine, but when work becomes less predictable and more mutable, employees must learn how to adapt. Infosys, the Indian technology services company, for example, trains employees on learning skills like creativity. In one workshop, employees were tasked with reimagining the digital retail experience through experimenting with enlivening a physical retail space. This training intends to enhance what former research and design head Sanjay Rajagopalan calls "learning velocity," the speed with which one turns a good idea into a great one.[20]

Telecommunications giant AT&T offers "nanodegrees," short courses that build employees' learning skills. Microsoft has incorporated into its performance review criteria assessments of how well employees learn from each other. Companies are betting that although technology can master tasks with largely static features and can integrate changes over time (as machine learning algorithms already do), humans might prove superior at adapting to a constantly changing work landscape.

As we've established, sociability and variability are important skills to master in an increasingly automated age. But performing tasks that involve sociability and variability are also cognitively demanding and may feel inauthentic to some people. In the sections to follow, I explain how employees and companies can maximize these two skills. Promoting these skills enhances employees' well-being as they distinguish themselves from automata and benefits organizations in ways beyond the potential cost savings of automation. I also describe the limitations of this two-skill strategy and then offer a third solution to complement sociability and variability, which can help rehumanize one's workplace life as well as life beyond one's organization.

Mastering Sociability

Increasing the social quality of work—namely, the degree to which people feel connected, understood, capable of understanding others, and driven to help others—I believe requires three distinct tasks: enhancing employees' social skills like empathy, highlighting the social impact of employees' work (how their work affects beneficiaries), and strengthening social affiliation (mutual recognition, cooperation) among employees. These three tactics vary in their applicability depending on the industry and the company, but any workplace can enhance performance on at least one of them. We examine evidence for the importance of each of these three in turn.

Enhancing employees' social skills is considerably challenging and, as the next chapter illustrates, machines may eventually coopt certain social skills. Nonetheless, training in such aptitudes, particularly in displaying empathy, can both enhance the social quality of work and improve performance and customer satisfaction.

There are few domains where empathy is more important than in customer support. Although Frey and Osborne's automation report gives customer service representatives a 55 percent chance of becoming automated, people still prefer customer service humans to robots. Surveys show overwhelmingly that consumers (even tech-savvy millennials) prefer engaging with live human beings rather than robots for customer service, although they consistently report being disappointed in customer service.[21] That is, people want other people to resolve their customer service issues but often dislike these interactions with fellow human beings. Almost half of 1,000 respondents in a representative consumer survey stated that they would happily use a chatbot for customer service as long as it was effective.[22] Empathy is essential to keep humans employed in customer service; without it, people will begrudgingly settle for the robots.

Companies that prioritize empathy in customer service win consumer loyalty as well. For example, Telefonica Germany, the German outpost of the multinational telecommunications company, implemented an empathy training program and saw customer satisfaction reports increase by 6 percent in six weeks.[23] The content of empathy training varies considerably across contexts and can focus on building specific skills such as listening and understanding others' emotions or can focus on role-playing how another person might feel. The limited empirical research available suggests that empathy training does boost empathy in medical professionals, social workers, and even criminal populations.[24] However, even less work has examined quantitatively the effects of empathy training in corporate contexts.

To address this issue, let's examine several lines of evidence outside of training per se that do suggest that empathy benefits organizations. One comes from the Global Empathy Index, a metric that a United Kingdom–based consultancy developed to evaluate companies on empathy. The index combines survey data, social and financial feeds, and textual analysis of companies' social media interactions to score empathy on metrics like employee perceptions of their CEOs, ethical practices, and sensitivity to customer needs. The companies that ranked in the top ten (e.g., Audi, LinkedIn) of the 2015 index generated 50 percent more earnings and increased in value over twice as much as companies that ranked in the bottom ten (e.g., RyanAir, Vodafone).

Other evidence on this point comes from a 2007 study by the Center for Creative Leadership. This survey of 6,731 managers from 38 countries found that leaders whose subordinates rated them as highly empathic also received higher job performance ratings from their bosses.[25] A 2014 study by research organization Catalyst examining 1,512 employees from six different countries also found that employees who perceived their managers to be altruistic leaders performed better on innovation and team citizenship (e.g., helping colleagues with their work, picking up the slack for absent colleagues).[26] Altruistic leadership in this context refers to empathic behaviors including sacrificing personal interests to empower others and learning from their criticism. The results of these different studies point to a common conclusion—that is, ensuring that employees consider the needs of others improves performance, both for employees and companies more broadly.

Outside of direct training, how do companies successfully promote empathy, keep humans top of mind, and maintain an altruistic leadership style among their top executives? The answer is currently murky given that organizations only recently have begun to recognize the importance of sociability, but we'll take a look at several organizations that provide some clues.

One method of increasing the social character of work (increasing feelings of empathy, connection, and impact) is through highlighting to workers the human customers that their work serves. This type of thinking epitomizes human-centered design (also called "design thinking"), which has pervaded various industries and organizations for the past thirty years. Consulting firm IDEO is the company most responsible for popularizing design thinking, having used this philosophy to completely reimagine industrial, digital, organizational, product, and business design. For example, for one project, IDEO designed a mobile application called Moneythink to train low-income teenagers in financial literacy. Because a critical step in design thinking is gaining empathy for the user behind any product, the team behind this app toured Chicago neighborhoods where these teenagers lived. By understanding how social the experience of money is for these teenagers—typically they receive money on social occasions like birthdays and spend money in social situations as well—IDEO added a social component to the app to make it more user friendly.

In a consumer goods context, Procter & Gamble has used design thinking to develop its highly successful floor-cleaning device, the Swiffer. Ethnographic teams studied how people typically clean and found that most people swept their floors before they mopped and spent as much time rinsing their mops as they did cleaning with them. When the Swiffer eliminated these time-consuming aspects of cleaning by introducing a disposable towel as the mop component, it became a multimillion-dollar best seller. Design thinking forces companies to get into the minds of their customers not simply to sell them something (as advertising does) but also to provide an optimal product that fulfills their needs.

Not only does design thinking improve product design, whether for mobile apps or household goods, but it can also give employees a greater sense of purpose. Neil Stevenson, a former IDEO executive, described to me this experience in working on a project with a paint company.[27] IDEO's goal was to help people choose paint colors. Although Stevenson found the project mechanistic at first ("the definition of a boring project . . . literally watching paint dry"), he discovered a spark in the ethnographic work of studying people buying paint. He told me, "I was hanging out in the aisles of hardware stores with a camera and I got this photo of a husband and wife and she was slumped over and he was looking at the paint. This was the theater of the paint aisle—she wants an emotion, he wants a paint color." At that moment, Stevenson realized, "That became the problem. Satisfying both of those users. By having that experience and seeing those people, I became infused in the project. I got some skin in the game." This type of investment enhanced his sense of purpose toward the project.

On this point of purpose, design thinking is philosophically akin to prosocial motivation. Adam Grant, whose work on this topic is highlighted in chapter 5, has described how organizations across industries have successfully motivated employees by reminding them of their impact on other people. For companies like restaurant chain Olive Garden, circulating customers' letters of appreciation to the wait staff makes the employees feel valued. For technology companies like Microsoft, the practice of "end user training" has dominated the industry to improve product design and development.[28] Typically, this training brings engineers and developers together with the customers who actually use their product to hear customers' concerns and to understand their pain points. This training helps employees develop empathy for customers' issues and to generate creative solutions that address their needs.

Medical schools have undertaken innovative end user methods to connect future physicians with their patients. One study led by physician Lesley Latham asked undergraduate medical students to wear, for twenty-four hours, a temporary tattoo that simulated a psoriatic lesion and found that this experience dramatically increased empathy for psoriatic patients.[29] Prior to wearing the tattoo, study participants rated the physical and mental impact of psoriasis and eczema to be far lower than other diseases. After wearing the tattoo, these medical students rated the impact of psoriasis and eczema to be much greater, on par with the impact of arthritis, diabetes, and heart disease.

So far, we have discussed the importance of directly training or enhancing employees' social skills and highlighting the social impact of work for employees. Beyond these two steps, strengthening connections between colleagues is essential to rehumanizing work, as these relationships have waned in recent decades. The number of Americans reporting they have a coworker in their core social network dropped from 48 percent in 1985 to 30 percent in 2004.[30] A 2010 report similarly indicated that only 30 percent of people report having a close friend at work.[31] Building connections doesn't mean that employees have to become best friends but simply that they develop relationships based on mutual respect and recognition of each other's work.

One simple way to rebuild these relationships is through creating incentives that benefit the collective rather than the individual. Some companies such as fast-food chain Pret A Manger have adopted the logic of prosocial bonuses (described in chapter 5). Pret gives new employees £50 vouchers when they pass specific training milestones, stipulating that they must spend it on colleagues who have helped them along the way. Several technology companies such as Medium, Google, Shopify, and Valve allow employees to reward each other in a peer-to-peer fashion. Google's peer-to-peer bonus system, for example, enables employees to send each other bonuses up to $175 to express gratitude for help received. These programs enable employees to explicitly recognize and appreciate each other.

Other organizations employ peer recognition systems that are less focused on money. For example, Colorado's Douglas County library system asks employees to nominate each other for outstanding accomplishments (like starting a reading program for special needs children).[32] The library honors these employees at a special dinner and gives them a paid day off. Festivities like this are relatively cheap and easy ways to make employees feel valued and to acknowledge each other, strengthening social connection.

The benefits of sociability raise the question of what could possibly be the downside to enhancing the social nature of our work. Beyond enhancing productivity, motivation, and product design, feeling socially connected is a boon to mental health.[33] The problem is that for some of us being social, including speaking with others, engaging with others, gauging others' emotions, considering others' perspectives, or merely relinquishing one's privacy to spend time with others, simply exhausts us or feels inauthentic.

A recent study of Finnish university students used smartphone technology to examine how socializing affects exhaustion. Over a twelve-day period, psychologists Sointu Leikas and Ville-Juhani Ilmarinen surveyed participants on their phones at various points of the day (about what they were doing and how they felt) and sent them a personality assessment.[34] This assessment categorized some participants as introverts and some as extroverts. What Leikas and Ilmarinen found was that behaving in an extroverted manner—that is, talking and meeting with others—made people happier in the moment but fatigued three hours later. And this effect persisted for both introverts and for extroverts, who naturally seek out more social situations. This study suggests that the momentary well-being benefits of social interaction can be offset by its depleting effects.

Even socializing and interacting with others online can be fatiguing. Therapist and psychoanalyst Patricia Blatt describes how Facebook, Twitter, and Instagram adversely affect adolescents, stating, "Social media has created a new sense of impulsivity and urgency, it can make them feel overwhelmed by what is happening in the world, and all of these factors can be fatiguing and can impact how they sleep."[35] Research has also begun finding evidence of "social media fatigue," which is "the tendency to become overwhelmed by information on social media sites." Ironically, this fatigue is more common among people who feel most capable of using social media and who might be using it to the point of burning out.[36]

A separate issue is that many people may simply not identify with being social (talking with others, deeply engaging with others, or exchanging personal information with others)—it is not a core part of who they are. Although estimates of extroverts and introverts in the population vary, one widely cited estimate from Susan Cain's 2013 book *Quiet* is that 33 percent to 50 percent of Americans are introverts.[37] Still, other work suggests that a considerable percentage of us are ambiverts, toggling between extroversion and introversion.[38] In addition, people with social anxiety or those on the autism spectrum might feel completely incapable of taking on work that requires increased social capacities like empathy, perspective-taking, and recognizing others' emotions. For these individuals, social interaction is demanding both cognitively and emotionally.

Other work demonstrates the arduous nature of empathy, the process that enables effective social interaction. Occupations that require empathy such as nurses, therapists, and even professional fund-raisers produce high emotional burnout. The excessive need to provide care for others in these jobs can also contribute to *compassion fatigue*. This term, popularized by psychologist Charles Figley, refers to the emotional and physical stress that comes from overly identifying with a patient's or client's trauma.[39] Even in jobs that do not explicitly require care, empathy is cognitively demanding because getting inside of another mind draws on finite working memory, our capacity to hold and process information.[40] These findings suggest that advice to master sociability needs to be counterbalanced with approaches that offset feelings of exhaustion and inauthenticity. Before turning to that approach, we address the other primary skill experts claim is automation-proof: variability.

Mastering Variability

In addition to promoting sociability, humanizing work requires promoting variability—that is, fewer routines, fewer scripts, and fewer short-term goals. Variability seems particularly important given the trends cited above showing that routine work is most susceptible to automation. What promoting variability looks like in practice is less clear, but one prominent example comes from online retailer Zappos, which famously eliminated scripts for their customer service representatives. As Zappos CEO Tony Hsieh states, "We don't have scripts, because we want our reps to let their true personalities shine during every phone call, so that they can develop a personal emotional connection with each customer."[41] Customer service work might not necessarily seem like glamorous work, but it can become meaningful and even humanizing when it enables workers to connect emotionally with a customer and address that customer's needs. As a result of this method, Zappos has built a unique customer service empire that distinguishes the company from other online retailers.

Increasing variety not only increases efficiency and customer satisfaction, but it also enhances employee motivation. Several lines of work show that humans crave variety, including the most influential theory of effective job design, the job characteristics model. This theory, developed by organizational behavior scholars Richard Hackman and Greg Oldham, describes three essential task-related factors that boost feelings of meaningfulness and, hence, motivation: (1) task significance—the degree to which the task has an impact on others, akin to prosocial impact described above, (2) task identity—the degree to which the task produces an identifiable piece of work, and (3) skill variety—the degree to which the task requires a variety of skills and activities to be completed.[42] Over the forty years since the development of this model, skill variety remains an essential predictor of how engaged people feel with their work. Furthermore, research shows worker perceptions of skill variety in their jobs have increased since 1975 whereas task identity and task significance have remained steady.[43]

A 2007 meta-analysis of 259 studies involving 219,625 participants also showed the positive effects of task variety, that is, how much one's job involves a diverse set of tasks.[44] This analysis showed that task variety predicts increased satisfaction with one's job, one's supervisor, and one's compensation. Another recent study also showed that skill variety and task variety differentially benefit older and younger workers. Task variety benefited older workers by reducing burnout and desire to quit one's job.[45] Skill variety, on the other hand, benefited younger workers by reducing their desire to quit.

Research by operations scholar Bradley Staats and psychologist Francesca Gino illustrates the importance of variety at work in a highly specialized context. Their research examined two and a half years of home loan processing data from a Japanese bank to assess worker productivity in processing mortgage loan applications.[46] The critical question Staats and Gino asked was which factor better enhanced productivity: specialization or variety.

Mortgage processing, as it turns out, is a job that involves seventeen distinct tasks ranging from performing a credit check to verifying an applicant's income tax. Therefore, Staats and Gino measured specialization in terms of how often workers performed one of these tasks repeatedly (i.e., over and over) and variety in terms of how often workers switched from task to task. They found that over periods of several days, variety strongly enhanced productivity measured in terms of employees' efficiency and speed in processing applications.

Other recent work demonstrates that switching back and forth between two different tasks enhances creative performance on these tasks.[47] In these studies, led by psychologist Jackson Lu, participants received instructions to perform such tasks one at a time (e.g., generate as many alternative uses for a brick as possible for four minutes, then generate as many alternative uses as possible for a toothpick for four minutes), or to switch back and forth between tasks (e.g., brick-toothpick-brick-toothpick). Those who switched back and forth produced more creative responses because they fixated less on a single task, which often impedes creative thought.

Despite variety's benefits for productivity and creativity, mastering variability—like mastering sociability—can be arduous. Behaving in a nondeterministic manner is simply something humans struggle to do. One example of this comes from Iran's 2009 presidential election, in which Mahmoud Ahmadinejad won in a landslide, prompting skepticism over the results. Bernd Beber and Alexandra Scacco (who were political science graduate students at the time) investigated the possibility of election fraud by systematically examining the province-by-province vote totals for different candidates.[48] Specifically, they examined the last two digits of each vote total and found that these numbers differed considerably from numbers that would have occurred naturally (and randomly). For example, they found more 7s and fewer 5s than would have occurred by chance. Beber and Scacco also found similar evidence for manipulated numbers in 2007 elections in Senegal and Nigeria.[49] People intending to falsify the vote totals would do well to generate numbers that resemble those that would occur naturally. Yet even those attempting to sway globally influential elections could not overcome the human tendency toward deterministic behavior.

These election fraud findings are consistent with research demonstrating humans' difficulty with behaving randomly. For decades, psychologists have assessed randomness ability through various methods, asking people to generate letters or words, arrange symbols, press computer keys, or produce sequences of coin flips. In virtually all cases, people produce certain outcomes more than others, indicating a deviation from true chance behavior. In one classic example, psychologist Paul Bakan asked participants to generate sequences of three coin flips that they would expect to occur if flipping an unbiased coin (e.g., heads, then heads, then tails). Participants consistently generated sequences that included at least one heads and one tails even though heads-heads-heads and tails-tails-tails sequences were just as likely to occur.[50] Furthermore, 80 percent of those participating generated heads for the first coin flip. Decades of research following these early studies suggests that because humans are drawn to systematic patterns and misunderstand what randomness is, they struggle to behave truly variably.

A more recent study, led by mathematician Nicolas Gauvrit, suggests that people's ability to generate randomness maps on to other critical cognitive abilities and peaks in early adulthood.[51] Gauvrit and colleagues administered several tasks (e.g., produce a series of coin flips, select cards that would appear in a random shuffle of a deck) to 3,429 participants. For each task, Gauvrit measured participants' "algorithmic randomness," a comparison between what humans produce and what computers produce by chance, finding that randomness ability peaks at age twenty-five and sharply declines after age sixty, mimicking the rise and fall of general cognitive skills. This research again suggests that asking employees to produce less routine work may not be such a simple request.

Beyond humans' difficulty in producing randomness, embracing variability faces another challenge: multitasking, like sociability, can be cognitively costly and can even temporarily impair one's natural intelligence. A 2011 McKinsey report on information overload among CEOs and other executives warns, "Always-on, multitasking work environments are killing productivity, dampening creativity, and making us unhappy."[52] Although work cited above demonstrates the productivity benefits of variety in work, when people handle too many various tasks simultaneously, multitasking can become burdensome.

As an academic psychologist, I constantly experience the strain of multitasking. In addition to teaching, consulting, and performing administrative tasks for my university and department, much of my work involves collaborating on various research projects simultaneously. These projects involve working with multiple people from different disciplinary backgrounds at different ranks (from undergraduate research assistant to full professor) in geographically disparate places. They employ multiple methodologies ranging from examining patients with brain lesions to neuroimaging to conducting laboratory experiments to digging into existing large data sets. My professional survival depends on my ability to multitask, to juggle multiple projects at once, and to generate novel research questions. It is a recipe for burnout, which I have attempted to combat temporarily by writing a book. When I griped to a mentor about a research project with a distant collaborator that required mastering several new methodological tools and analytic procedures, he said, "Why don't you just cut all ties?" Even though I recognize that not everyone can do this, his life-changing advice saved my professional sanity.

A broad literature on task-switching also shows how juggling even simple tasks depletes cognitive resources. Early work by psychologist Arthur Jersild demonstrated that people took longer to perform math tasks that involved switching between operations (adding, subtracting) than repeating the same operation over and over.[53] Not only is task-switching cognitively depleting, but it even impairs performance on tasks where people are already proficient. Psychologists Renata Meuter and Alan Allport conducted studies showing that asking bilingual people to switch between using their first (dominant) language and their second (nondominant) language actually impaired their use of their first language.[54] These findings suggest that training skilled individuals to perform a second task can impair performance on the task for which they are experts.

Outside of the laboratory, systems and operations scholar Diwas KC demonstrated the perils of multitasking for emergency department doctors.[55] KC examined an emergency department that saw 145,935 patients and measured multitasking by simply counting how many patients a physician cared for at a given moment. He then assessed patient outcomes and found that excessive multitasking meant a longer time before patients were discharged, fewer correctly detected diagnoses, and more patients returning to the emergency department within twenty-four hours. A conceptually similar study of Italian judges showed that judges who worked on fewer different cases at a time completed more cases per quarter and completed their cases more quickly.[56] If workers and organizations do not manage it appropriately, the cost of variability on work can outweigh its benefits.

Real Leisure

Sociability and variability represent two skills necessary to humanize work. Yet, if both are cognitively and emotionally costly, then one additional solution must offset these consequences. Such a solution must be mentally restorative and enable people to regain their authentic selves. As most business schools and the leadership industry focus on increasing engagement, it gives me great pleasure to be the rare business school professor to recommend increasing employee disengagement as the solution. I believe people must work less and base their identities and self-worth less on their jobs.

Embracing work to boost feelings of personal meaning and self-esteem has led us to overwork ourselves. Psychologist Chris Hsee and colleagues recently empirically documented this tendency to embrace busyness and avoid leisure, what they term "idleness aversion."[57] Hsee's studies gave participants a choice between idleness and busyness such as completing a survey and waiting out the remaining time of the study (idly) or completing a survey and delivering it to a faraway location (thus keeping busy). Most people consistently chose whichever task kept them busier, even when that task was more arduous. Other work by Hsee and colleagues has shown that when people are incentivized for their work, they overearn.[58] That is, rather than working until they have earned rewards that they will actually consume, people work until they are exhausted, accumulating rewards mindlessly. In doing so, they miss opportunities to mentally recharge.

Other recent work by Ed O'Brien and Ellen Roney suggests that people believe they only deserve leisure once labor is completed.[59] In these studies, people receive both the opportunity to experience some leisure activity (e.g., eat snacks, get a massage) and to perform labor (e.g., take a midterm exam). They also get to determine the order in which they would like to engage in these two activities. O'Brien and Roney found that participants consistently choose labor before leisure, believing that the looming work would distract from their enjoyment of leisure. In fact, regardless of whether leisure occurs before or after work, participants find it equally enjoyable. This research suggests our intuitions about leisure are misguided and that we believe leisure is something we can enjoy only once work is done.

These beliefs are particularly pervasive in the modern Silicon Valley–driven organizational landscape that attempts to incorporate fun, social life, and leisure into work. This was extremely apparent when a friend and former Facebook employee toured me around Facebook's corporate campus in Menlo Park, California. The campus resembled Disneyland's "Main Street USA" as Facebook recruited Disney consultants to help design it. My friend showed me the various snack-stocked kitchens around the campus, the multicuisine cafeteria, the pop-up hamburger station, the likes of which have become standard Silicon Valley workplace fare. There was an entire printmaking shop where employees could make art and a fully transparent glass office where CEO Mark Zuckerberg held a meeting in plain sight. At one point, my guide had to slip away to a physical therapy appointment on campus with the in-house physical therapist. There was also a campus center where one could visit a doctor, a bank, a music studio, and a video arcade. All office spaces were open with few self-contained cubicles.

Of course, these accoutrements were intended to increase employees' sense of fun, relaxation, and convenience. However, when I asked my guide how he got anything done in this environment, he responded instantaneously, "It's impossible. I have to take all my work home." Attempts at workplace-incorporated leisure can hamper productivity and contribute to what has come to be known as the "24-7 workplace."

Companies increasingly expect employees to be "on" at all hours of the day, to bring their work home with them, or work at offices where labor and leisure are fused. The question is implicit: If there is a health center, a physical therapist, and a bank at work, why would you ever have to leave?

Several companies have tried to combat the 24-7 workplace by offering flexible vacation policies. Vacation is essential, and research shows that it improves productivity, worker success, and workplace happiness.[60] Beyond its restorative power, a generous vacation offering allows companies to communicate to employees that (a) we care about your well-being and (b) we trust you to get your work done. Both of these are humanizing messages.

In its early days, crowdfunding company Kickstarter let managers give as many days off to employees as they wished but, after six years, they capped the policy at twenty-five days a year, suspecting it had been affecting employees negatively. Other companies like Netflix, Virgin America, and Best Buy have at various points implemented unlimited vacation policies with mixed results. Many of my MBA students who have worked at companies with similar policies suggest employees end up taking less time off than they would have otherwise. Noted management scholar Lotte Bailyn suggests, "People take less time off because they feel they're not sure if this is really a commitment to them or that this is more a PR thing."[61] Many of my students agree, also telling me that when companies have unlimited vacation policies, it can become competitive to see who can take the least time off. A 2014 survey conducted by Glassdoor.com supports this point, showing that American employees, on average, only take half of their days off, and 61 percent of these employees report working while on vacation.[62] One of the Glassdoor.com researchers on this project, Katie Denis, noted that millennial women in particular "tend to have more pronounced guilt and feel they don't want to burden people with their time away."[63] Distrust, competition, and guilt all contribute to people's aversion to taking free time off even when companies grant it.

Some companies are improving at forcing their employees into vacation, experimenting with creative policies to do so. Technology company FullContact, for example, pays workers a $7,500 stipend to take a family vacation with one stipulation: employees are not allowed to work while on vacation. If they find employees doing any work or opening a single work email while on a company-sponsored vacation, employees must return the entire stipend. Applications increased, and turnover rates dropped shortly after the company implemented the policy.[64]

Other companies simply make vacation mandatory. Social media platform Buffer, anticipating the problems with unlimited vacation policies, initially paid employees $1,000 to take vacation. After they discovered 57 percent of their employees took less than fifteen days of vacation, they implemented a mandatory three-week-vacation policy.[65] Jobs website Anthology gives employees two weeks of vacation on top of holidays, plus an additional "bank" of five days. If an employee has not taken any vacation time in the past three months, the company forces the employee to use a "bank" day.[66]

Other companies have tried to combat the work obsession by reducing email outside normal working hours. Electrical parts distributor Van Meter, for example, shuts off employee email accounts when employees take vacation. German automobile maker Daimler has gone further, offering employees a program that automatically deletes emails they receive while on vacation. This program sends an autoreply to the sender explaining that the email will be deleted and provides contact information of another employee to email if the matter is urgent. In this same spirit, France passed a law in January 2017 banning work email after hours. This law requires companies with over fifty employees to grant their employees the "right to disconnect" from work email after leaving work in the evening. More recently, the

South Korean government rolled out an initiative that will automatically shut down its employees' computers at 8 p.m. on Fridays, to prevent overworking into the weekend. The strictness of these measures to force people toward leisure speaks to humans' obsession with labor. These examples also illustrate that the affinity for work and busyness is not exclusively an American phenomenon.

In another attempt to infuse work with freedom, several companies have implemented regimented work-based "free time." Google's "20% time" is the most famous example, such that it almost needs no explanation. Google founders Larry Page and Sergey Brin pioneered the 20% time policy in 2004 to give Google employees 20 percent of their time to spend doing whatever they like. This policy birthed products like Google Maps, Gmail, and Adsense, all of which produce significant revenue. Yet in 2013, Google decided to crack down on the policy and as of 2015 only 10 percent of employees were using it. Several ex-Googlers I have spoken to call the policy a myth and former Google employee-turned-Yahoo CEO Marissa Mayer stated, "I've got to tell you the dirty little secret of Google's 20% time. It's really *120%* time" (italics mine).[67] In other words, the policy nudged people into working beyond their normal duties instead of taking time off from their daily responsibilities to operate freely.

Other attempts to infuse leisure into work involve social events such as retreats, catered lunches, holiday parties, networking mixers, and happy hours (commonly called "mandatory fun"). As I have written elsewhere, these events often fail to improve cohesion and engagement for several reasons: people tend to cluster with those they know (instead of truly "mixing"), they awkwardly fuse business and personal relationships, and these events keep people's conversations focused on work.[68] I discussed the mandatory fun phenomenon with someone we'll call Laura, an employee at a nonprofit focused on workforce development for young adults. She described her experiences by writing me, "We have a decent amount of forced work bonding . . .

We'll have a lot of happy hours and there's definitely a work drinking culture." She noted often people working in nonprofits experience "traumatic bonding between employees" and that working with troubled youth "does actually require a degree of closeness and emotional bonding between the staff." She added, "On one hand, it is nice to have the support of people that you feel genuinely close to, but it also becomes suffocating. It'll be like 'have a difficult day, go to happy hour and get drunk and exhausted together, come back to work the next day still drained.'" Laura's experience illustrates how, despite the benefits of bonding, work-related socializing fails to provide true restorative leisure.

Organizations design initiatives for free time and socializing to fight exhaustion, burnout, and job dissatisfaction, yet simply sending people home might be more effective. This occurred to me when my brother (a medical resident at the time) told me how medical schools have increasingly sought to address emotional burnout among doctors and nurses. He described frequently seeing advertisements for various "resilience training" sessions intended to combat the pressures of the medical environment, particularly in critical care units where mortality and morbidity are high. Ironically, he told me, much of this training involves ruminating on stressful experiences, reliving difficult interactions with patients, and of course remaining at work. Such resilience programs seem to have some benefits for reducing burnout.[69] However, I would like to see their effects compared to sleep, watching TV, playing a game on their phone, or anything that pulls employees away from their actual jobs.

Taking leisure seriously and championing disengagement are necessary weapons to fighting a work-obsessed culture in which people increasingly fuse their personal identities with their labor. Furthermore, committing seriously to leisure will offset the demands of increasingly complex twenty-first-century work that involves multiple skills including sociability and variability. Doing so will require brave leadership from company leaders because it means forfeiting control over employees' time and placing it in employees' hands instead. In one recent promising experiment, New Zealand trusts firm Perpetual Guardian simply gave employees one day off per week, for two months. The firm gave workers four-day weeks while paying them for five days and found that stress decreased, job satisfaction increased, and productivity and performance remained strong. The company now wants to make the four-day workweek permanent, a promising step forward.[70]

* * * *

BECAUSE HUMANIZATION involves recognizing others as thinking, feeling beings, humanizing work requires organizations to provide work that recognizes employees' thoughts and feelings. This means giving people meaningful and challenging work and compensating them sufficiently, but as this chapter illustrates, it also involves something more. It involves ensuring employees do not feel disposable, mechanical, or commoditized in the face of automation—people have a deep need to be and feel irreplaceable. To avoid these experiences organizations must provide work that engages employees' most distinctively human skills while providing sufficient leisure time to detach people's identities from their jobs. Leisure itself, I would also argue, is a skill that robots can never master and, therefore, experiencing leisure whether through resting, listening to music, or simply letting one's mind drift enables people to feel "more than" automata.

As we see in the next chapter, despite the recommendations here for how to humanize work in the automation age, we must also accept that the rise of the machines will not reverse course. Therefore, we must learn how to effectively partner with these machines to retain our humanity in their presence.

CHAPTER 7

Building Human-Machine Partnerships

MY WIFE AND I RECENTLY WALKED OUR SON AROUND THE neighborhood and surprisingly found ourselves locked out when we returned. We called a locksmith company and they sent over a sixteen-year-old kid to help us. As the locksmith fiddled with our backdoor, I admired his surgical precision and pondered the future of his profession.

According to Frey and Osborne's 2013 analysis, locksmiths have a 77 percent likelihood of losing their jobs to automation. Already, a company called KeyMe has automated a primary function of locksmiths. Convenience stores like 7-Eleven house KeyMe kiosks where customers can pay $3.50 to scan the key that they want to copy. KeyMe then stores the digital file of each key on its online database, so that if customers find themselves locked out, they can log in to a kiosk using a fingerprint scan and pay another $20 to get a new key cut immediately, obviating the need to destroy their locks. Several roboticists have also developed robots capable of picking or breaking locks in a matter of seconds. These advancements suggest that human locksmiths' days are numbered.

However, in talking with the locksmith, one aspect of his job stood out to me as a particularly difficult task to automate. The first thing he asked me before tampering with the lock was whether we had a window open (it was a chilly day, and we did not). He explained to me that every time he arrives at a job, he first asks residents if they have an open window, and often the answer is yes. Residents far prefer scaling their houses or climbing a tree to jam themselves through a window than breaking their locks to get inside. This insight, I believe, gives the human locksmith superiority over a robot, as I know of no robot primarily tasked with completely disregarding the job it was programmed to do in order to develop a solution outside of its expertise.

"Aha!" an automation evangelist might respond. "Given machines' vast capability to learn from human performance, the automated locksmith would certainly come to learn about the benefits of open windows, and would add this to its repertoire of questions to ask before beginning the lock-breaking process!" And although plausible, it is also precisely why humans will likely stave off automation for longer than predictive models suggest. Machines almost always will be catching up with and learning from humans rather than the other way around. That is, machines need humans.

Although countless articles have expressed both anxiety and excitement over how humans and machines might collaborate in the automated future, there is little clarity over how these bonds will actually form. Here we explore this issue in greater depth.

As work becomes more mechanized, several possible solutions to this societal shift have emerged. All proposals are on the table, from universal basic income to support workers who lose their jobs to automation to Bill Gates's proposed "automation tax" on anyone who develops a robot that replaces human workers. The most optimistic vision of the automated future involves a division of labor whereby humans complete tasks for which they are uniquely suited while robots perform everything else. But what do these partnerships actually look like? Here I describe three prescriptive templates: (1) let robots and humans play to their respective moral strengths; (2) let robots handle the dull, rote, and mechanical work to give humans more interesting work; and (3) let robots reduce the emotional burdens that humans face in their jobs. We examine each one in turn.

Playing to Moral Strengths

In the context of decision making, people expect robots to be utilitarian entities that make choices based on cold, cost-benefit calculations. People expect humans, on the other hand, to follow "deontological" moral rules such as "do not actively discriminate against another person."[1] These expectations indeed reflect machines' and humans' unique moral strengths. Robots' moral advantage is their "blindness" to context. However, research shows humans prefer deontological decision makers who consider subjective factors related to harm and injustice to perfectly utilitarian decision makers.[2]

In work explicitly examining people's aversion to machines making moral decisions, psychologist Yochanan Bigman and Kurt Gray found that people indeed preferred humans instead of machines to make moral decisions in medical, military, and legal contexts, yet people were receptive to machines in an advisory role.[3] In one study asking participants whether a doctor, a computer system named Healthcomp (capable of rational, statistics-based thinking), or a doctor advised by Healthcomp should decide about pursuing a risky surgery for a child, a majority of people favored the doctor advised by the machine. Thus, one method of optimizing human-machine partnerships is letting robots guide decision processes through intensive utilitarian calculations and letting humans ultimately correct for any additional moral violations.

My colleague, sociologist Brian Uzzi, has written about this first prescription while discussing housing rental company Airbnb's response to racial discrimination complaints.[4] Airbnb's issues have included hosts sending racist messages to potential renters and denying or canceling renters' plans based on their race, as well as a report showing hosts were less likely to rent to individuals with stereotypically African American–sounding names. Uzzi describes how machine learning algorithms could scour user-generated text on the Airbnb website or on Twitter to identify "red flag" phrases that tend to predict discriminatory patterns of behavior from property hosts. Humans may not be able to identify the precise words that predict such behavior, and they definitely do not have the time to comb through countless terabytes of text-based data looking for red flag terms. This algorithmic search process, however, as Uzzi describes, is insufficient on its own to prevent large-scale discrimination. Such an effort would require comparing an algorithmic search process to information about property hosts through vetting them, as well as ensuring the algorithm is not developing its own biases (more on this below). The vetting process would involve asking hosts if they have a history of prejudiced behavior and favor certain races more than others. Here, human discrimination and diversity experts would need to design surveys and other methodological tools to obtain information directly and accurately from these hosts. And this is where humans would have to decide on the moral rule whereby we consider another person to be racially prejudiced or discriminatory. Machine learning can pinpoint hot-button words to identify people at risk of discriminating, but confirming these suspicions requires a human being asking people directly about their behavior and attitudes toward discrimination.

There exist several cases where machines left unchecked have produced more rather than less race-based and gender-based discrimination. For example, a *Bloomberg News* report found that Amazon's data-driven approach to determine where to offer Amazon Prime (a service that offers same-day delivery on products) neglected majority black neighborhoods in major American cities.[5] Amazon responded by describing how it uses various data points (including distance to order fulfillment centers and number of existing Prime members in a region) to determine algorithmically which neighborhoods are Prime eligible (and this was the reason, Amazon claims, black neighborhoods were excluded).[6] Yet consumers were not satisfied with this response, prompting human beings at Amazon to reverse course, admitting that the algorithmic process is unfair. Once these racial disparities became apparent, Amazon agreed to provide Prime services to the appropriate neighborhoods in Boston, New York, and Chicago.

Communications scholar Safiya Umoja Noble directly examines how algorithms fortify inequality in her book *Algorithms of Oppression: How Search Engines Reinforce Racism*.[7] Noble came to her topic after a Google search of the term "black girls" immediately returned to her results full of pornography featuring black women. Noble describes this discovery, writing, "Black girls were still the fodder of porn sites, dehumanizing them as commodities, as products and as objects of sexual gratification." When Noble searched Google asking "why are black women so . . . ," the autocompleted results were disparaging (e.g., "loud," "lazy," "rude"), whereas equivalent searches on "white women" were far more complimentary.

Noble describes several other examples of machine-learning-driven discrimination including Google's photo-organizing service tagging images of black people as gorillas. Again, once Google identified this glitch, human engineers fixed it. Similarly, when computer scientists Joy Buolamwini and Timnit Gebru presented research showing that algorithmic facial recognition software from Microsoft and IBM struggled to recognize black women's faces in particular, representatives from both companies responded that they would fix this issue.[8]

Machine discrimination occurs because computer programs can learn and produce gender- and race-based biases just as humans can. Research by computer scientist Aylin Caliskan illustrated this by using a machine learning program to scan massive amounts of text across the internet to learn the proximity of associations between different words (e.g., "dog" often occurs frequently next to "cat" but less frequently alongside "macaroni").[9] Her research found that machines trained on human-generated data (text) develop similar racial and gender-based associations as do humans, with pernicious consequences.

Caliskan's program associated African American names more with negative terms and European American names with more positive terms, a racial bias that commonly emerges in humans. The program also associated female-related words with family-related words and male-related words with career-related words. These biases are problematic because algorithms such as these form the basis of many online tools including Google Search's autocomplete function. As Noble found, searching phrases like "women are . . ." or "Chinese people are . . ." prompts Google to offer off-putting terms (e.g., "women are like children") because Google's algorithms learn through association. Caliskan also demonstrated this phenomenon by using Google Translate to translate a genderless phrase "bir doctor" in Turkish to English. The software translated the phrase to "he is a doctor," associating this professional term with males rather than females. Recently I just tried translating the same phrase, and it now translates appropriately to "a doctor," suggesting, again, that human beings at Google identified and corrected the issue.

Microsoft also inadvertently demonstrated machines' capacity for bias when it unleashed an artificial intelligence bot on Twitter to chat like a typical teenager in real time. The bot, named Tay or Taybot, mined publicly available text online to "learn" how to converse on Twitter, but within twenty-four hours of its release, it began spouting bigoted tweets such as "GAS THE KIKES RACE WAR NOW." Again, it took humans to flag this inappropriate behavior and shut the entire program down. The partnerships I am describing here require humans to do what they can exclusively do better than machines: decide the moral code we want to live by and teach machines accordingly. Because most of us have decided we want our moral code to exclude inequities based on race or gender, it is up to humans to identify when machine output appears to perpetuate these inequities and to correct course.

These examples of language-based biases are trivial when compared to the ways that machine learning has begun to influence more consequential decisions. Public interest website ProPublica published an exposé on how courtrooms have begun using algorithms to predict a criminal defendant's risk of future crime.[10] These programs calculate risk scores that humans then use to determine everything from assigning bail bond amounts to deciding whether or not to grant parole.

In contrast to the ProPublica article, computer scientist Jon Kleinberg and colleagues built a machine learning algorithm that can make better bail-granting decisions than human judges.[11] Kleinberg's research shows that an algorithm that learns based on human judges' prior decisions (in this case, five years of New York City arrests data), and accounts for various defendant characteristics (e.g., demographics, type of criminal charge, prior criminal record, or whether a defendant reoffends after being granted bail) could reduce crime without increasing jailing rates or reduce jailing rates without increasing crime. Implementing this particular algorithm would considerably reduce jailing rates of African American and Hispanic individuals.

The ProPublica exposé on such an algorithm (not Kleinberg's, but a tool called COMPAS—Correctional Offender Management Profiling for Alternative Sanctions) revealed something more pernicious: increased racial bias in criminal sentencing. The report showed that, for example, the sentencing formula that Broward County, Florida, used from 2013 to 2014 misidentified black defendants as future criminals almost twice as often as white defendants. Even after accounting for defendants' criminal history and criminal charge, the formula identified black defendants as 77 percent more likely to commit a future violent crime.

COMPAS used 137 questions ranging from queries like "Are there gangs in your neighborhood?" to "About how many times have you been fired from a job?" to "Is it difficult for you to keep your mind on one thing for a long time?" The relationship between these items and the risk of reoffending is murky, but one thing is clear: it will certainly require human beings to help determine the types of situations and personality traits that best predict criminal behavior to ensure these that decisions are morally just.

Let Robots Do Robotic Work

Beyond humans and machines dividing up moral decision-making, a second way to structure human-machine partnerships is to let robots do dull, routine work with humans taking on tasks that involve variety and spontaneity. Henry Wang, a former venture capitalist who has worked on investments in several early-stage AI companies, characterized these differences to me by noting, "A robot's mind cannot wander," whereas "the data you capture as a human being is broader and more random."[12] Given this distinction, humans and robots could complement each other using their opposing expertise, with robots mastering scripts, rules, and the routine while humans focus on variety, anomaly, and improvisation.

One question is whether such partnerships can emerge if robots have begun fully displacing workers in the "routine" jobs examined in chapter 6. Historically, we can observe the example of the automatic teller machine (ATM) and the bank teller. The machine performs the exceedingly rote job of counting and dispersing money whereas human bank tellers can handle more complex transactions while managing customers' concerns about their personal finances or the security of the bank. Eric Schmidt, executive chairman of Alphabet, attempted to assuage worries over automation and unemployment by noting that introducing ATMs in fact increased employment of bank tellers. However, Schmidt failed to explain that this primarily resulted from ATMs enabling banks to lower costs and open more branches, thereby employing more tellers.[13] Now that bank branches are declining (in part because ATMs are becoming more sophisticated and because many manage their money through mobile banking), this trend is unlikely to continue.

A more promising domain where humans and machines could split more routine and less routine work is cybersecurity. Several organizations have begun using machine learning to identify security risks by scrolling through endless data and using pattern recognition to flag potential threats. This task of identifying and storing patterns across millions of lines of data certainly qualifies as robotic work that few humans would enjoy. The problem is that these computerized systems produce too many false positives, tagging risks or attacks that turn out to be mundane behaviors. This is where humans come in—in particular, analysts who are capable of finding nuance and outliers in the data.

A study from MIT's Computer Science and Artificial Intelligence laboratory demonstrates how humans and machines can work together to optimize this task.[14] The MIT team developed a platform that could detect 85 percent of cyberattacks and reduce false positives to 5 percent through the following procedure: the platform sifts through gobs of data to identify any suspicious activity. It then reports a sample of its findings to human analysts. The analysts look in the sample to see if anything that the platform identified as a cyberattack is actually a false positive (something that the platform identifies as a virus may actually be anomalous). Then the human analysts feed that information back into the platform, which it uses to perform its next search for cyberattacks. Through this iterative process, the platform learns and improves its performance. The researchers suggest that an otherwise unsupervised machine would produce closer to a 20 to 25 percent false positive rate—not very promising.[15] Meanwhile, humans working alone would produce too many false negatives, missing critical security threats.

Cybersecurity provides a beacon of hope for human-machine collaboration. This is because (a) cyberattacks have become more sophisticated and thus require more human input, and (b) the cybersecurity field currently faces a human talent shortage. A 2015 report by Cyber-Security Ventures estimated that 3.1 million cybersecurity job openings would be available by 2021.[16] This trend suggests some optimism for humans and machines working together. As machines become capable of handling bigger and bigger data sets, we can let them do the dull, heavy lifting of scouring the web and matching patterns, while humans dig into what the patterns actually mean.

Another promising domain for this type of human-machine partnership is law. Law firms have begun employing technology that scans documents and aggregates data to determine which information is relevant for a particular case. This rote task of sifting through countless documents is the type of work that typically causes lawyers' hours to balloon; these new technologies seem poised to save lawyers significant valuable time. For example, in a *New York Times* article, bankruptcy lawyer Luis Salazar describes using an artificial intelligence program to find cases that best match the one he is currently pursuing.[17] As the program accomplished instantly the same task that took Salazar ten hours, he remarked, "It's kind of scary. If it gets better, a lot of people could lose their jobs." However, machines seem unlikely to master the art of persuasive argumentation and negotiation that is the core of human legal work. At least not yet.

Emotional Labor

Beyond partitioning principles of moral decision making or splitting up routine and nonroutine work, a third possible work arrangement between humans and machines is to divide emotional labor. Given that tasks involving empathy and emotion regulation can be depleting, offloading some of this work onto robots could restore our wherewithal to perform emotional labor as well. In an essay titled, "Let Robots Handle Your Emotional Burnout at Work," science writer Meeri Kim suggests robots could mitigate the negative consequences of emotional labor, including burnout and compassion fatigue.[18] This recommendation is counterintuitive considering research I have already described showing people dislike the idea of robots performing emotional tasks. However, designing robots that convey the proper emotional cues can mitigate this aversion (a topic to which I return below).

Kim suggests that jobs requiring social interaction are the most emotionally burdensome, noting, "Professions that require emotional labor, which involves inducing or suppressing emotion for the sake of a job, continue to see unprecedented levels of attrition, especially among customer service representatives, flight attendants, doctors, nurses, school teachers, and hotel employees." She also describes a humanoid customer service robot named Pepper that operates in one of these emotion-laden domains. Pepper is a baby-faced robot that operates in retail stores and hospitals. Currently, Pepper provides only limited responses and primarily communicates through text message. This rudimentary functionality enables Pepper to answer small queries, which is helpful for customers who are double-parked and just need to know which store aisle contains shampoo. However, once Pepper resolves these basic queries, humans can offer more customized and direct responses as to which shampoo is best for dandruff or whether a particular brand is on sale.

Some successful examples of how to divide this emotional labor come from phone-based customer service software. Customers despise the gauntlet of questions they must answer before actually talking to a human being. A *Harvard Business Review* article by Accenture consultants discusses how technology can alleviate this experience.[19] For example, they describe a Canadian financial services firm that uses a biometric program to identify the customer by voice, eliminating authentication questions altogether and improving customer service routing by 50 percent. They also describe a European Bank that uses biometrics to identify high-profile clients as their conversation progresses on the phone. This system has reduced call handling time, on average, by fifteen seconds, with 93 percent of clients rating the system positively. These systems can reduce the frustrations that customers typically offload onto innocent customer service agents, contributing to these agents' burnout. By eliminating the emotional burdens of the job, technology can free up customer service agents to handle more substantive inquiries beyond verification. As described in chapter 6, empathy will be essential for humans to remain employable in customer service, and if robots can manage the small frustrations like user authentication, they can free up humans to empathize with more complex customer issues.

Beyond phone-based customer service, domains that explicitly require social care and understanding could benefit from dividing emotional labor between humans and machines. For example, several companies are developing robots for socioemotional tasks ranging from therapy to preschool instruction to eldercare. People's general resistance to robots in emotional domains makes them a tough sell, but with the right features in place, they can succeed. Take, for example, the therapeutic robotic seal called Paro. In addition to being cuddly, socially responsive, capable of generating emotions, and able to learn people's names, Paro is most importantly nonhuman, which makes it seem nonthreatening and nonjudgmental. Research has shown that elderly individuals who interact with Paro show improved mental health and physical activity levels, although I know of no evidence suggesting such care robots can fully substitute for human companionship.[20]

What role can humans play then if robots become capable of assisting with care? This is the question I asked Ai-jen Poo, executive director of the National Domestic Workers Alliance.[21] Poo is a labor organizer who has devoted her career to fighting for domestic workers including eldercare workers. As the automation age coincides with a boom in the elderly population, Poo has begun thinking as much as anyone about how robots might collaborate with human caretakers. Poo told me, "There's a lot of things that technology will make it easier such as helping sort medications." She also mentioned how robotic technology could improve on the Hoyer lift (she calls it an "outdated piece of machinery") to physically transfer limited mobility individuals into a car or a bathtub. However, Poo also believes there is "an artificial distinction between manual labor and emotional labor." As she mentions, "The importance of touch and the intimacy that comes with that human contact is an important part of care." Poo's point resonates with other commentators warning that the decline of literal human touch in our daily lives is also contributing to declines in mental health.[22] As we saw in chapter 2, human touch can spur compassion, generate cooperation, and even reduce pain, and machines cannot provide a substitute.

Given the importance of human touch, it appears that caretaking robots are best used to give human caretakers a breather. Employing robots for key tasks can help people in emotionally demanding empathic work avoid burnout and compassion fatigue. In addition, despite the promise of therapeutic robots like Paro, emotion-laden human-machine partnerships only work if humans will engage with machines and, in some cases, treat them as they do other humans. Thus, enabling these partnerships requires designing technology in humanizing ways that attracts users rather than repels them. And this goes not only for work robots but also for robots performing mundane tasks from shopping to commuting to helping us stick to our exercise routines. In the following sections, we explore the research on robot design to understand the essential design principles for optimizing human engagement.

Optimal Design for Humanized Technology

A few years ago, an engineer from General Motors emailed me and asked if I was interested in studying the self-driving car. General Motors, like all the other forward-thinking automobile and technology companies, was developing its own version of a self-driving car and wanted a psychologist's point of view. In particular, the engineer wanted my colleagues and me to answer a simple question: Would people actually like such a vehicle?

General Motors then purchased us a very fancy and realistic driving simulator so that we could conduct a simple experiment.[23] We programmed the simulator to approximate driving in three separate ways for three separate experimental conditions. In one condition, participants drove as they normally would on any road, controlling steering, braking, speed, and changing lanes. In an autonomous condition, the vehicle controlled these features. In an anthropomorphic condition, the vehicle drove autonomously (as in the autonomous condition), but we also added three simple features. We gave the car a name ("Iris"), a gender (female), and a voice—Iris narrated the drive similar to a GPS system.

All participants drove the car through two courses: one basic driving course around a simulated city and one course that forced all participants to experience an unavoidable accident where a car backed out of a driveway and hit them. In addition, throughout the study, we measured trust in the vehicle in three ways. (1) We asked people to report how much trust and confidence they felt toward the car during the first course and how much they liked the car. (2) We measured their heart rate when they got into the accident in the second course to assess physiological arousal. (3) We videotaped their reactions to the accident and research assistants rated how startled the participants looked. These measures captured both self-reported trust in the car's competence and trust in terms of participants' comfort with the car.

Such measures enabled us to ask whether people would respond more favorably to driving normally or driving autonomously. And would the addition of human features make any difference?

We found that people reported trusting the car more and appeared less startled by the accident (both in their videotaped responses and in their heart rate change) in the anthropomorphic condition as compared to the autonomous and normal conditions. We also asked participants to indicate how much their car should be punished and blamed for the accident, and people held the car in the autonomous and anthropomorphic conditions more responsible. This response is unsurprising given that, in the normal condition, the car itself had very little to do with the accident. Yet interestingly, blame and punishment dropped in the anthropomorphic condition compared to the autonomous condition, suggesting participants gave the car the benefit of the doubt when it appeared more humanlike. Despite looming fears about the safety of self-driving vehicles, and despite people's attachment to driving, people responded much more positively overall to the conditions where the car drove autonomously. And people responded even more positively when the car had a voice, name, and gender.

This study echoes the research presented in chapter 3 on how humanness engenders moral care. It demonstrates that mere humanness can encourage trust and affiliation with technology, allowing people to preserve their own humanity in the presence of robotic agents.

Addressing the Uncanny

Considering the methodological and time constraints for our self-driving car study, we could only add the most minimal of humanlike cues—gender, name, and voice. When I have presented this work publicly, people have asked whether adding excessively humanlike features might pose a threat to users or provoke discomfort, to which I have responded, "Sure."

Many are familiar with the concept of the "uncanny valley," robot-icist Masahiro Mori's 1970 observation that as robots become more humanlike in appearance, people feel more positively toward them until a certain point where robots become uncannily humanlike.[24] At this point, people become repulsed. Entities that fall within this val-ley include not only robots but also animated characters such as Tom Hanks's conductor in *The Polar Express*—Hanks's character appears just a bit too much like the real Hanks to fit into the human or non-human category, creating a discomfort that repels viewers.[25] In Mori's original essay, he describes a prosthetic hand that looks humanlike but feels dead and cold. This is where the discomfort emerges.

A 2016 viral video featuring legendary Japanese filmmaker and ani-mator Hayao Miyazaki illustrated this phenomenon. The video depicts Miyazaki listening to a group of student programmers showing him an animation created by an artificial intelligence program. In the animation, a zombie with discernibly human features writhes across the floor in a manner unlike any human. An exasperated Miyazaki responds, "Whoever creates this stuff has no idea what pain is what-soever. I am utterly disgusted," adding, "I strongly feel that this is an insult to life itself."[26]

In my many years of trying to study the uncanny valley, I have never truly figured out its practical importance. I have also observed that empirical tests of the phenomenon sometimes fail to produce its predicted pattern.[27] As it turns out, Mori's original title of his essay, "Bukimi No Tani," does not translate to "uncanny valley" (a mistranslation popularized by American authors) but rather is bet-ter encapsulated by the phrase "valley of eeriness." This more gen-eral phenomenon implies a simpler point: more humanness is not always better. Despite the overarching argument in chapters 2 and 3 that humanness enhances perceptions of meaningfulness, value, and morality, it appears that excessive human resemblance can also be off-putting. Indeed, technology theorist Nicholas Carr explains that one reason consumers have readily adopted robotic smart speakers (e.g., Amazon Echo, Google Home, Apple HomePod) in their homes is these speakers do not resemble humans. "Lacking human characteristics," Carr explains, "smart speakers avoid the uncanny valley altogether."[28]

In the next several sections, we will see how designing technology for effective human-machine interaction involves knowing which human cues to select. Considerable research has examined how to humanize machines optimally, presenting them as humanlike enough to engage users but not too uncanny to repulse them. Let us explore that research now.

Voice Unlocks Humanness

As demonstrated by the success of vocally communicative smart speakers and our insights from the earlier self-driving car study, voice can humanize technology to positive ends. It may in fact be the most important feature for conveying humanness without spurring revulsion.

Renowned human-computer interaction expert Clifford Nass and his student Scott Brave wrote in their 2005 book *Wired for Speech* about the voice's critical function for anthropomorphic technology. Nass and Brave describe how voice engages people with technology, stating that "over the course of 200,000 years of evolution, humans have become *voice-activated* with brains that are wired to equate voices with people and to act on that identification . . . Because humans will respond socially to voice interfaces, designers can tap into the automatic and powerful responses elicited by all voices . . . to increase trust, efficiency, learning, and even buying."[29] They suggest that voice is a fundamental cue to an entity's human likeness, and research since has shown this cue engages us in several positive ways.

Research outside of technology use led by psychologists Juliana

Schroeder and Nick Epley has shown how voice conveys credibility. In their studies, they asked professional recruiters and participants role-playing hypothetical employers to evaluate job candidates making a pitch.[30] These observers watched, listened to, or read pitches that candidates delivered through video, audio-only, or text-only means. Participants rated candidates as smarter and more competent when they heard the candidates' voices (either through audio or video means) compared to merely reading their pitches, even though the information conveyed in the pitches was exactly the same. What is more, Schroeder and Epley found video pitches were no better than audio-only pitches. Thus, their studies show that voice, rather than visual appearance, is critical to conveying credibility. In other work, Schroeder and Epley showed that adding voice (but not video) to a script of computer-generated text made people more likely to judge that a human being generated the text.[31] This work suggests that voice critically engages people and that observable appearance provides little added benefit beyond voice in communicating the presence of an intelligent mind.

Deroboticizing the Robotic

Voice is a critical humanizing cue for robot design, but how should designers optimize robot behavior? I believe a certain degree of spontaneity might be the key. As I discussed earlier in this chapter as well as in chapter 6, we tend to prize technology for its rote, predictable nature, whereas we value other humans' ability to deviate from scripted behavior. However, programming a certain degree of unpredictability in machines can increase our engagement with them.

This instruction might sound counterintuitive, but for proof, take a study of toddlers' responses to a humanoid robot in a childhood education center.[32] The study involved observing children interacting with the robot over a five-month period in three distinct phases. During phase 1, the researchers introduced the robot, which displayed its full behavioral repertoire, including walking, dancing, sitting, standing, lying down, giggling, and making hand gestures. Over this time period, the quality of children's interactions with the robot steadily improved as rated by the researchers. However, in phase 2, the researchers programmed the robot to behave predictably, mostly just dancing alone; the quality of interaction with the toddlers deteriorated substantially. When, in phase 3, the researchers reintroduced the robot's full behavioral variability, interaction improved again with the toddlers now treating the robot as a peer rather than an inanimate object. They were fully engaged.

Some of my own research, noted in this book's introduction, also supports this point. It demonstrates that robots that behave in minimally unpredictable ways can encourage people to want to make sense of the robot's behavior.[33] This sense-making motivation then prompts people to humanize the robot. For example, we programmed a computerized robot to respond to yes or no questions with consistent patterns (mostly yes or mostly no) or with unpredictable patterns (50 percent yes, 50 percent no). When the robot behaved unpredictably, people were more likely to treat it like a human being. In subsequent work, we showed that encouraging people to think about nonhuman entities as humanlike also made people feel that they better understood the entity. Our work suggests that a little bit of unpredictability spurring humanization can enhance interactions with technology.

The idea here is not to program robots to behave randomly but rather to introduce subtle variability outside of the robot's specified task to keep people engaged. Minimal unpredictability motivates people to make sense of that unpredictability through humanizing it. In this way, making robots a tad less robotic can improve our interactions with them.

One example of what such a robot would look like is Mimus. Mimus is an industrial robot that computational design scholar Madeline Gannon developed and programmed to behave in an unconstrained fashion. A description on Mimus's website reads, "Mimus has no preplanned movements: she is programmed with the freedom to explore and roam about her enclosure."[34] On display at the London Design Museum, Mimus can mimic the movements of observers, respond to gestures by moving closer or farther away, explore its environment, or simply get bored and shut down. Mimus's description follows: "Ordinarily, robots like Mimus are completely segregated from humans as they do highly repetitive tasks on a production line. With Mimus, we illustrate how wrapping clever software around industry-standard hardware can completely reconfigure our relationship to these complex, and often dangerous, machines. Rather than view robots as a human adversary, we demonstrate a future where autonomous machines, like Mimus, might be companions that co-exist with us."

How Mimus would work in an actual industrial setting is still unclear. Would workers respond more amicably to an industrial robot that took occasional breaks to interact with them? Would human employees more quickly solve a problem that a machine cannot address if they are more attuned to that machine's diverse behaviors? I would certainly welcome the experiment to test whether an ounce of machine spontaneity could facilitate better human-machine interactions on the factory floor.

Humans in Charge

The goal of designing a robot for which human employees feel responsible is to empower employees. This goal also addresses a consistent concern about the rise of intelligent technology—namely, that it will threaten humans' autonomy. We humans, as it turns out, generally like to call our own shots, control our situations, and experience choice and independence in our daily actions. When technology threatens our autonomy, we might discard it even when it offers us convenience. One potential solution to this threat is making robots more childlike. Given that threats to autonomy are already a broad concern for aging adults, introducing robots that aid them in small tasks might exacerbate these concerns. If the robots doing the caregiving could also receive care, such a relationship could give elderly individuals a sense of responsibility and empowerment.

I asked Tandy Trower about this possibility.[35] Trower is, as of writing, CEO of Hoaloha Robotics, after having spent twenty-eight years at Microsoft where he successfully launched the Windows operating system and other iconic products. In 2005, he joined Microsoft founder Bill Gates's strategic staff and then led Microsoft's initiative on robotics. He left Microsoft in 2009 to start Hoaloha, which specializes in developing social companion robots for the elderly that can perform various tasks from retrieving objects to scheduling reminders for users to call their grandchildren. Trower wrote to me, "It is very important that our user regard our robot as being in a subordinate, but not 'servant' role. This is important not only to ensure that the user feels in control (a basic tenet of good design), but also helps sets expectations appropriately. . . . Our approach starts with the paradigm center[ing] on a good companion, and our model is the role of conventional 'sidekick.' In almost every case, Barney to Fred, Boo Boo to Yogi (yes showing my age here), Robin to Batman, etc. there is a dominant partner and a subordinate one. In our scenarios, the user is the dominant partner. We reinforce this in several ways. First, our design presents our robot more as a youthful/child-like personality. When it introduces itself, it notes that it doesn't know very much and requires interaction with the user to get better." Trower clearly understands the importance of granting the user autonomy and giving the user an opportunity to care for others.

Designing eldercare robots to be subordinate or childlike follows the same logic of giving elderly individuals other opportunities for mastery. A famous 1976 study of nursing home residents by psychologists Ellen Langer and Judith Rodin showed that giving elderly individuals the responsibility to care for a houseplant increased their activity, alertness, and general happiness, as compared to a group given a plant under the care of the nursing home staff.[36] Granting responsibility through plant care gave these individuals a sense of agency in their lives that critically enhanced well-being. By the same token, giving elderly individuals responsibility to "care" for a childlike robot could create a sense of mastery even as the robot is in place to assist them.

One radical example of a successful childlike robot is the Blab-droid, which is barely a robot at all. Developed by artist and roboticist Alexander Reben, the Blabdroid is a cardboard robot on wheels whose face resembles that of a wide-eyed infant. The Blabdroid also speaks in a child's voice. In a panel I sat on with Reben to discuss the future of artificial intelligence, he noted that he specifically used cardboard instead of plastic and metal because it makes the robot "feel more familiar and more vulnerable."[37] Reben also presented a film for which he sent various Blabdroids out in the world across several continents, equipped with video cameras, to document humans' responses to its inquiries. He programmed the robot to get "stuck" in public places and to request help and thereby demonstrated that passersby consis-tently showed a willingness to provide assistance. More impressively, Reben programmed the Blabdroid to ask strangers sensitive questions (e.g., "Who do you love most in the world?" or "What is something you have never told a stranger before?") and found people willingly divulged their deepest secrets to the Blabdroid. People's comfort with the Blabdroid's childlike appearance seemed to put them at ease and make them willing to collaborate with it. Reben's experiment also demonstrated that the most effective design for a robot interacting with humans does not need to be technologically sophisticated.

Matching Tasks and Users

Beyond designing robots that preserve humans' autonomy, it is also crucial to customize them to the particular task they are performing and to the user for which they are performing. Research consistently demonstrates that doing this optimizes the user's experience. Demonstrating the importance of task matching, Michael Norton and I found that people preferred robots designed to appear capable of cognition to perform cognitive tasks (e.g., data analysis) whereas they preferred robots designed to appear more capable of emotion for more social tasks (e.g., social work).[38] We drew on work showing that people perceive robots with "baby-faced" features such as a small chin and wide eyes to have greater emotional capability compared to robots with more masculine and mature facial features. In our studies, people preferred the more baby-faced robot for more emotional tasks. This finding also provides an answer to how to mitigate people's discomfort with robots taking on emotional labor—that is, make the robot appear capable of emotion.

Research led by psychologist Jennifer Goetz also shows the importance of matching robot appearance to its specified task.[39] In one study, Goetz and colleagues designed two-dimensional robots to be more humanlike or more machinelike, and asked college students which robots they preferred for jobs that were more or less social in nature. Jobs for which participants preferred more humanlike robots were more social in nature such as aerobics instructor and museum tour guide. Jobs for which participants preferred more machinelike robots were jobs that were less social such as a customs inspector or lab assistant. A subsequent study by these researchers found that people complied more with a robot that instructed them to stick to an exercise routine when the robot behaved seriously rather than playfully. This was because the task itself was not playful, but rather one that required discipline, the match between the robot personality and the task made users more engaged.

Along these lines, an experiment by psychologist Gale Lucas and colleagues showed what robot psychotherapy might look like. Lucas and colleagues showed that designing a virtual human to appear capable of emotional understanding increased participants' comfort with the robot conducting a mental health screening interview, a situation rife with emotion.[40] In this paradigm, the virtual human, which could detect specific emotions and respond in real time, appeared on a computer screen to conduct a semistructured interview. In Lucas's experiment, the mental health screening interview varied across two conditions. In one condition, participants believed the virtual human was fully automated, and in another condition, they believed human researchers in the next room were controlling it. Participants answered interview questions, such as "Tell me about an event or something that you wish you could erase from your memory," and evaluated the interview process overall. When participants believed that other humans were absent from the process and that they were interacting with artificial intelligence alone, they disclosed more personal information and reported less fear of being evaluated negatively. In other words, when the robot appeared independently capable of emotional intelligence, people engaged with it more naturally and effectively.

Other work by Clifford Nass and colleagues also shows the importance of not only matching the robot to the task but also matching the robot to the user. In particular, Nass's work has shown the benefits of matching technological agents' voices to the users' emotional states and personalities. In one study, Nass's research team measured participants' personalities to classify them as introverts or extroverts, and then asked them to peruse an Amazon.com-like book-buying website.[41] The website included information and reviews about books delivered by a vocal agent. In varying conditions, Nass manipulated the agent's voice to sound more extroverted or introverted, producing speech with higher quickness, loudness, mean frequency, and frequency range to mimic extroverted speech and lowering these qualities to produce more introverted speech.

After exploring the website, participants rated each book reviewer agent, and both introverts and extroverts rated the agent whose voice matched their personality higher on credibility, liking, and review quality. Both groups also reported more interest in purchasing books from the website when there was a personality match. A follow-up study found similar results using an online auction website modeled off eBay.com. Nass and colleagues programmed an extroverted or introverted voice—manipulating the same dimensions of quickness, loudness, frequency, and frequency range as in the book recommendation study—to describe collectible auctions and found participants preferred the voice that matched their personality.

To take this idea further, Nass and colleagues conducted another study that used a driving simulator to examine matching machines and users on emotional state.[42] In this study, the researchers first manipulated participants' moods by playing film and TV clips that either communicated happy or sad themes to put the participants in a good or bad mood. Then all participants drove a simulated course narrated by a "virtual passenger" GPS system. For half of the participants, the voice of the virtual passenger spoke with a happy, energetic tone while for the other half of participants the virtual passenger spoke with a subdued, sadder tone. Participants could speak back to the virtual passenger, and the amount of that speaking served as a measure of engagement. Afterward, participants completed a questionnaire evaluating the overall experience. The researchers also counted how many accidents participants got in during the simulation and how attentive they were while driving, measured by their reaction time to driving-specific tasks.

As predicted, matching users and agents on emotional state greatly improved users' driving experience. When a happy-sounding virtual agent accompanied happy drivers and when a sad-sounding agent accompanied sad drivers, participants got in fewer accidents, reported more alertness, and responded more quickly to events on the road even while they communicated more with the virtual passenger. Emotion-matching enhanced user engagement and safety.

Together, these findings suggest the importance of robot customization for work, leisure, shopping, commuting, and more. Knowing the task that the robot will perform and knowing who the user is can enable robot designers to tailor the robot to the specific user experience, optimizing the human-machine relationship.

* * * *

SIX MONTHS before beginning this book, I attended an academic conference in Tel Aviv. The experience of traveling to Tel Aviv was largely bereft of human beings. From my home in Chicago, I used the Uber app on my phone to request a ride to the airport, bypassing the old system of having to call and talk to a cab dispatcher. I put my headphones on in the cab and listened to a Kamaiyah album instead of talking to the driver. During the ride, I pulled up my boarding pass on my phone so that I could avoid any gate agent or boarding pass–dispensing machine at the airport and headed straight to the security line.

I took an initial flight from Chicago O'Hare to Newark where I had a four-hour layover. The Newark airport offers a fantastic and novel (to me) dining experience. Simply sit down at any table, view the menu presented on an iPad affixed to that table, select on the iPad what you would like to eat, and a server delivers it to your table with minimal interaction. You pay using the iPad when you are finished.

After eating my spaghetti Bolognese and drinking a diet Coke, I realized I had forgotten my phone charger, and with little time before my next flight, I found a vending machine that dispensed electronic devices. Using the machine precluded me from waiting in a store line or navigating overeager salespeople. When it was finally time to board my Tel Aviv flight, as luck would have it, the seat next to mine was empty. This was as human-free an experience as one could possibly have on an international journey.

One need not be an introvert to find the experience I described above as enjoyable. Even the most gregarious among us appreciate both freedom and efficiency during travel. Yet as I began to dive deeper into the research required for this book, I realized that a human-less experience is greatly deficient compared to a more human one, even if it comes at the expense of convenience. As technology becomes more advanced, travel and other basic activities will become even more human-free (and the experience described here will likely sound quaint to future readers). Human beings will become less relevant, as navigating the complexity of others' feelings, desires, wants, needs, and opinions will become less of a necessary activity. Therefore, it is incumbent upon us to push back against automation or to at least make our interactions with technology more human.

We might also ask, given humans' desire to connect socially with others, why would so many of us prefer a human-less experience in the first place? As we've already seen, interacting with humans is mentally demanding and empathy is one of the hardest tasks in our cognitive repertoire. Because of our limited capacity for deep social engagement, we often discard or overlook other humans who do not reside within our immediate social circle (those who differ from us in psychologically significant ways). In the next two chapters, we learn how to improve relationships with these socially distant others, as well as with those closest to us.

CHAPTER 8

Seeing Human amid Conflict

IF HUMAN-MACHINE CONFLICT REPRESENTS SOCIETY'S NEW-
est challenge, intergroup conflict represents its oldest. Conflict
between ethnicities, nationalities, religions, ideologies, and tribes has
raged for millennia and research on such intergroup conflict largely
provided the foundation for my (relatively young) home discipline,
social psychology.

A flurry of intergroup conflict research followed the Second World
War, with social psychologists in subsequent years attempting to
explain events such as the Holocaust, Bosnian genocide, or Rwandan
civil war. Yet perhaps social psychology's most important insight on
intergroup conflict came from a summer camp. Psychologists Muzafer
Sherif and Carolyn Sherif famously studied competing factions of
Boy Scouts of America campers in Robbers Cave State Park in Oklahoma in the early 1950s.[1] Among several important findings, their key
contribution was showing that they could reduce conflict between
these groups by highlighting shared goals between them. Decades
of research that followed focused on the benefits of superordinate
goals (that supersede any particular group's interests) including goals
to fight a common enemy or to create a common identity. Common

identity, common goals, and common villains highlight the human needs of "them" to reveal that they are surprisingly like "us."

Before scrutinizing these common ground–oriented attempts at creating shared humanization, let us first look at dehumanization's role in intergroup conflict more broadly. Of course, conflict can occur without dehumanization, but I believe it is central to conflict. Let's revisit some fundamental assertions to explain why.

To return to the definition of dehumanization established in the introduction, dehumanization represents the failure (either deliberately or not) to consider another person as having a mind capable of thinking and feeling. Dehumanization, therefore, can enable violence and other forms of aggression in the following way: given our strong aversion to harming other humans, construing an out-group as lacking emotion or reason means that aggression toward that out-group does not constitute harm any more than slamming a notebook on a table does. In addition to enabling harm, people also use dehumanization to justify intergroup violence post hoc, excusing aggression already done (e.g., "they were not really humans, so the crime is not so severe").[2] This sort of post hoc dehumanization can then license subsequent violence toward the group, as it is easier to be aggressive toward someone that you have already mistreated.

As merely one of several mechanisms underlying conflict, I believe dehumanization is nonetheless fundamental to intergroup conflict because of how we cognitively process the self and others. A set of core psychological mechanisms leads us to dehumanize other people virtually by default, leading to outsized dehumanization of out-groups. Let's look at how these mechanisms operate sequentially.

First, people inherently perceive themselves to have greater mental capacity than others. This phenomenon is what Nick Epley, Juliana Schroeder, and I have collectively termed the *lesser minds problem*.[3] This problem occurs not merely because we think we are mentally superior to or smarter than others but also stems from a basic feature of cognition—that is, we have direct access to our own minds but not to other people's minds. As a result of this indirect access to other people's minds, these other minds seem lesser—that is, dimmer, weaker, more inadequate—than our own. Several lines of research document this phenomenon across various judgments about others' mental states. For example, studies show that people perceive themselves to have more free will than others.[4] People also believe they experience embarrassment more frequently than others.[5] And people believe that they are more capable of rational thought (i.e., being impermeable to cognitive bias) than others.[6] That we perceive our capacities for intention, emotion, and reason as more robust than others' means that we fundamentally see ourselves as more human than other people.

To test this phenomenon yourselves, if you are reading this book in a coffee shop, on a train, or at home with family, take a moment to ask yourself how you feel right now and what you think about the information I just described in the previous paragraph. Now, identify the closest person nearby and ask yourself how that person is feeling right now and what he or she is thinking. The difference in difficulty between these two tasks is the essence of the lesser minds problem. Others' minds are less visible to us than our own and, by contrast, appear more superficial.

And yet we do not perceive all other minds as equally lesser. People view in-group minds, those minds belonging to members of our family, religion, country, and ethnicity, as similar to themselves and, therefore, as being reasonably human.[7] Getting into the minds of in-group members is somewhat manageable because we share experiences, histories, and values with these people that allow us to easily approximate their mental states. By contrast, out-groups are inherently dissimilar from our in-group in appearance, values, shared history, and cultural norms, making those minds harder for us to access. And because of the simple contrast effect between those who look and act like us and those who do not, we mostly view out-groups as less mentally capable and thus less human than in-group members.[8]

This contrast between in-group and out-group represents the second psychological mechanism that produces intergroup dehumanization. What the lesser minds problem and this in-group–out-group contrast phenomenon demonstrate is that animosity between groups is not necessary for dehumanization to occur. (Animosity does, however, exacerbate the contrast between in-group and out-group.) These processes simply result from how vision and attention operate—that is, we are more capable of noticing the mental complexities of the self than of others. Because perceiving out-groups as less than human is an inherent psychological tendency, dehumanization tends to be the starting point from which intergroup interaction occurs, establishing the ideal conditions for conflict to proceed.

As noted in the introduction, real, blatant intergroup dehumanization is not a relic of the past when violence was more frequent and severe. Government leaders and military members strategically use dehumanizing rhetoric toward out-groups to highlight the contrast between "us" and "them" and to perpetuate conflict among their constituents. The current Israeli-Palestinian conflict, for example, is rife with dehumanization of this type, with Israeli Prime Minister Benjamin Netanyahu in recent years likening Muslims and non-Israeli Middle Easterners as "wild beasts"[9] and "dangerous animals."[10]

Historian Roberta Strauss Feuerlicht illustrated this dehumanization in describing a 1981 report on the Israeli military's treatment of Arabs on the West Bank. In this report, issued by the Israeli League for Human and Civil Rights, Feuerlicht details "information that came from Israeli army reservists who were troubled by what they had experienced. One reservist reported that when his unit arrived in Hebron they participated in an orientation session on the Arabs. The orientation instructed them that Arabs 'are not like human beings' and should be treated like 'animals.'"[11] Pervasive dehumanizing rhetoric in this conflict contributes to its intractability because it lessens the moral burden of harming other humans.

Dehumanizing rhetoric also thrives in other long-standing conflicts such as Hindu-Muslim tension in India. In late 2017, Yogi Adityanath, chief minister of India's most populous state Uttar Pradesh, called Muslims a "crop of two-legged animals that has to be stopped."[12] Such description is intended to spur his militant Hindu youth organization to avenge what they perceive to be past wrongs perpetrated by Muslims. When delivered by a powerful politician such as Adityanath, these statements fuel the fire of long-standing bitterness between certain Hindus and Muslims in India.

Dehumanization of this type also plagues Myanmar, where the military has undertaken large-scale ethnic cleansing of the majority-Muslim Rohingya people. This conflict stems from post–World War II fallout, after the Rohingya fought on behalf of the British, whereas many Buddhists, who represent Myanmar's majority population, fought on behalf of the Japanese against the British. In a 2017 *New York Times* article describing how high-ranking Buddhists encouraged this conflict over several decades, Jeffrey Gettleman writes, "Some influential Buddhist monks said the Rohingya were the reincarnation of snakes and insects and should be exterminated, like vermin."[13] This demonizing view of Rohingya as a pest, in need of extermination, has fueled reactionary responses from the Rohingya with horrific violence resulting.

Beyond these prominent stories, scientific evidence for such intergroup dehumanization is widespread and multifaceted.[14] For example, from chapter 1 we've seen research showing that people see out-groups as less evolved and more animalistic than in-groups. People often believe in-group members can experience uniquely human emotions such as nostalgia and optimism, whereas out-group members can only experience baser emotions such as panic and fright, which people often believe are emotions shared with lower animals. Related work shows that people across different ethnicities perceive their out-groups to lack traits considered uniquely human or essential to human nature.[15]

Dehumanization also dominates stereotypes and perceptions of racial and ethnic minorities. Psychologist Philip Goff and colleagues have shown that people associate images of apes more readily with black faces than with white faces.[16] Goff's research has also shown that news articles written about black convicts contained more ape-related words than equivalent news articles about white convicts. Some of my work with psychologists Kelly Hoffman and Sophie Trawalter has contributed to a broad literature demonstrating a different form of racially biased dehumanization: Observers view black people to experience less pain and require less pain treatment than white people, even when the cause of harm is the same.[17] Interestingly, Goff's work and our work show that both white and nonwhite participants demonstrate these racial biases, suggesting the effects may not result from bias alone. Nonetheless, these dehumanizing perceptions contribute to exacerbating the interracial divide in consequential ways. For example, so robustly do people underestimate nonwhites' experience of pain that, according to one study, pharmacies in nonwhite neighborhoods understock opioid analgesics compared to pharmacies in primarily white neighborhoods.[18]

As another illustrative example of this racial bias in a medical context, consider African American tennis icon Serena Williams. Shortly after giving birth to her daughter, Williams nearly died because of inattention to her reports of pain.[19] Williams describes how she began experiencing shortness of breath and asked a nurse for a CT scan and blood thinner to treat what she believed to be blood clots. The nurse assumed she was confused, and a doctor soon arrived only to perform an ultrasound of her lower body. After an inconclusive ultrasound, she finally received the CT scan, which indeed revealed blood clots in her lungs. Williams's encounter is sadly emblematic of medical professionals' propensity to overlook the pain of black patients,[20] a tendency that may even contribute to African American women dying at a disproportionate rate after childbirth.[21]

Related to racial bias in perceptions of pain, other work I conducted with Hoffman and Trawalter documented a separate form of racial dehumanization toward African Americans specifically among white participants. We found evidence of white participants *superhumanizing* black people.[22] For example, in one study we asked white participants this question: Between a white individual and a black individual, who is more capable of superhuman abilities like suppressing hunger and thirst or surviving a fall from an airplane? Participants consistently selected black individuals a majority of the time. Although such depictions might appear on the surface complimentary, note that superhumanization still involves denying people core mental states and categorizing them as something other than humans. Furthermore, we found this tendency to cast black people outside the human realm as god-like or spirit-like contributed to perceiving black people as less afflicted by physical pain.

Common to all these different forms of dehumanization is denying racial out-groups and minorities a complex inner mental life. By denying this inner life, people can more easily justify and perpetrate prejudice and discrimination. Author Toni Morrison characterized the inherently dehumanizing nature of racism in noting that its mundane character carries an additional consequence: "The function, the very serious function of racism," Morrison stated, "is distraction. It keeps you from doing your work. It keeps you explaining, over and over again, your reason for being. Somebody says you have no language and you spend twenty years proving that you do. Somebody says your head isn't shaped properly so you have scientists working on the fact that it is. Somebody says you have no art, so you dredge that up. Somebody says you have no kingdoms, so you dredge that up. None of this is necessary. There will always be one more thing."[23] Denying a group's "reason for being," their language, their art, or their kingdoms simply rejects that group's capacity for human achievement and represents them as lesser minds.

Finding Common Humanity

The examples above illustrate how the lesser minds problem initiates dehumanization and how the intergroup divide exacerbates this problem. Other minds are less accessible than our own and therefore appear lesser. Out-group minds are even more distant from and dissimilar to the self and therefore appear *considerably* lesser. If these processes represent the steps to dehumanizing out-groups, then the solution to reducing intergroup dehumanization seems simple: focus on reducing the social distance between people, making them more self-like and, thus, perceptibly more human. Although the recommendation sounds easy, in practice it is far messier. Important research has shown the benefits of trying to find common humanity across groups and subsequent work has provided an important caveat to the idea of common humanity as a panacea. We examine both in turn.

Recently, a student of mine demonstrated—better than any scientific study—the power of recognizing common humanity as a solution to dehumanization. I often meet my most fascinating students while teaching our executive MBA (EMBA) program. Students in this program are typically in their late thirties or early forties who are going back to school while working. These are financially successful people in executive-level positions in industries like financial services, communication and information technology, and manufacturing. A particular student stood out, however, because he had a unique background as a Special Operations Soldier, or Green Beret.

When I told my EMBA class I was writing a book about humanization and dehumanization, this student (who I'll call David)
approached me after class with extensive insights on both topics.
David was not just a Green Beret, but in fact had a twenty-year career
in the military with nine combat deployments. These included the
United States' first deployment to Afghanistan after September 11,
2001, to fight the Taliban as well as several deployments to Iraq under
Operation Iraqi Freedom.

I was most interested in David's experiences with dehumanization—
how the military makes people comfortable with killing. He told me
about how, whether intentional or not, dehumanization encompasses
the military culture, even in the language used to describe combat.
Soldiers refer to enemy combatants as "targets," or more simply, the
"objective area." He mentioned the phrase "mowing the grass" that
refers to the practice of killing and capturing insurgent groups, knowing that others will grow into those same insurgent positions. He also
described how killing becomes professionalized. "As a Green Beret,"
he told me, "you're the NBA, NFL of the military; this is what you
do," adding that, "the operator feels no pain." If killing is simply part of
your job, then it becomes routinized; to break from that routine would
be disobeying your role.

He also described humor as a form of dehumanization, telling me
of colleagues who once found the hand of a suicide bomber shortly
after detonating. As they stared at the hand on the ground, one of
them picked it up and began high fiving it. David clearly recognized
the grimness of this event but also noted how it diffused the tension
of the moment.

Despite the necessity of dehumanization in his line of work, David
noted humanization was a far more effective tactic. He described
how gaining familiarity with the other side led him to realize that
"one man's terrorist is another man's freedom fighter." He added, "You

have a far greater reach on the battlefield if you treat them how you want to be treated; if you don't treat them as idiots because they don't speak the language." In other words, productive exchanges with the other side begun once he stopped considering them as mindless. He described the humanizing process in practice, stating, "You meet with mullahs, and hear their grievances and you meet with those people where they are. I talk about my family, I show pictures of my kids, and they talk about their family."

David's insight complements our research showing this tendency to focus on outgroups' perceived hatred rather than their capacity to love their own drives conflict. As described in chapter 1, Liane Young, Jeremy Ginges, and I found that amid political conflict, American Democrats and Republicans believe out-group hate motivates the other party rather than in-group love. We also found the same pattern among Israelis and Palestinians.[24] When we surveyed nationally representative samples of Israelis and Palestinians to ask them what motivated their own group to support conflict and what motivated the other group, both replied similarly. Palestinians and Israelis each said that their group was more motivated by love (of their own side) whereas the other group was more motivated by hatred (of the other side). We also found that the strength of this perceived hate-love asymmetry predicted opposition to conciliatory action such as peaceful negotiations, or, in the case of Israelis, voting for a two-state solution. When, in one study, we incentivized one side in a conflict to recognize that their out-group was driven by in-group love, they became more optimistic about reaching a resolution and more willing to negotiate. As in our research, my Green Beret student felt most optimistic in uncovering the other side's motivation to protect their own and care for their families.

Strategies such as these that reduce social distance through finding common humanity can typically be divided into three categories: creating shared goals, creating shared enemies, and highlighting shared identity. Let's look at the evidence for each one.

Shared Goals

Sherif and Sherif's summer camp research powerfully demonstrated how shared goals, in this case the need to manage shared problems, created interdependence. In one of their famous experiments, they created the conditions for two groups of campers to butt heads upon arriving to the camp. These groups named themselves the Eagles and the Rattlers and quickly developed in-group hierarchies and social norms, persistently pranking, taunting, and name-calling the other group whenever they interacted.

Once the researchers (posing as camp counselors) introduced situations that evoked shared goals, this tension dissipated. For example, in one instance, the counselors artificially created a water shortage and suggested both groups work together to investigate a leaky pipe system. Once the groups solved the shortage through jointly fixing a water tank, they celebrated together, and the Rattlers let the Eagles drink ahead of them without taunting. (Prior to this event, the Rattlers often jeered the Eagles with the juvenile exclamation, "Ladies first!")

A second situation involved selecting a movie to watch at the camp. Both groups wanted to watch the classic pirate film *Treasure Island*, but counselors told them securing the film required members of both groups to contribute money. After jointly funding the movie screening, the two groups ate dinner together peacefully, a rare occasion. In another staged event, one of the camp's staffers called for several campers—both Eagles and Rattlers—to pull his truck up a hill using a rope. After completing this feat, the boys cheered together, exclaiming, "We won the tug-of-war against the truck!" Although the Sherifs' experiment may not meet the requirements of today's psychological research for ethical or methodological rigor, it provided an important and lasting insight:[25] that is, two warring groups recognizing shared goals and needs can create interdependence, stimulating cooperation and affiliation.

Programs intended to connect people from opposing backgrounds often introduce shared activities to try to foster interdependence. For example, Israel's Peres Center for Peace has developed a sports school that brings Palestinian and Israeli children together to play soccer on mixed-ethnicity teams, with the largest trophy awarded to the team that treats the opposing teams with the most respect.[26] A Brandeis University incubator brings young Palestinian and Israeli adults together to work with each other in developing start-up companies. Palestinian entrepreneur Abeer al-Natsheh describes the benefit of this program bringing the two groups together at an "economic level" where presumably politics are less focal.[27] And one of the most prominent programs of this type, Seeds of Peace, closely resembles the Sherifs' original setting by providing an American summer camp where Israeli and Palestinian children live for the summer and participate in shared activities, or "peace games," designed to bring the groups closer together.

Shared Enemies

Although highlighting shared goals can effectively resolve conflict, doing so is often difficult because conflict originates from divergent goals. This is where a separate type of commonality can help reduce intergroup dehumanization: namely, identifying shared enemies. Psychologist Jonathan Haidt, for example, has suggested that common threats could solve political discord between American liberals and conservatives. He states, "Common ground is often very hard to find . . . we [should] start by looking for common threats because common threats make common ground."[28] This suggestion is intuitive to those of us who remember the bipartisan bond that formed following the World Trade Center attacks on September 11, 2001. By identifying Al-Qaeda and Osama bin Laden as the clear culprits, American identity subsumed people's Democratic and Republican identities, and an ideologically diverse set of individuals supported war against the Taliban.

In championing the idea of shared enemies, Haidt has even opined optimistically about an asteroid heading toward Earth that would unite conservatives and liberals toward the greater cause of saving human life. He has founded an organization dubbed "the asteroids club" to bring ideologically dissimilar people together to discuss common threats.

The cinematic version of Haidt's suggestion occurs in the film *Independence Day*, where extraterrestrials from space threaten to attack Earth. President Thomas Whitmore, played by Bill Pullman, delivers a memorable speech noting the uniting power of this new common enemy, stating, "In less than an hour, aircrafts from here will join others around the world. And you will be launching the largest aerial battle in the history of mankind. 'Mankind.' That word should have new meaning for all of us today. We can't be consumed by our petty differences anymore. We will be united in our common interests." While I would prefer avoiding attack whether by aliens or asteroids, I appreciate that these threats can highlight something shared across humanity: our mortality.

Contemporary research in more constrained contexts also illustrates how shared enemies can lessen conflict by highlighting competitors' common interests. In one surprising set of studies, organizational behavior scholar Ting Zhang and colleagues showed in a competitive negotiation the presence of a hostile mediator can serve as a shared enemy, transforming foes into friends.[29] Typically, a mediator's role in conflict settings is to reduce hostile emotions. In an initial study assessing people's predictions about mediators, Zhang found that people indeed predicted that a kind mediator would be more help-ful than a hostile mediator. In subsequent studies, she placed peo-ple in competitive negotiations to test whether people's predictions were accurate—that is, whether the negotiation would proceed more smoothly with a kind mediator versus a hostile one.

Participants in Zhang's studies played competitive counterparts in various business negotiations. Their task was to reach an agreement, and in different experimental conditions they encountered either a kind or hostile mediator to begin the negotiation. The kind mediator said things like, "Hi, I'm Jamie. I'm your mediator for today. I can't decide what happens in this dispute or how you resolve issues. My job is just to help people who are in conflict, like yourselves." The hostile mediator said things like, "Hi, I'm Jamie. I'm your mediator for today. I can't decide what happens in this dumb dispute or how you resolve issues. My job is just to help people who are incapable of reaching agreement, like yourselves." Zhang then found that those who nego-tiated in the presence of a hostile mediator reached agreements more easily than those in the presence of a kind mediator. One of Zhang's studies revealed that seeing the mediator as a shared enemy was criti-cal to improving outcomes, with participants stating that they believed their negotiation counterpart shared a negative opinion of the hostile mediator. Thus, these studies show how shared enemies can highlight shared interests, creating common ground between adversaries.

Other research by psychologist Jennifer Bosson and colleagues also highlights the benefits of shared enemies. Their work did not exam-ine conflict but instead showed that sharing a negative attitude about another person fosters connection among friends and strangers.[30] Fur-thermore, shared negative attitudes promoted connection more than did shared positive attitudes, supporting Haidt's idea that common ground might emerge most easily through shared enemies. Bosson's studies asked participants to recall attitudes that they shared with their closest companion and found that participants recalled significantly more shared negative attitudes about people than positive attitudes, sometimes by a factor of four. In other words, shared enemies created bonds better than shared allies did, perhaps because shared enemies created a sense of a shared in-group and shared humanity.

Shared Identity

Shared goals and shared threats increase intergroup empathy and reduce social distance in part through creating a common identity. In many ways, common identity represents the key to diminishing dehumanization across intergroup lines because, as research demonstrates, common identity can eliminate these lines altogether.

My favorite example of how superordinate identity can generate intergroup compassion comes from a study of self-identified Manchester United soccer fans. The study, led by psychologist Mark Levine, tested whether a small set of male Manchester United fans would help a stranger who was wincing in pain after slipping and falling.[31] Levine's research staff staged the accident in front of study participants who had been instructed to travel from one university building to another. The research team employed an actor (portraying the stranger) to appear injured just as participants crossed his path. Critically, in three different experimental conditions, the stranger wore different T-shirts: a T-shirt with the logo of participants' favorite soccer team (Manchester United), a T-shirt with the logo of their least favorite soccer team (Liverpool FC), or an unbranded T-shirt.

Prior to encountering the stranger in pain, all participants also wrote a short essay that served as a separate experimental manipulation to highlight different aspects of identity. In one treatment, participants wrote about the ways they identified with their team, Manchester United. In another treatment, they wrote about the ways that they identified with soccer fans more broadly. Thus, the first treatment highlighted their in-group identity as Manchester United fans, but the second treatment highlighted a superordinate identity— soccer fan—one shared even with Liverpool FC fans.

As may have been expected, when the experimenters covertly observed participants encountering the injured stranger, they found that participants who had reflected on their Manchester United identity stopped to help in almost every case that the stranger wore their favorite team's shirt. In the other two T-shirt conditions, these participants rarely helped.

Conversely, when participants had first reflected on their broader soccer fan identity, they helped the stranger with the Liverpool FC T-shirt a majority of the time. Although the study involved only eighty-seven participants, it nicely illustrates how highlighting a broader identity ("soccer fan" versus "Manchester United fan") can make ostensible outsiders seem more like us, thereby enabling our compassion.

Psychologists Samuel Gaertner and John Dovidio have summarized the bulk of research on superordinate identity and formulated it into "the common in-group identity model." Their model explains how intergroup conflict dissipates when opposing groups recategorize "us" and "them" as "we."[32] They and their colleagues have also conducted several studies on racial bias to illustrate the model's utility. For example, in one study, they showed that white University of Delaware students complied with black students' help requests more when these black individuals wore University of Delaware paraphernalia, highlighting their common university identity.[33]

Other work by Gaertner, Dovidio, and colleagues assessed racial attitudes of nearly 1,400 high school students at a multicultural high school consisting of black, Chinese, Hispanic, Japanese, Korean, Vietnamese, and Caucasian students (a considerable portion being Jewish).[34] Students answered questions about each of these ethnicities as well as questions about their general experiences and perceptions of the school. Some questions asked whether they perceived the student body as "one group," "two groups," "separate individuals," or different groups playing on the "same team." Students who reported perceiving the student body as "one group" or on the "same team" also reported more favorability and less bias toward students of races different than their own.

Although the idea of highlighting identity beyond one's race is intuitively appealing, it may not be practical. This approach to racial harmony, also called the "color-blind approach," can make some individuals, particularly racial minorities, feel erased. This issue came up in talking with Raianna Brown, an African American dancer, choreographer, industrial engineering student, and former Georgia Tech football cheerleader who gained viral fame in late 2017 after kneeling alone during the national anthem. Brown's protest followed that of NFL quarterback Colin Kaepernick, who began kneeling during the national anthem in 2016 to protest racial injustice in the United States (more on the response to Kaepernick below). I contacted Brown for this book after hearing her describe her protest against racial injustice in terms of humanization and dehumanization. In a *Teen Vogue* interview, she stated, "We're not going to stand for this treatment of people of color and lack of recognition of humanity of other people."[35] When I asked her about how the anthem protests have prompted calls for greater racial unity and color blindness, she said, "I think sometimes we get so politically correct that unity and not seeing color diminish the experiences of people who are different . . . When people say they don't see color, it means they are diminishing my experience as a black woman." Here Brown indicates how even well-intended attempts to establish common humanity can feel dehumanizing.

Limits to Togetherness

Brown's experience begins to illuminate the limits of forging common bonds and seeing everybody as a unified mass. Shared goals, common enemies, and superordinate identity would seem to reduce dehumanization because they highlight mutual similarity, which could solve the lesser minds problem. Yet these methods are not silver bullets—not only do they sometimes fail to bring people together, but they sometimes also spur further intergroup resentment.

The Palestinian-Israeli summer camp, Seeds of Peace, described above illustrates this ineffectiveness. Psychologist Phillip Hammack worked at the camp and examined its effects by interviewing students after they returned home to Israel and Palestine. Hammack's interviews revealed that any positive effects were short-lived and that participating in the camp largely left attitudes toward the Palestinian-Israeli conflict unchanged. One Palestinian teenager, Ali, told Hammack a year after attending Seeds of Peace, "We got so much done at camp. We had even solved Jerusalem! I made Israeli friends. But when I went back home, I just realized that this is wrong. You can't be talking to them! You can't be making friends with them. They're killing you! . . . I don't believe in peace. I believe peace is like giving up." An Israeli teenager, Roai, told Hammack, "They want the world to see the Israelis as bad people, but I know that what they say is not true. Like in Lebanon, they say Sharon ordered the Sabra and Shatilla massacres, and it's not true! . . . I didn't change my mind about anything listening to the Palestinians, but it was interesting."[36] These interviews reveal the tenuous nature of conflict resolution strategies that simply focus on bringing groups together to establish commonality.

Other research also demonstrates mixed effects of attempts to connect groups through increased contact.[37] Political scientist Ryan Enos demonstrated the pernicious effects of intergroup contact in studying whites' attitudes toward Spanish-speaking immigrants. In a naturalistic experiment, Enos randomly assigned Spanish-speaking confederates (hired for his study to act as commuters) to congregate in various Boston area train stations. These were stations frequented by Caucasian commuters from otherwise racially homogenous neighborhoods.

Enos surveyed willing participants a few days following this subtle intervention and found a striking result. Those who unwittingly encountered Spanish speakers on the train platform responded more negatively toward immigration, reflecting greater prejudice toward those with whom they interacted.[38] Although chapter 3 describes how exposure to out-group members can enhance attitudes toward that out-group, Enos's study reinforces an important caveat: intergroup contact only has beneficial effects if it allows people to consider the minds of out-group members and connect with them. If contact with out-group members triggers threat—either through activating negative stereotypes or concerns about competition over scarce resources—then superficial contact can exacerbate conflict.

Other studies have shown that even direct expressions of empathy between warring groups can backfire. An experiment by psychologists Arie Nadler and Ido Liviatan asked Jewish Israeli participants to watch a key Palestinian politician deliver a speech.[39] Some participants saw a speech where the politician expressed empathy, stating, "Palestinians do not have a monopoly on suffering . . . Israelis also experience much suffering." This expression of empathy intended to represent Palestinians and Israelis on equal footing, with the same goal, for peace. Other participants saw a similar version of the speech but one that contained no meaningful expression of empathy. After viewing the speech, both groups of participants answered questions about Palestinian-Israeli relationships.

Participants who saw the high-empathy speech expressed more willingness to reconcile than those who viewed the no-empathy speech but with an important qualification. This effect only emerged for participants who reported (before viewing the speech) high trust with the Palestinians, for example, stating that Palestinians are peaceful and are adhering to the Oslo Peace accords. When initial trust was low, the effect actually reversed such that the high-empathy speech reduced participants' willingness to reconcile compared to the no-empathy speech. That is, if trust is lacking between groups, expressions of empathy can be more harmful than no empathy at all. How could this be?

The Power of Power

Nadler and Liviatan suggest that one important feature of their particular study setting, the Israeli-Palestinian conflict, is the power asymmetry between groups. Israelis simply have more authority and resources than Palestinians; thus, these two represent high-power and low-power groups, respectively. Indeed, attempts at uniting people to recognize common humanity often fail because of inattention to power. Through observing recent geopolitical conflicts and examining the literature on intergroup processes, I have come to believe that power is the most important topic in the social sciences and the key to understanding group life and group conflict. Power also explains why highlighting shared goals, shared enemies, and shared identity fails to bring people together to recognize shared humanity.

As an example of how power interferes with intergroup reconciliation, we can look at the literature on superordinate identity. Although Dovidio and Gaertner popularized the common in-group identity model, they discovered years later (along with their graduate student at the time, Tamar Saguy) how power asymmetries complicate common identity. They then refined their model to acknowledge that low-power groups (often the minority group) and high-power groups (often the majority group) want different things out of that shared identity. In general, high-power groups prefer that members of both groups assimilate to the dominant superordinate identity, akin to the color-blind mind-set. By contrast, low-power groups prefer maintaining their minority identity and developing a dual identity that incorporates aspects of both their minority and superordinate identities.[40]

Take, for instance, the context of immigration in which a minority group of migrants encounters a majority group of existing citizens in a given country. Many current American citizens favor the view of the United States as a "melting pot" that integrates people from different ethnicities to adopt an overarching American identity with specified American values and norms. However, ethnic minorities might not experience the cultural acceptance implied by the melting pot metaphor and, therefore, toggle between an American identity and a separate ethnic minority identity. African American thinker W. E. B. Du Bois famously wrote in 1903 about African Americans' struggle with this dual identity following slavery, stating, "One ever feels his twoness."[41] More recently, writer and immigrant Tasnim Ahmed wrote in a 2014 *Harvard Crimson* editorial, "America still isn't the melting pot it claims to be. Instead, it's a compartmentalized storage unit, with Whites in the biggest compartment . . . the word 'assimilation' is profane . . . it implies that I am forced to transform myself to accommodate others."[42] These views highlight how groups that differ in power approach identity differently.

Dutch psychologist Jan Pieter Van Oudenhoven and colleagues studied these diverging approaches in the context of immigration. They surveyed Moroccan and Turkish immigrants to the Netherlands, as well as Dutch majority individuals, about how immigrants might adapt to Dutch society.[43] While Dutch majority participants supported an assimilative strategy in which new immigrants identify with the dominant Dutch culture and downplay their original national cultures, Moroccan and Turkish immigrants strongly preferred to integrate both the dominant culture and their original national culture into their identities. In other words, these two groups have very different ideas about how to establish a "we" out of "us" and "them."

It is worth keeping these findings in mind when conflict between political parties, ethnicities, or work groups begins to intensify. When commentators call on these groups to find resolutions, it is easy to predict which group will suggest "overcoming our differences," call for unity, or ask both sides to find empathy. Rarely is it people low in power or minority group members who make these calls. Instead, it is the high-power and majority groups are those who call for unity. Martin Luther King Jr. famously wrote his "Letter from Birmingham Jail" in response to a newspaper editorial titled, "A Call for Unity," written by eight white Alabama clergymen.[44] The clergymen had criticized King's protest tactics during the fight for African Americans' civil rights, writing, "We further strongly urge our own Negro community to withdraw support from these demonstrations, and to unite locally in working peacefully for a better Birmingham." The strategic use of Birmingham as a superordinate identity did little to quell King's protests and sparked a forceful rejection of the pastors' suggestion to unite.

In a more contemporary example, consider the National Football League's (NFL) response to quarterback Colin Kaepernick's kneeling protest during the national anthem. When Kaepernick's protest prompted other NFL players to kneel as well, team owners and league president Roger Goodell became concerned. Rather than embracing Kaepernick's stance, the owners and Goodell pushed back, fearing that the protest was hurting NFL television ratings and game attendance. Several owners released statements calling for "unity," and Goodell issued a message stating, "The NFL and our players are at our best when we help create a sense of unity in our country and our culture."[45] Again, such calls for unity amid conflict came from those in positions of power. In contrast, groups that lack power express relative comfort with maintaining separate identities instead of unifying. In the aftermath of conflict, many low-power groups often resonate with Chimamanda Ngozi Adichie's sentiment cited in this book's introduction: "The responsibility to forge unity belongs not to the denigrated but to the denigrators."[46]

Understanding that power asymmetries are endemic to intergroup conflicts clarifies the need to account for power in trying to reduce social distance and dehumanization. Several lines of research have demonstrated how power differences drive conflict and how these differences hamper conflict resolution. For example, in competitive negotiations, high-power and low-power groups disagree even on bureaucratic details like the order of the meeting agenda. When selecting an agenda, low-power groups prefer to discuss the most important issues first whereas high-power groups prefer to start with discussing less consequential issues and then easing into the more contentious ones.[47]

In studying agenda ordering, Nour Kteily and colleagues found that Palestinian participants were more willing to accept an invitation to negotiate with Israelis when the invitation explicitly stated these negotiations would discuss consequential issues (e.g., the Palestinian right of return and the potential of a future Palestinian state) first rather than last. Israelis showed just the opposite pattern—they were most willing to negotiate when the invitation presented consequential issues later in the agenda and least willing to negotiate when these issues appeared first. Kteily also replicated these findings in a study with participants role-playing administrators and unionized graduate students in a university labor dispute. Those playing grad students were most willing to negotiate when the agenda first discussed the tough issues whereas mock administrators preferred to negotiate these issues last, revealing again how power differences complicate merely getting people to the table.

Kteily's findings emerge in part because of a robust tendency for low-power groups to focus on changing the status quo and high-power groups to focus on maintaining the status quo. Additional work led by Tamar Saguy bears this out. Saguy brought into the laboratory two Israeli ethnic groups that differed in power and status, the Ashkenazim (the relatively higher-power group) and Mizrahim (the relatively lower-power group). She asked them about intergroup relations and their preferences for discussing various topics with a member of the other group.[48] Some of the topics focused on commonalities between the groups and some focused on the power asymmetry between the groups. Mizrahim participants reported more motivation to change the status quo of the current power asymmetry and, as a result, preferred talking about power differences more than talking about commonalities. A broader literature supports this finding, demonstrating that most people like power; thus, groups with power want to keep it whereas groups lacking power seek more of it.

Saguy's findings also capture what I consider to be the first rule of power: those who have it don't want to talk about power, whereas those who lack power do want to talk about it. Low-power groups see conflict through the lens of power, whereas high-power individuals, by choice or by blindness, often fail to see power as the source of intergroup struggle. These different emphases create vastly different agendas.

The research on power then begs the question of how to create shared goals, shared enemies, or shared identity when groups diverge on what those goals, enemies, or identities look like. How can people forge a common humanity out of such diverging agendas? Typically, history's most horrific instances of power-asymmetric intergroup dehumanization such as American slavery or the Holocaust ceased as a result of further bloodshed, but emerging psychological findings suggest that other methods are possible.

Perspective-Taking versus Perspective-Giving

Few studies have empirically examined customizing conflict resolution approaches to high- versus low-power groups. One of the few studies to do so has uncovered a critical distinction between perspective-giving and perspective-taking: low-power groups warmed to high-power out-groups after expressing their difficulties to the high-power groups. High-power groups, on the other hand, became more empathetic toward low-power groups after hearing that side's perspective and the difficulties the other side has experienced.

The work examining these hypotheses, by psychologists Emile Bruneau and Rebecca Saxe, involved structuring dialogues between differing groups, including white Americans in Arizona and Mexican immigrants.[49] In these interactions, conducted over Skype, participants received instructions either to summarize the struggles of their own group or to respond to that statement by summarizing the other side's struggles in their own words. In essence, participants occupied the role of perspective-taker or perspective-giver. Bruneau and Saxe surveyed participants after this exchange and found that whereas high-power groups benefited from perspective-taking, low-power groups benefited from having their perspective taken. Mexican immigrants reported more positive attitudes toward white Americans after expressing their difficulties whereas white Americans reported more positive attitudes after receiving and processing them. Saxe and Bruneau replicated these findings with Palestinian and Israeli participants as well.

Other work conducted in Colombia has replicated the benefits of perspective-giving for members of communities afflicted by violence between guerrilla and paramilitary groups and the government.[50] Victims of violence given an opportunity to express themselves to ex-combatants developed more positive attitudes toward the group that formerly plagued their communities. Again, these results demonstrate that for low-power groups, being heard can have vast and humanizing effects.

These findings echo a phrase that kept reappearing as I researched intergroup conflict for this book: "We just want to be heard." Whether reading about young Brazilian students protesting corrupt government officials,[51] Malaysian soccer fans protesting the governing body of Malaysia's national football team,[52] or University of Michigan students protesting racism on campus,[53] I consistently encountered this rallying cry from subjugated groups explaining their collective efforts to those in power. When high-power groups hear this cry and begin to listen, a path to reconciliation begins to appear.

One radical approach to enabling a marginalized community to express its voice comes from an organization called Project Row Houses. Project Row Houses is a small community of shotgun houses in Houston's Third Ward. In the early 1990s, artist Rick Lowe purchased and restored the dilapidated houses, transforming them into art studios and exhibition spaces. Project Row Houses now invites artists, many of whose work focuses on African American identity, for residencies in the studios where they can create, show their work, and engage with the neighborhood. The platform has redefined art as a social practice as Project Row Houses integrates seamlessly with the Third Ward surroundings. It is a site of both artistry and activism, offering services for single mothers, neighborhood children, and other community members.

Project Row Houses also serves as a living, breathing example of how to humanize individuals whose lives, in Lowe's words, have been "reduced to a stereotype." As he explained to me over email, "Often artists working in communities are marginalized from the 'mainstream' art world and activists are marginalized because of the perceived irrelevance of their voice. Once again, Project Row Houses' origin was in re-contextualizing place and people in a way to show their relevance and value. Instead of pushing at the door of the art world to be heard, Project Row Houses offers opportunities for artists to have meaningful connections with people and place that are authentic forcing the art world to acknowledge them."[54] In radically transforming people's conceptions of what art is—in this case, it is a thriving community— Project Row Houses has provided a radical way for a marginalized group to be heard and recognized by a broader population. Lowe's platform enables African American artists and activists to become visible and valued, not by seeking access from a high-power group (i.e., the mainstream art community) but by expressing themselves on their own terms and forcing the larger art world to recognize them.

Needing Status versus Needing Reputation

Part of why expressing one's voice (perspective-giving) and listening to others' voices (perspective-taking) differentially benefit low-power and high-power groups is that these processes satisfy different core needs. Several lines of research demonstrate what these needs are and how they differ within power-asymmetric conflict. For example, research led by psychologist Hilary Bergsieker demonstrated that in interracial interactions, minority race individuals like blacks and Latinos desire respect and want whites to see them as competent.[55] Majority race individuals (i.e., whites), conversely, primarily want blacks and Latinos to like them and see them as moral. These studies show how groups differing in societal power differ in what they want out of an interaction.

Work by psychologists Nurit Shnabel and Arie Nadler suggests a similar pattern. They showed that in the aftermath of conflict, victims (who lack relative power) focus on needing to restore their lost status, whereas perpetrators (who possess relative power) focus on needing to restore their tarnished reputations.[56]

Shnabel and Nadler's experiments placed participants in either a victim or perpetrator role in various settings—for example, a waitron denied permission by a superior to take off a New Year's Eve shift. They examined the needs of perpetrators and victims and both parties' willingness to reconcile. Following exposure to the conflicts, low-power victims sought power and status from their superiors whereas these high-power perpetrators sought to restore their moral image to their victims. More critically, Nadler and Shnabel found that when victims and perpetrators could satiate these respective needs for moral restoration and for power— when perpetrators communicated an empowering message to their victims or when victims communicated acceptance to the perpetrators—both expressed more willingness to reconcile. Satisfying these different needs brought people closer together and made them more willing to pursue a shared understanding.

Belief in Change

One additional factor toward establishing shared humanity resonates with both high-power and low-power groups: activating the idea that people can change. The lay belief that people can't change and "you can't teach an old dog new tricks" implies that trying to resolve disagreement is fruitless. If one's adversary is unchangeable, why even try to negotiate? By the same token, research suggests, believing that others can change makes reconciliation efforts seem worthwhile.

Psychologist Eran Halperin and colleagues demonstrated the power of malleability beliefs in the Israeli-Palestinian conflict.[57] Although this conflict is fundamentally power-asymmetric, Halperin's studies found that both Israelis and Palestinians expressed greater willingness to compromise for peace when experimenters convinced them that the other side could change. In these studies, Israeli Jews, Palestinian citizens of Israel, and Palestinians in the West Bank read an ostensibly scientifically validated article about aggressive social groups. Depending on experimental condition, the article portrayed such groups as having either a fixed nature (stuck in their ways) or a malleable nature (capable of changing). Notably, the article did not mention any specific group such as Israelis or Palestinians. Afterward, participants answered questions about the opposing group and about compromise—for example, Israeli Jews answered questions about willingness to evacuate settlements or to compromise over Jerusalem's status, whereas Palestinians answered questions about a proposal to establish Israel as a Jewish state but with autonomy for Palestinian citizens. When participants read about groups' malleability, they believed the article's conclusions and expressed warmer attitudes toward the out-group. These positive feelings then increased their support for pursuing compromise solutions for peace.

Although simply intended to change minds about the possibility of peace, Halperin's malleability induction, in my view, has an additional humanizing effect. Presenting people as fixed in their ways makes them seem scarcely different from automata; that is, their behavior appears scripted, routine, and inert. As we learned in chapters 6 and 7, people consider humans to be more variable and spontaneous entities than machines. Framing social groups as capable of change therefore points to these groups as possessing a fundamentally human quality. People believe that a key aspect of being human is not only the capacity for mind but also the capacity to change one's mind.

Reframing Values

As the work presented here demonstrates, sometimes groups have fundamentally different agendas because of differences in power and status. Other times, their agendas differ because of their core values. Research on ideological conflict illuminates how to simply manage groups with fundamentally differing moral values. This work, led by psychologists Matthew Feinberg and Robb Willer, concerns conflict between liberals and conservatives, groups that navigate ongoing power asymmetries with sometimes liberals feeling more powerful and sometimes conservatives feeling more powerful.[58]

Feinberg and Willer tested a method that they call "moral reframing" for bringing liberals and conservatives closer together on contentious policy issues. Their method was based on Jonathan Haidt's moral foundations theory, which describes how liberals and conservatives prioritize different principles when determining whether something is right or wrong; these moral values also fundamentally shape liberals and conservatives' opposing worldviews.[59] For example, liberals value social justice and equality more whereas conservatives value loyalty and national pride more. Such values tend to clash during debates on policy issues ranging from immigration to military intervention.

Feinberg and Willer examined whether framing an issue in terms of the preferred moral principles of an individual's particular ideology would change the individual's mind on that issue. For example, in one study, they found unsurprisingly that framing military spending in terms of ensuring American global superiority leads conservatives to favor military spending more than liberals. However, when they framed military spending as helping the disadvantaged to overcome poverty and inequality—an argument that couched military spending in terms of social justice and equality—liberals supported military spending almost as much as conservatives did. In another study, they asked liberals and conservatives about same-sex marriage. In a neutral experimental condition, the expected political differences emerged such that liberals supported same-sex marriage more than conservatives. However, when the researchers framed the issue in terms of loyalty and national pride, moral foundations tied to conservatism, conservatives expressed much greater support. Framing the issue by noting "same-sex couples are proud and patriotic Americans" prompted conservatives to support same-sex marriage to virtually the same degree as liberals. In other work, Feinberg and Willer showed that although conservatives typically devalue pro-environment policy issues, framing them in terms of a conservative value—purity—produced far more conservative support for environmental issues.[60] These studies suggest that reframing a contentious issue in terms of the other side's values can begin to bridge the ideological divide, providing an important insight for resolving power-asymmetric conflict: You should feel free to present your own agenda, but by framing it in terms of the other side's values, reconciliation is more likely.

* * * *

THE APPROACHES described in this chapter suggest that attempts to uproot intergroup dehumanization must acknowledge the differing minds that exist across ideological, ethnic, and racial lines. Working toward finding common humanity can get us only so far, and ironically, we are more capable of achieving unity when we recognize people's distinct humanities—namely, the multitude of others' experiences, opinions, beliefs, and desires that differ across political parties, tribes, ethnicities, and religions.

Poet and scholar Audre Lorde has written about the necessity of difference for bridging racial, gender-based, age-based, and social class divides. In one notable work, Lorde states, "Certainly there are very real differences between us of race, age, and sex. But it is not those differences between us that are separating us. It is rather our refusal to recognize those differences, and to examine the distortions which result from our misnaming them and their effects upon human behavior and expectation."[61] The expectation Lorde speaks of is to reject and overcome difference—in fact, as much of the research in this chapter suggests, we can reduce social distance between people by appreciating difference instead.

CHAPTER 9

Humanizing Close Relationships through Critical Distance

IN THE CONTEXT OF CONFLICT, WE SEEK TO REDUCE dehumanization among bitter enemies by reducing social distance. The goal in these efforts is to enable individuals in conflict to understand what the other person understands and to feel what the other person feels. Taken to the extreme, feeling what another person feels is the ultimate expression of empathy. However, this type of self-other merging that often occurs when considering the experiences of loved ones can result in a less than humanizing response.

Decades of research led by psychologist C. Daniel Batson finds that feeling the pain of another person often evokes personal distress; this distress then leads us to disengage from that person.[1] Walking past a homeless person in December and recognizing that person is freezing while we are warm can lead us to offer a coat or shelter out of compassion. However, taking on another person's pain as our own—that is, vicariously experiencing their bitter cold—makes us less capable or willing to help.

Furthermore, research suggests this tendency to feel what another person feels occurs more frequently when considering close others versus distant ones. For example, work led by psychologist Meghan Meyer and colleagues shows that empathizing with a stranger's pain rather than a friend's pain, in fact, leads people to process that person's feelings more effectively, without confusing those feelings with your own.[2]

Author Octavia Butler's science fiction novel, *Parable of the Sower*, illustrates this condition of mentally merging with close others. The novel's protagonist is a young woman named Laura who is afflicted with "hyperempathy," a delusional disorder that causes her to share the pain of those around her. Laura describes how her "brother Keith used to pretend to be hurt just to trick me into sharing his supposed pain." She states, "Once he used red ink as fake blood to make me bleed. I was eleven then, and I still bled through the skin when I saw someone else bleeding . . . Keith only tricked me into bleeding that once, and I beat the hell out of him for it."[3] Although to many, "feeling another's pain" represents the ultimate empathic expression, Butler clearly understands and portrays the unpleasantness of this experience.

Work led by neuroscientist Laura Müller-Pinzler has documented self-other merging with close others in the context of mundane "pains" as well. In her work, sixty-four German participants underwent neuroimaging while observing sketches of friends or strangers involved in mildly embarrassing situations, such as realizing they do not have enough money to pay the cashier at a grocery store.[4] Participants also observed sketches of friends and strangers in neutral situations like returning a book to the library. Müller-Pinzler found that observing embarrassing situations compared to neutral situations activated areas within the mentalizing network, suggesting participants were considering the thoughts of each protagonist. However, brain areas indicating emotional distress activated more when observing friends' embarrassing situations compared to strangers' embarrassing situations. These data suggest that participants "felt" the embarrassment of their friends but not that of strangers. In other words, in considering friends to be extensions of the self, we vicariously experience their social pain.

Work led by psychologist Constantine Sedikides extends this phenomenon to taking on the failures of friends and family. His studies showed that when close others underperform on a shared, two-person creativity task, people take the blame for this underperformance. However, when they complete this task with a stranger, they do not take on this shared blame.[5]

Other research on this sort of mind-melding within close relationships presents another problem as well: we often err in assessing what our closest companions believe—but not what strangers believe—because we egocentrically confuse close others' beliefs with our own.[6] Research led by psychologist Kenneth Savitsky demonstrated this phenomenon by first asking people to communicate ambiguous phrases such as "What have you been up to?" to strangers or spouses (this phrase could communicate suspicion or simply reflect interest in another's well-being). Then participants reported how clearly they conveyed the message. Participants believed they communicated these phrases more clearly to their spouses than to strangers. However, experimenters also asked addressees how they interpreted the message and found that speakers' communication accuracy did not differ between close partners and total strangers. In other words, speakers better understood the minds of strangers, appreciating that there could be some ambiguity for these unfamiliar listeners. For close partners, participants heard the meaning of the message in their own minds and egocentrically assumed their spouses could hear this meaning as well.

What these studies suggest is that people indeed consider close friends and romantic partners to have minds but often see these minds as unsophisticated. Frequently, they see the minds of close others as simply a reproduction of their own minds. This concept surfaces in the Velvet Underground song, "I'll Be Your Mirror," which frontman Lou Reed wrote about his college girlfriend Shelley Albin. In Reed's biography, *Transformer*, author Victor Bockris writes, "When

Lou wrote a poem or a story, Shelley found herself doing a draw-ing or a painting that perfectly illustrated it. She had been sent to a psychiatrist in her teens for refusing to speak to her father for three years [Reed's relationship with his father was similarly fraught]. Lou wrote 'I'll Be Your Mirror' two years later about Shelley. And Shelley was Lou's mirror. Just as he had rushed a fraternity, she, much to his delight, rushed a sorority."[7] In other words, Albin saw Reed in herself.

In my view, this type of self-other merging fails to consider the other person as a distinct human being and instead conceptualizes the other as simply a reflection of the self. The studies described above show that, if anything, people are more adept at considering the dis-tinct humanity of strangers than others to whom they are close—that is, they consider less familiar individuals to have distinct minds, sep-arate from themselves.

At this point, let me make three clarifications. First, although I state that people are more adept at considering the distinct humanity of strangers, this is only true of common strangers; once strangers become categorized as clear out-group members, these individuals become more fully dehumanized as we saw in the previous chapter.

Second, I have argued that people tend to see close relationship partners as a reflection or extension of the self, which represents a failure to see them as fully distinct humans with fully distinct mental states. Yet, given people's familiarity and depth of experience with close relationship partners and their thoughts, feelings, and ideas, people also are capable of humanizing these relationship partners more than strangers. It is simply that the former type of processing, this self-other merging, *only* occurs with close others, and it represents a form of dehumanization with some troubling consequences that we will explore momentarily.

The third clarification is that indeed dehumanization of close oth-ers is not as problematic as dehumanization that enables genocide, for instance. In fact, some research suggests this failure to distinguish one's own mental states from one's partners can even benefit close relationships. Consider research led by psychologist Sandra Murray that surveyed dating and married couples with standardized questionnaires asking them to describe their own values, everyday feelings, and traits as well as to describe the values, everyday feelings, and traits of their partners.[8] The researchers also measured participants' reports of relationship satisfaction, frequency of arguing, and how much they felt their partner understood them.

Several interesting findings emerged. The first was tremendously unsurprising: couples are egocentric. Participants reported their partners' personalities to be highly similar to their own, well beyond similarities that existed in reality. If a participant rated himself as patient and open-minded, driven by ambition and success, and typically happy, he was likely to report his partner to be this way as well. The finding that was surprising, however, was that this erroneous egocentrism produced greater relationship satisfaction because it made people feel understood. In other words, if I believe that my wife and I share the same values, I'm more likely to feel that she really "gets me," which enhances our relationship (even if my belief is an illusion).

Despite the positive consequence of Murray's "kindred spirits" effect, few people truly enjoy feeling like a mere mirror of their partners. Emerging evidence suggests that, at least in the United States, people want something more from their close relationships. In particular, they want a partner who helps them express their true selves, and this self-expression fundamentally contradicts being treated as a replica.

My colleague, psychologist Eli Finkel, summarizes evidence for this increasingly pervasive drive for self-authentication as a relationship goal in his book, *The All-or-Nothing Marriage*. In previous historical eras when people married primarily for basic needs such as food, shelter, and safety, or good old-fashioned love, Finkel's thesis is that now people marry with the goal of finding self-actualization through their partner. Finkel writes, "Our primary emphasis here is on pursuing self-discovery and personal growth *through marriage* . . . As such, our spouse's ability to provide effective support requires precisely tailored actions oriented toward our unique needs and circumstances" (italics original).[9] "Unique" is the key term here, as in unique from one's partner. If good relationships were just about matching, we would be satisfied the moment we determine a shared set of interests, values, and activities with our partner. Yet the best relationships are those that involve personal growth and evolution for both parties.

On this point of growth, I was struck by one commenter on an internet dating message board who wrote, "I was actually interested in a girl who shared a lot of the same ideals and interests as myself, once. But it didn't take getting to the officially dating stage to come to the conclusion that I would be bored out of my fucking skull. There was zero debate, zero friction, zero growth . . . Echo chambers are nice when you feel the need to be reassured of your own viewpoint, but they don't expand your world in the slightest. There's only so many times I can have the same conversation with myself before I start going stir-crazy."[10] Although this viewpoint is extreme, it illustrates the limits of personal growth when one's partner simply appears as a reflection of the self. Renowned marriage expert and psychotherapist John Gottman puts it more soberly: "It's diversity that makes relationships interesting. We are not looking for our clones."[11]

Extensive research led by psychologist Abraham Tesser also suggests that feeling overlap with a friend or romantic partner can even threaten our self-esteem when that person outperforms us in a personally important domain (e.g., an athletic pursuit or a school subject in which we see ourselves as expert). However, no equivalent threat occurs when a stranger outperforms us in a self-relevant domain. Tesser's decades of research reveal that this threat derives from the sense of merged identity we experience with close others.[12] This sense of oneness is what activates unfavorable comparisons to our own performance, making us feel bad. By contrast, people discount strangers' performance in these domains as less identity relevant and less threatening. In other words, when we care about a task, we internalize close others' performance on that task often without enjoying their success. Tesser's work has also shown the happiest couples are those that avoid these threats by distributing power and decision-making based on complementary domains of expertise rather than ones that overlap.[13] That is, relationships thrive when partners consider each other's distinct expertise.

Work by psychologists Jacquie Vorauer and Tamara Sucharyna illustrates other negative consequences of failing to differentiate your own mind from your partner's mind.[14] Their studies measured how close participants felt toward a friend or romantic partner by asking them whether they would describe their relationship in terms of overlapping circles or more like two concentric circles that did not touch. They also prompted participants to think about this person in one of several ways. Some conditions asked participants to actively consider the person's mind through perspective-taking, and other conditions asked them to "take a neutral perspective, being as objective as possible" with no perspective-taking instructions. Vorauer and Sucharyna then measured various relationship outcomes including relationship satisfaction and how much they think their partner really knows their traits, values, and preferences.

Vorauer and Sucharyna found that when people described their relationship in terms of overlapping circles *and* adopted their partners' perspectives, they assumed greater perceived transparency. That is, they believed their partners really knew their traits, values, and preferences, which turned out to be a vast overestimation of what their partners actually knew. Remaining detached instead of attempting to take their partners' perspective mitigated this bias and inaccuracy. In a final study, the researchers found that perspective-taking during a tense discussion with their partner led people to overestimate the transparency of their negative feelings to their partner, prompting participants to report reduced relationship satisfaction. Overall, their studies showed that attempting to access a close other's mind compared to remaining objective led people to overestimate their partner's ability to "get them," resulting in greater relationship conflict. This finding is also consistent with research showing that the best way to resolve marital problems is for both parties to take a detached perspective on the conflict, writing about the conflict from the point of view of a third party outside the marriage.[15]

At this point, it is worth it for us to reorient and ask the following question: If considering the mind of another person is the essence of humanization, why would considering the mind of a close other lead people astray compared with remaining detached? The answer is that when trying to get into the mind of a close other, feeling a sense of self-other overlap with that close other causes people to behave ego-centrically. Instead of considering the mind of a close other as a distinct mind, one perceives it as indistinguishable from one's own mind, attentive to one's own preferences, values, and traits. By remaining detached, people are able to better distinguish their own minds from their partner's minds.

In other work along these lines, Vorauer and psychologist Matthew Quesnel showed that perspective-taking in close relationships particularly harms individuals low in self-esteem.[16] In this work, participants completed a self-esteem scale, and as in Vorauer and Sucharnya's work, took their partner's perspective or considered their partner without attending to mental states. Participants low in self-esteem who took their partner's perspective reported feeling less love from their partner and less relationship satisfaction. Ironically, this attempt to get into the other person's mind simply made people with low self-esteem more preoccupied with themselves as objects of evaluation. Low-self-esteem individuals who considered their partners' minds came to confuse feelings toward themselves with their partners' feelings toward them. That is, participants who felt negatively about themselves intuited that their partners felt similarly about them. When low-self-esteem individuals did not engage in perspective-taking, perceptions of love and relationship quality did not suffer. These findings again suggest adverse consequences when we consider a close other's mind without distinguishing that other mind from our own.

Whereas the key to bridging intergroup divides requires reducing the social distance between "us" and "them," optimizing and rehumanizing close relationships require the opposite. Seeing one's close friend or romantic partner as fully human necessitates establishing some critical distance and detaching from the other person to see that person as distinct from the self. We can fully see our friends and partners' humanity by distinguishing their minds from ours while still remaining close through occupying the same reality, sharing the same principles, and experiencing our actions as interdependent.

Navigating this delicate balance of relationship closeness without confusing the self with other protects against several negative consequences described here. These consequences include distress in response to a close other's pain or embarrassment, egocentric errors in understanding what a close other believes (or believes about you), and feelings of threat when a close other succeeds on your turf. These effects tend to detract from the relationship itself, and so detaching one's mental life from one's partners can produce longer-lasting friendships and marriages.

In fact, this separation is essential to how substance abuse rehabilitation programs recommend family members help addicts— Alcoholics Anonymous (AA) calls it "detaching with love." Hazelden Betty Ford Foundation, the country's leading alcohol and drug treatment center, published an article contrasting this form of detachment with "overprotection" that includes enabling behaviors like "calling in sick for your husband if he is too drunk to show up for work."[17] In other words, overprotection involves taking on a partner's addiction as though it was one's own.

Detaching with love, on the other hand, effectively distinguishes one's humanity from the humanity of one's partner. Hazelden Betty Ford's recommendations include asking questions like, "What are your needs beyond the needs of the alcoholic or addict? How can you take care of yourself even if the person you love chooses not to get help?" and warns against being overly "tuned in to someone else's feelings." Tuning out a loved one's feelings in a time of need might seem counterintuitive, but what this really means is distinguishing your feelings from the feelings of your loved one. AA's methods and those of Hazelden Betty Ford also document a critical benefit to this strategy: empowering addicts to own their decisions while critically protecting the mental wellness of the concerned party. This approach is humanizing as it critically recognizes the addict's mind in granting him or her agency and the capacity for thoughtful decision-making.

Detaching with love is also necessary for people tasked with treating sick or addicted individuals. Larissa MacFarquhar's book, *Strangers Drowning*, which details the lives of "extreme do-gooders," describes this separation in the context of professional counselors. She states, "At first the social worker may become too emotionally involved with his clients, so that when they fail he suffers, both because they are unhappy and because their failure is his failure, too. It's hard to spend his days confronting devastating problems that he cannot fix—the misery and helplessness rub off on him . . . Gradually, he learns to be more detached."[18] Without this critical distinction between themselves and their clients, social workers, like concerned family members, suffer the pain of individuals for whom they have come to care so much.

Psychologist Paul Bloom also argues empirically for this detachment that recognizes close others as distinct humans with distinct needs and feelings. In his book *Against Empathy,* he criticizes specifically "affective empathy" whereby people adopt the emotions of others. Bloom's solution to this tendency is "rational compassion," which he states does not "require mirroring of others' feelings" and instead involves "simply caring for people, wanting them to thrive."[19] Despite Bloom's broad definition, his research empirically distinguishes the mirroring phenomenon from this more general concern for others' well-being.

Along with Matthew R. Jordan and Dorsa Amir, Bloom tested his prescriptions by surveying people about their proclivity for vicarious concern toward others as well as for a more detached concern.[20] Questions assessing vicarious concern asked people whether the following situations characterized them: "If I see someone vomit, I will gag" or "If I see someone who is excited, I will feel excited myself." Questions assessing a detached concern ask about situations such as, "When I see someone being taken advantage of, I feel kind of protective toward them" and "I sometimes try to understand my friends better by imagining how things look from their perspective." Critically, the questions assessing vicarious concern involve situations in which the observer and the target share the same emotion (e.g., disgust or excitement). Alternatively, the questions assessing detached concern reflect situations in which the emotions differ (e.g., the target feels "taken advantage of" versus the perceiver "feeling protective"). Their research found that detached concern for others predicted more generosity toward others than vicarious concern. Although Bloom was not studying close relationships per se, his work points to the possibility that we often do better for others if we consider their emotions as distinctly their own rather than feel them directly.

The work shown above on the negative effects of self-other mind-merging holds similar implications. It shows that people can at times process strangers' mental states more effectively than friends' mental states because they don't confuse them with their own. And it shows that viewing your partner objectively can inhibit the negative consequences of perspective-taking. Finding this critical distance with people with whom you are close is the only way to appreciate their minds as robust and sophisticated rather than an unsatisfying replica of your own.

* * * *

BEST FRIENDS and partners are those who feel like they are extensions of ourselves, but the best relationships both for our partners and ourselves are those in which we can recognize the other person's distinct humanity. I realize this can all sound a bit mind-bending—to say that the ideal state of affairs is a relationship in which both partners incorporate aspects of each other into themselves but neither projects their own mind onto the other—but let me return to the science of close relationships to better explain this view.

In particular, I want to turn to the work of psychologist Art Aron, the preeminent scholar of close relationships. He has produced an essential model of psychology's thorniest topic—namely, love—which suggests that including the other in your self-concept is an initial step toward experiencing love. That is, self-other overlap is critical for establishing relationship closeness. However, in Aron's model, relationships do not blossom into fulfilling love unless this inclusion of the other in the self produces a sense of self-expansion. That is, by including the other in your own self-concept, you grow as a result. At this stage, you must consider your partner as distinct from yourself, as self-expansion occurs through our partners exposing us to novel and exciting activities. Put differently, love comes from a close relationship with an individual who takes us outside of our own minds.[21] As you can see, that even humanizing our closest friends and family requires such effort speaks to how hard the task of humanization is more broadly. In the epilogue that follows, I again emphasize the difficulty of seeing human, and we look to three essential components involved in mastering this most arduous task.

Time, Connection, and Mattering

ARISTOTLE FAMOUSLY REFERRED TO HUMANS AS "SOCIAL animals," yet this portrayal mischaracterizes humans as naturally social rather than social because they recognize the need to expend effort engaging with others. As noted throughout this book, extensive research confirms that our capacity to humanize—to consider other minds—is finite because we each have finite cognitive resources. As humans, we need time to draw on and deploy these resources in effective ways.

Humanization requires time, and this poses a problem because many of us increasingly experience what organizational behavior scholar Leslie Perlow calls a "time famine."[1] In fact, every rehumanization solution I have offered, including the basic process of humanization itself (i.e., considering others' minds), requires time. To rehumanize the workplace, individuals must develop new, cognitively demanding skills like sociability and variability. (Remember the suggestion to balance skill development with dedicated time for disengagement from work). To rehumanize our interactions with technology, we must learn how to collaborate with machines and divide labor effectively. To rehumanize relationships with enemies and competitors, we must not only find common ground through shared goals, shared enemies, or shared identity but also establish common ground around power asymmetries. And rehumanizing relationships with close friends and romantic partners requires the most work of all: disentangling our own humanity from theirs, despite our feelings of self-other overlap.

Given that these strategies tend to require effort suggests the need for a dramatic societal-level mind-set shift, one that values time above all else. You would think that the automation age would make finding time and choosing time easier than ever before. Beyond the prospect of technology taking over our work, technology's ability to fast-track tasks from purchasing theater tickets to conducting bank transactions should give us a time surplus rather than a dearth of it. Yet, as I suggest in chapter 6, given our penchant for busy-ness, the experience of free time makes us uncomfortable and we return to the activities that society has deemed fundamentally purposeful, namely work.

In considering the importance of pursuing time, what is most critical is that we not fear that time will deprive us of purpose or meaning. If used in the service of humanizing others, time can create perhaps the greatest source of psychological well-being and good health: social connection.

Throughout this book, I have described the power of humans to generate meaning and morality and to inspire and motivate, yet I have saved the greatest power for last. It is humans' capacity, through forming social relationships, to literally reduce mortality. Evidence for the life-extending power of social relationships comes from several sources, but the clearest data come from a meta-analysis conducted by psychologist Julianne Holt-Lunstad and colleagues in 2010.[2] This meta-analysis of 148 studies including over 148,000 participants assessed the links between social relationships and physical health and found that people reporting stronger social relationships have a 50 percent greater chance of survival than people who report weak relationships. The effect of social relationships on mortality in this analysis was stronger than the effects of quitting smoking, abstaining from alcohol, getting a flu vaccine, or engaging in physical exercise. Holt-Lunstad and colleagues confirmed these findings with a follow-up meta-analysis in 2015 of studies on social isolation and mortality.[3]

Holt-Lunstad's findings echo a similar paradigm-changing 1988 study demonstrating that social isolation poses a health risk on par with smoking, obesity, or high blood pressure.[4] Work conducted by my mentor John Cacioppo and summarized with William Patrick in their book *Loneliness* similarly documents countless negative health effects of simply feeling alone.[5] Social connection, on the other hand, counteracts these negative effects.

What is the mechanism by which human relationships affect physical health? Research suggests several, but the most well-established explanation is that they do so through affecting our mental health. Social relationships are a major determinant of happiness,[6] and according to Cacioppo and Patrick, they also reduce stress, the primary source of cortisol release that impairs our immune functioning. We can probe this issue even further, however, to ask, well, why do social relationships increase happiness and reduce stress?

Based on my years of thinking about this topic, the best answer I have come up with is that social relationships make us feel like we matter, and mattering is the essence of feeling human. When people devote time to understanding and acknowledging our feelings, our fears, our desires, and our points of view, we feel a sense of purpose, and we feel seen—no longer invisible. Indeed, the reason why social isolation seems to drive extreme behaviors ranging from terrorism to drug addiction, as research suggests, is because people are seeking alternate sources of happiness, purpose, and connection to something larger than themselves.[7] Research also shows that when people experience ostracism and exclusion, they feel less than fully human.[8]

The formula, then, for shifting toward the more person-oriented society described by Martin Luther King Jr. is that we need to find time, which enables social connection and feeds the sense that we matter. My concern is that time, connection, and mattering are in short supply, but this book seeks to suggest ways we can replenish these resources to rehumanize the world around us.

If nothing more, I hope to have made three things clear. Our tendency to see other people in their full humanity is declining. Seeing human is psychologically important. And rehumanizing the world around us is possible. As I want to make clear here, rehumanization is hard, and I only hope we expend the effort to reverse dehumanization's course.

This concluding and somewhat dissatisfying note recalls the earliest memory of my life when I was four years old in preschool. During some unstructured playtime, the lot of us twenty kids had gotten unruly, and my dear teacher Ms. Cecil, seeking to bring us to order, shouted, "Children, stop what you're doing, you're all behaving like a bunch of animals." Some unexplored confidence inside me drove me to respond, "Well, humans are animals."

My classmates all went silent, shocked I had talked back to the teacher. Cutting through the hushed room, Ms. Cecil asked me defiantly, "Are you an animal?" Although wishing to continue the argument on scientific grounds, the terror of Ms. Cecil singling me out led me to respond meekly, "No." Class activity resumed as we formed a semicircle around the front of the room for story time. However, my response still troubles me to this day because the "correct" answer to Ms. Cecil's question seems to reside between yes and no.

I wish I could say that this experience led me to my current scholarly pursuit of studying what it means to be human, but the truth is that it led me to a more mundane insight: seeing human is a flexible process. This means the choice is up to us. We can create time to expend the mental energy necessary to see others in their full humanity, or let the current fragmented moment pull us apart as isolated bodies, united only as members of a common animal species.

Acknowledgments

I wish to thank everyone involved with this book from inception to finished product. First, I thank my agent Max Brockman for helping me crystallize my scattered thoughts into a meaningful narrative. I thank my editor Quynh Do for her wisdom and guidance in teaching me what it means to write a book. I thank my mentors John Cacioppo and Nick Epley for helping me articulate the ideas that form the basis of everything here.

I thank Eliza Myrie for her editorial and research skills that gave this book vitality, Chloe Keywell, Alanna Lazarowich, and Tom Mayer for their assistance along the way, and the Kellogg School of Management and the Russell Sage Foundation for their institutional support.

I thank everyone who gave me feedback and insight on this project from the proposal stage to the book's completion: Adam Grant, Carol Dweck, Robert Cialdini, Brad Keywell, Jamil Zaki, Jonah Berger, Kurt Gray, Mike Norton, Allison Wood Brooks, Emily Witt, Nour Kteily, Eli Finkel, Adam Galinsky, Robb Willer, and Karen Huang. My deepest gratitude goes to everyone willing to talk to me to offer their unique insights on these topics: Raianna Brown, Theodore Bruckbauer, Glenn Greenwald, Wayne Hsiung, Seth Leibson, Rick

Lowe, John LaBree, Woody Marshall, Sharmila Mulligan, Ai-Jen Poo, Josh Safdie, Neil Stevenson, Matt Besser, Tandy Trower, Henry Wang, and Nathan Yee.

Beyond the pages of this book, I owe so much of who I am to a core group of scholars and friends who have contributed to my intellectual development over the years: Jamil, Kurt, Liane Young, Diana Tamir, and Hal Hershfield. I also want to thank all of my coauthors, colleagues, and students who have given me consistent insights that have helped me grow in my research and thinking.

Finally, I thank Mom and Dad, Josh Waytz, Rachel Datz, David Waytz, Annie Jacobsen, and Asha and Krishna Murthy for their encouragement and support. And I thank Megha, Amartya, and Tulsi for their love.

Notes

Introduction

1. Colby Itkowitz, "What Is This Election Missing? Empathy for Trump Voters," *Washington Post*, November 2, 2016, https://www.washingtonpost.com/news/inspired-life/wp/2016/11/02/what-is-this-election-missing-empathy-for-trump-voters.

2. Michael Lerner, "What Happened on Election Day," *New York Times*, http://www.nytimes.com/interactive/projects/cp/opinion/election-night-2016/stop-shaming-trump-supporters.

3. Chimamanda Ngozi Adichie, "Now Is the Time to Talk about What We Are Actually Talking About," *The New Yorker*, December 2, 2016, http://www.newyorker.com/culture/cultural-comment/now-is-the-time-to-talk-about-what-we-are-actually-talking-about.

4. George E. Newman and Paul Bloom, "Physical Contact Influences How Much People Pay at Celebrity Auctions," *Proceedings of the National Academy of Sciences* 111, no. 10 (2014): 3705–8, doi:10.1073/pnas.1313637111.

5. Jennifer J. Argo, Darren W. Dahl, and Andrea C. Morales, "Positive Consumer Contagion: Responses to Attractive Others in a Retail Context," *Journal of Marketing Research* 45, no. 6 (2008): 690–701, http://journals.ama.org/doi/abs/10.1509/jmkr.45.6.690.

6. Thomas Kramer and Lauren G. Block, "Like Mike: Ability Contagion through Touched Objects Increases Confidence and Improves Performance," *Organizational Behavior and Human Decision Processes* 124, no. 2 (2014): 215–28, doi:10.1016/j.obhdp.2014.03.009.

7. Julian Huxley, *New Bottles for New Wine: Essays* (London: Readers Union, 1959); Carl Sagan, *Cosmos* (New York: Random House, 1981).

8. B. Martín-López, C. Montes, and J. Benayas, "The Non-economic Motives behind the Willingness to Pay for Biodiversity Conservation," *Biological Conservation* 139, no. 1–2 (2007): 67–82, doi:10.1016/j.biocon.2007.06.005.

9. Adrian Franklin, *Animals and Modern Cultures: A Sociology of Human-Animal Relations in Modernity* (London: Sage, 1999).

10. Laurel D. Riek et al., "How Anthropomorphism Affects Empathy toward Robots," *Proceedings of the 4th ACM/IEEE International Conference on Human Robot Interaction—HRI 09* (2009): 245–46, doi:10.1145/1514095.1514158.

11. Rozina Sini, "Does Saudi Robot Citizen Have More Rights Than Women?" BBC News, October 26, 2017, http://www.bbc.com/news/blogs-trending-41761856.

12. Edward-Isaac Dovere, "How Clinton Lost Michigan—and Blew the Election," *Politico*, December 14, 2016, http://www.politico.com/story/2016/12/michigan-hillary-clinton-trump-232547.

13. Jonah Berger, *Invisible Influence: The Hidden Forces That Shape Behavior* (New York: Simon & Schuster Paperbacks, 2017).

14. "Protective Mother Wrestles Lost Polar Bear," *The Globe and Mail*, April 23, 2018, http://www.theglobeandmail.com/news/national/protective-mother-wrestles-lost-polar-bear/article703773/.

15. Ye Li and Margaret S. Lee, "Comparing the Strengths of Self-Interest and Prosocial Motivations," *YeLi.Us*, July 1, 2011, http://yeli.us/papers/Li Lee2011ProsocialMotivation.pdf.

16. Studs Terkel, *Working: People Talk about What They Do All Day and How They Feel about What They Do* (New York: New Press, 1974), xxxiii.

17. Adam Waytz and Michael I. Norton, "Botsourcing and Outsourcing: Robot, British, Chinese, and German Workers Are for Thinking—Not Feeling—Jobs," *Emotion* 14, no. 2 (April 2014): 434–44, doi:10.1037/a0036054.

18. "The Worldwide Employee Engagement Crisis," Gallup.com, January 7, 2016, http://www.gallup.com/businessjournal/188033/worldwide-employee-engagement-crisis.aspx; "Job Satisfaction: 2014 Edition," The Conference Board, https://www.conference-board.org/publications/publicationdetail.cfm?publicationid=2785¢erId=4.

19. Rebecca Rifkin, "In U.S., 55% of Workers Get Sense of Identity from Their Job," Gallup.com, August 22, 2014, http://www.gallup.com/poll/175400/workers-sense-identity-job.aspx.

20. "Future of Technology May Be Determined by Millennial Malaise, Female Fans and Affluent Data Altruists," Intel Newsroom, October 17, 2013, https://newsroom.intel.com/news-releases/future-of-technology-may-be-determined-by-millennial-malaise-female-fans-and-affluent-data-altruists/.

21. Karl Marx, *Capital: A Critique of Political Economy* (London: Penguin Books in Association with New Left Review, 1976).

22. Murtaza Hussain, "Former Drone Operators Say They Were 'Horrified'

by Cruelty of Assassination Program," *The Intercept*, November 19, 2015, https://theintercept.com/2015/11/19/former-drone-operators-say-they-were -horrified-by-cruelty-of-assassination-program/.

23. Steven Pinker, *The Better Angels of Our Nature: Why Violence Has Declined* (New York: Viking, 2011), 389.

24. Steven Pinker, "Frequently Asked Questions about *The Better Angels of Our Nature: Why Violence Has Declined*," (n.d.) http://stevenpinker.com/pages/ frequently-asked-questions-about-better-angels-our-nature-why-violence -has-declined.

25. "Harmony Korine," interview, *WTF with Marc Maron* (audio blog), August 3, 2015, http://www.wtfpod.com/podcast/episodes/episode_625_-_harmony_ korine.

26. Personal communication, March 30, 2018.

27. Greg Milner, "Death by GPS," *Ars Technica*, May 03, 2016, https:// arstechnica.com/cars/2016/05/death-by-gps/.

28. Adam Waytz et al., "Making Sense by Making Sentient: Effectance Motivation Increases Anthropomorphism," *Journal of Personality and Social Psychology* 99, no. 3 (2010): 410–35, doi:10.1037/a0020240.

29. Fyodor Dostoyevsky, *The Idiot*, trans. Henry Carlisle and Olga Carlisle (New York: Signet Classic, 1969), 577.

Chapter 1: The Dehumanizing Shift

1. David A. Fahrenthold and Jose A. DelReal, "'Rabid' Dogs and Closing Mosques: Anti-Islam Rhetoric Grows in GOP," *Washington Post*, November 19, 2015, https://www.washingtonpost.com/politics/rabid-dogs-and-muslim -id-cards-anti-islam-rhetoric-grows-in-gop/2015/11/19/1cdf9f04-8ee5-11e5 -baf4-bdf37355da0c_story.html.

2. "PM Blames Calais Crisis on 'Swarm' of Migrants," ITV News, July 30, 2015, http://www.itv.com/news/update/2015-07-30/pm-a-swarm-of -migrants-want-to-come-to-britain/.

3. Randall Bytwerk, "The Poisonous Mushroom," *German Propaganda Archive*, (n.d.) http://research.calvin.edu/german-propaganda-archive/story2.htm.

4. Jim Malewitz, "Miller Facebook Post Compares Refugees to Rattlesnakes," *Texas Tribune*, November 19, 2015, https://www.texastribune .org/2015/11/19/miller-facebook-post-compares-refugees-rattlesnake/.

5. Aleksandar Hemon, "The Deadly Treatment of Refugees in Europe," *Rolling Stone,* February 9, 2016, http://www.rollingstone.com/politics/news/ the-deadly-treatment-of-refugees-in-europe-20160209.

6. Nour Kteily et al., "The Ascent of Man: Theoretical and Empirical Evidence for Blatant Dehumanization," *Journal of Personality and Social Psychology* 109, no. 5 (2015), doi:10.1037/pspp0000048.

7. Nour Kteily and Emile Bruneau, "Backlash: The Politics and Real-World Consequences of Minority Group Dehumanization," *Personality and Social Psychology Bulletin* 43, no. 1 (2016), doi:10.1177/0146167216675334.

8. Medea Benjamin, "Israel's Lesson to Palestinians: Build More Rockets?" *AlterNet*, December 5, 2012, https://www.alternet.org/news-amp-politics/israels-lesson-palestinians-build-more-rockets.

9. Victoria M. Esses et al., "Justice, Morality, and the Dehumanization of Refugees," *Social Justice Research* 21, no. 1 (2008), doi:10.1007/s11211-007-0058-4.

10. Victoria M. Esses, Stelian Medianu, and Andrea S. Lawson, "Uncertainty, Threat, and the Role of the Media in Promoting the Dehumanization of Immigrants and Refugees," *Journal of Social Issues* 69, no. 3 (2013), doi:10.1111/josi.12027.

11. Gordon Hodson and Kimberly Costello, "Interpersonal Disgust, Ideological Orientations, and Dehumanization as Predictors of Intergroup Attitudes," *Psychological Science* 18, no. 8 (2007), doi:10.1111/j.1467-9280.2007.01962.x.

12. Andrea Pitzer, *One Long Night: A Global History of Concentration Camps* (London: Hachette UK, 2017), 13, 92, 186.

13. Donald Trump, June 19, 2018, https://twitter.com/realdonaldtrump/status/1009071403918864385.

14. "Polish Opposition Warns Refugees Could Spread Infectious Diseases," *Reuters*, October 15, 2014, https://www.reuters.com/article/us-europe-migrants-poland/polish-opposition-warns-refugees-could-spread-infectious-diseases-idUSKCN0S918B20151015.

15. Stephen Michael Utych, "A Matter of Life and Death: Essays on the Value of Human Life in Politics," PhD diss., Vanderbilt University, 2015.

16. Shekhar Aiyar et al., "Refugee Surge in Europe," *Proceedings of the Refugee Surge in Europe: Economic Challenges*, International Monetary Fund, 2016, https://www.imf.org/external/pubs/ft/sdn/2016/sdn1602.pdf, 14.

17. Edward C. Baig, "Steve Jobs' Biological Father Was Syrian Migrant, Some Note," *USA Today*, November 16, 2015, https://www.usatoday.com/story/tech/columnist/baig/2015/11/16/steve-jobs-biological-father-syrian-migrant-some-note/75899450/.

18. Michael Cavna, "Banksy's Striking New Mural Imagines Steve Jobs as a Syrian Refugee," *Washington Post*, December 11, 2015, https://www.washingtonpost.com/news/comic-riffs/wp/2015/12/11/we-all-know-steve-jobs-syrian-migrant-roots-but-banksy-brings-message-home/.

19. Chris Fuhrmeister, "Anthony Bourdain Hits Back at Donald Trump,

Defends Immigrants," *Eater*, October 29, 2015, https://www.eater
.com/2015/10/29/9638304/anthony-bourdain-donald-trump-immigration.

20. The definitions noted in this paragraph are summarized in the following
article: Martha J. Farah and Andrea S. Heberlein, "Personhood and Neuroscience: Naturalizing or Nihilating?" *American Journal of Bioethics* 7, no.
1 (2007): 37–48, doi:10.1080/15265160601064199.

21. Peter Singer, *Rethinking Life and Death: The Collapse of Our Traditional
Ethics* (Oxford: Oxford University Press, 1994), 180.

22. Michael Tooley, "Abortion and Infanticide," *Philosophy and Public Affairs* 2,
no. 1 (1972): 37–65, http://www.jstor.org/stable/2264919.

23. Joel Feinberg, "Abortion," in *Matters of Life and Death*, ed. T. Regan (Phil-
adelphia: Temple University Press, 1980), 188–89.

24. H. Tristram Engelhardt Jr., *The Foundations of Bioethics* (Oxford: Oxford
University Press, 1986), 138.

25. Shane Schweitzer and Adam Waytz, "Language as a Window into Mind
Perception: How Mental State Language Differentiates Body and Mind,
Human and Nonhuman, and the Self from Others" (2018), unpublished
working paper.

26. Heather M. Gray, Kurt Gray, and Daniel M. Wegner, "Dimensions of
Mind Perception," *Science* 315, no. 5812 (February 2, 2007), doi:10.1126/
science.1134475.

27. Nick Haslam, "Dehumanization: An Integrative Review," *Personality and
Social Psychology Review* 10, no. 3 (2006), doi:10.1207/s15327957pspr1003_4.

28. Jacques-Philippe Leyens et al., "The Emotional Side of Prejudice: The
Attribution of Secondary Emotions to Ingroups and Outgroups," *Personality and Social Psychology Review* 4, no. 2 (2000), doi:10.1207/
s15327957pspr0402_06.

29. Jason P. Mitchell, Todd F. Heatherton, and C. Neil Macrae, "Distinct
Neural Systems Subserve Person and Object Knowledge," *Proceedings of the National Academy of Sciences* 99, no. 23 (2002), doi:10.1073/
pnas.232395699.

30. Jason P. Mitchell, Mahzarin R. Banaji, and C. Neil Macrae, "General
and Specific Contributions of the Medial Prefrontal Cortex to Knowledge about Mental States," *NeuroImage* 28, no. 4 (2005), doi:10.1016/j
.neuroimage.2005.03.011.

31. James K. Rilling et al., "The Neural Correlates of Theory of Mind within
Interpersonal Interactions," *NeuroImage* 22, no. 4 (2004), doi:10.1016/j.neuro
image.2004.04.015.

32. Lasana T. Harris and Susan T. Fiske, "Dehumanizing the Lowest of the
Low," *Psychological Science* 17, no. 10 (2006), doi: 10.1111/j.1467-9280
.2006.01793.x; Lasana T. Harris et al., "Regions of the MPFC Differentially

Tuned to Social and Nonsocial Affective Evaluation," *Cognitive, Affective, and Behavioral Neuroscience* 7, no. 4 (2007): 309–16.

33. Adam Waytz et al., "Making Sense by Making Sentient: Effectance Motivation Increases Anthropomorphism," *Journal of Personality and Social Psychology* 99, no. 3 (2010), doi:10.1037/a0020240.

34. Jamil Zaki and Kevin N. Ochsner, "The Neuroscience of Empathy: Progress, Pitfalls and Promise," *Nature Neuroscience* 15, no. 5 (2012): 675.

35. Sara H. Konrath, Edward H. O'Brien, and Courtney Hsing, "Changes in Dispositional Empathy in American College Students over Time: A Meta-Analysis," *Personality and Social Psychology Review* 15, no. 2 (2010): 180–98, doi:10.1177/1088868310377395.

36. These constructs roughly approximate to "prosocial concern" and "mentalizing" in terms of Zaki and Ochsner's (2012) definition of empathy.

37. Jean M. Twenge, *Generation Me—Revised and Updated: Why Today's Young Americans Are More Confident, Assertive, Entitled—and More Miserable Than Ever Before* (New York: Simon & Schuster, 2014), 56.

38. Kali H. Trzesniewski and M. Brent Donnellan, "Rethinking 'Generation Me': A Study of Cohort Effects from 1976–2006," *Perspectives on Psychological Science* 5, no. 1 (2010): 58–75, doi.org/10.1177/1745691609356789.

39. Eunike Wetzel et al., "The Narcissism Epidemic Is Dead; Long Live the Narcissism Epidemic," Psychological Science 28, no. 12 (2017): 1833–47, doi.org/10.1177/0956797617724208.

40. Robert D. Putnam, "Bowling Alone: America's Declining Social Capital," interview, *Journal of Democracy* 6, (1995): 65–78.

41. Thomas H. Sander and Robert D. Putnam, "Still Bowling Alone? The Post-9/11 Split," *Journal of Democracy* 21, no. 1 (2010): 9–16, https://www.journalofdemocracy.org/article/still-bowling-alone-post-911-split.

42. Joe Cortright, "Less in Common," *City Observatory*, June 9, 2015, http://cityobservatory.org/less-in-common/.

43. Eric D. Gould and Alexander Hijzen, "Growing Apart, Losing Trust? The Impact of Inequality on Social Capital" (IMF working paper, International Monetary Fund, 2016).

44. N. Epley, A. Waytz, and J. T. Cacioppo, "On Seeing Human: A Three-Factor Theory of Anthropomorphism," *Psychological Review* 114, no. 4 (2007): 864–86, doi:10.1037/0033-295X.114.4.864.

45. S. Cacioppo et al., "Loneliness Clinical Import and Interventions," *Perspectives on Psychological Science* 10, no. 2 (2015): 238–49, doi:10.1177/1745691615570616; Stephen Marche, "Is Facebook Making Us Lonely?" *The Atlantic*, May 2012, 60–69.

46. Pew Research Center, "Social Isolation and New Technology," November 4, 2009, http://www.pewinternet.org/2009/11/04/social-isolation-and-new-technology/; D. Matthew et al., "Declining Loneliness over Time: Evidence

from American Colleges and High Schools," *Personality and Social Psychology Bulletin* 41, no. 1 (2015): 78–89.

47. Christian Welzel, *Freedom Rising* (New York: Cambridge University Press, 2013).

48. Henri C. Santos, Michael E. W. Varnum, and Igor Grossmann, "Global Increases in Individualism," *Psychological Science* 28, no. 9 (2017):1228–39, doi.org/10.1177/0956797617700622.

49. Michael J. Sandel, *What Money Can't Buy: The Moral Limits of Markets* (New York: Farrar, Straus and Giroux, 2012), 9.

50. Lasana T. Harris et al., "Assigning Economic Value to People Results in Dehumanization Brain Response," *Journal of Neuroscience, Psychology, and Economics* 7, no. 3 (2014): 151.

51. Alan P. Fiske, "The Four Elementary Forms of Sociality: Framework for a Unified Theory of Social Relations," *Psychological Review* 99, no. 4 (1992): 689–723.

52. Tara Palmeri, "Rich Manhattan Moms Hire Handicapped Tour Guides So Kids Can Cut Lines at Disney World," *New York Post,* May 14, 2013, http://nypost.com/2013/05/14/rich-manhattan-moms-hire-handicapped-tour-guides-so-kids-can-cut-lines-at-disney-world/.

53. Philip Bump, "Congress Sets a New Record for Polarization. Here's How — In 7 Charts," *Washington Post,* June 2, 2015, https://www.washingtonpost.com/news/the-fix/wp/2015/06/02/congress-sets-a-new-record-for-polarization-but-why

54. Jeffrey M. Jones, "Obama's Fourth Year in Office Ties as Most Polarized Ever," Gallup.com, January 24, 2013, http://news.gallup.com/poll/160097/obama-fourth-year-office-ties-polarized-ever.aspx.

55. Brandon Rottinghaus and Justin S. Vaughn, *Official Results of the 2018 Presidents & Executive Politics Presidential Greatness Survey,* https://sps.boisestate.edu/politicalscience/files/2018/02/Greatness.pdf; Kenneth T. Walsh, "Polarization Deepens in American Politics," *U.S. News & World Report,* October 3, 2017, https://www.usnews.com/news/ken-walshs-washington/articles/2017-10-03/polarization-deepens-in-american-politics.

56. Tim Groeling, "Media Bias by the Numbers: Challenges and Opportunities in the Empirical Study of Partisan News," *Political Science* 16, no. 1 (2013): 129–51.

57. Pew Research Center, "Partisanship and Political Animosity in 2016," June 22, 2016, http://www.people-press.org/2016/06/22/partisanship-and-political-animosity-in-2016/.

58. Pablo Barberá et al., "Tweeting from Left to Right: Is Online Political Communication More Than an Echo Chamber?" *Psychological Science* 26, no. 10 (2015): 1531–42, doi.org/10.1177/0956797615594620.

59. Adam Waytz, Liane L. Young, and Jeremy Ginges, "Motive Attribution Asymmetry for Love vs. Hate Drives Intractable Conflict," *Proceedings of the National Academy of Sciences* 111, no. 44 (2014): 15687–92, doi:10.1073/pnas.1414146111.

60. Ed O'Brien and Phoebe C. Ellsworth, "More Than Skin Deep: Visceral States Are Not Projected onto Dissimilar Others," *Psychological Science* 23, no. 4 (2012): 391–96, doi:10.1177/0956797611432179.

61. James L. Matherus, "Party Animals? Party Identity and Dehumanization," 2018, unpublished working paper; Leor M. Hackel, Christine E. Looser, and Jay Van Bavel, "Group Membership Alters the Threshold for Mind Perception: The Role of Social Identity, Collective Identification, and Intergroup Threat," *Journal of Experimental Social Psychology* 52 (May 2014): 15–23, doi.org/10.1016/j.jesp.2013.12.001.

62. Ben Jacobs, "Hillary Clinton Calls Half of Trump Supporters Bigoted 'Deplorables,'" *The Guardian,* September 10, 2016, https://www.theguardian.com/us-news/2016/sep/10/hillary-clinton-trump-supporters-bigoted-deplorables.

63. Donald J. Trump (@realDonaldTrump), "Animals representing Hillary Clinton and Dems in North Carolina just firebombed our office in Orange County because we are winning @NCGOP," Tweet, October 16, https://twitter.com/realDonaldTrump/status/787782613633208320.

64. Thomas Piketty, *Capital in the Twenty-First Century* (Cambridge: Belknap Press, 2014).

65. "World Inequality Database," accessed July 11, 2018, http://wid.world; Edward Wolff, "Deconstructing Household Wealth Trends in the United States, 1983–2013" (NBER working paper no. w22704, The National Bureau of Economic Research, September 2016); Emmanuel Saez, "U.S. Top One Percent of Income Earners Hit New High in 2015 amid Strong Economic Growth," Washington Center for Equitable Growth, April 10, 2018, http://equitablegrowth.org/research-analysis/u-s-top-one-percent-of-income-earners-hit-new-high-in-2015-amid-strong-economic-growth/; Chad Stone et al., "A Guide to Statistics on Historical Trends in Income Inequality," Center on Budget and Policy Priorities, February 16, 2018, https://www.cbpp.org/research/poverty-and-inequality/a-guide-to-statistics-on-historical-trends-in-income-inequality.

66. Paul Jargowsky, "Architecture of Segregation," Century Foundation, August 7, 2015, https://tcf.org/content/report/architecture-of-segregation/.

67. Susan T. Fiske, "From Dehumanization and Objectification to Rehumanization," *Annals of the New York Academy of Sciences* 1167, no. 1 (June 2009): 31–34, doi:10.1111/j.1749-6632.2009.04544.x.

68. Sundance, "John Stossel Interview with Labor Secretary Nominee Andy

Puzder," Last Refuge, December 9, 2016, https://theconservativetreehouse
.com/2016/12/09/john-stossel-interview-with-labor-secretary-nominee
-andy-puzder/.

69. Lea Hudson, "Commentary: Feeding 'the Animals' Makes Them Dependent,"
The Tennessean, September 18, 2016, https://www.tennessean.com/story/news/
local/cheatham/2016/09/18/feeding-animals-makes-dependent/90623538/.

70. Fiske, "From Dehumanization and Objectification to Rehumanization."

71. Andrew K. Przybylski and Netta Weinstein, "A Large Scale Test of the
Goldilocks Hypothesis: Quantifying the Relations Between Digital Screens
and the Mental Well-Being of Adolescents," *Psychological Science* 28, no. 2
(January 13, 2017): 204–15, doi:10.1177/0956797616678438.

72. Adam Waytz and Kurt Gray, "Does Online Technology Make Us More or Less
Sociable? A Preliminary Review and Call for Research," *Perspectives on Psychological Science* 13, no. 4 (2018): 473–91, doi: 10.1177/1745691617746509.

Chapter 2: Humans as Meaning Makers

1. Fred Katz, "Thunder Notes: Roberson Keeps Hugging, Drops Career High,"
Norman Transcript, February 24, 2017, http://www.normantranscript.com/
oklahoma/thundernotes-roberson-keeps-hugging-drops-career-high/
article_a6a6ac04-fb14-11e6-a23d-7348081810b8.html.

2. Frank N. Willis and Helen K. Hamm, "The Use of Interpersonal Touch in
Securing Compliance," *Journal of Nonverbal Behavior* 5, no. 1 (1980): 49-55,
doi:10.1007/bf00987054.

3. Chris L. Kleinke, "Compliance to Requests Made by Gazing and Touching
Experimenters in Field Settings," *Journal of Experimental Social Psychology*
13, no. 3 (1977): 218–23, doi:10.1016/0022-1031(77)90044-0.

4. April H. Crusco and Christopher G. Wetzel, "The Midas Touch: The
Effects of Interpersonal Touch on Restaurant Tipping," *Personality and
Social Psychology Bulletin* 10, no. 4 (1984): 512–17.

5. James A. Coan, Hilary S. Schaefer, and Richard J. Davidson, "Lending a
Hand: Social Regulation of the Neural Response to Threat," *Psychological
Science* 17, no. 2 (2006): 1032–39, doi:10.1111/j.1467-9280.2006.01832.x.

6. Sarah L. Master et al., "A Picture's Worth: Partner Photographs Reduce
Experimentally Induced Pain," *Psychological Science* 20, no. 11 (2009):
1316–18, http://dx.doi.org/10.1111/j.1467-9280.2009.02444.x.

7. Pavel Goldstein et al., "Empathy Predicts an Experimental Pain Reduction during Touch," *Journal of Pain* 17, no. 10 (October 2016): 1049–57,
doi:10.1016/j.jpain.2016.06.007.

8. Ryan W. Buell, Tami Kim, and Chia-Jung Tsay, "Creating Reciprocal Value

through Operational Transparency," *Management Science* 63, no. 6 (May 2016): 1673–95, https://doi.org/10.1287/mnsc.2015.2411.

9. Justin Kruger et al., "The Effort Heuristic," *Journal of Experimental Social Psychology* 40, no. 1 (2004): 91–98, doi:10.1016/S0022-1031(03)00065-9.

10. Adam Smith, *An Inquiry into the Nature and Causes of the Wealth of Nations* (1817).

11. Karl Marx, *Wage-Labor and Capital* (Moscow: Progress Publishers, 1847).

12. Angelina Hawley-Dolan and Ellen Winner, "Seeing the Mind Behind the Art: People Can Distinguish Abstract Expressionist Paintings from Highly Similar Paintings by Children, Chimps, Monkeys, and Elephants," *Psychological Science* 22, no. 4 (March 2011): 435–41, doi .org/10.1177/0956797611400915; Leslie Snapper et al., "Your Kid Could Not Have Done That: Even Untutored Observers Can Discern Intentionality and Structure in Abstract Expressionist Art," *Cognition* 137 (April 2015): 154–65, doi:10.1016/j.cognition.2014.12.009.

13. Nigel Reynolds, "Art World Goes Wild for Chimpanzee's Paintings as Warhol Work Flops," *The Telegraph*, June 21, 2005, http://www.telegraph.co.uk/ news/1492463/Art-world-goes-wild-for-chimpanzees-paintings-as-Warhol-work-flops.html.

14. Kurt Gray, "The Power of Good Intentions: Perceived Benevolence Soothes Pain, Increases Pleasure, and Improves Taste," *Social Psychological and Personality Science* 3, no. 5 (January 2012): 639–45, doi .org/10.1177/1948550611433470.

15. Robert Kreuzbauer, Dan King, and Shanka Basu, "The Mind in the Object—Psychological Valuation of Materialized Human Expression," *Journal of Experimental Psychology: General* 144, no. 4 (August 2015): 764–87, doi:10.1037/xge0000080.

16. Marianna Mairesse and Katie L. Connor, "Christian Louboutin: In His Shoes," *Marie Claire*, February 27, 2012, http://www.marieclaire.com/ celebrity/a6920/christian-louboutin-interview/.

17. Christoph Fuchs, Martin Schreier, and Stijn M. van Osselaer, "The Handmade Effect: What's Love Got to Do with It?" *Journal of Marketing* 79, no. 2 (March 2015): 98–110, doi.org/10.1509/jm.14.0018.

18. Gregory A. Hall, "Maker's Mark 'Handmade' Claim Allowed by Judge," *Courier-Journal*, July 29, 2015, https://www.courier-journal.com/story/ life/food/spirits/bourbon/2015/07/29/judge-dismisses-lawsuit-markers -mark/30830057/.

19. Veronika Job et al., "Social Traces of Generic Humans Increase the Value of Everyday Objects," *Personality and Social Psychology Bulletin* 43, no. 6 (April 2017): 785–92, doi.org/10.1177/0146167217697694.

20. Ulrich Kirk et al., "Modulation of Aesthetic Value by Semantic Context: An

fMRI study," *Neuroimage* 44, no. 3 (February 2009): 1125–32, doi:10.1016/j.neuroimage.2008.10.009.

21. James George Frazer, "The Golden Bough," in *The Golden Bough* (London: Palgrave Macmillan, 1990), 701–11.

22. Carol Nemeroff and Paul Rozin, "The Contagion Concept in Adult Thinking in the United States: Transmission of Germs and of Interpersonal Influence," *Ethos* 22, no. 2 (June 1994): 158–86, doi.org/10.1525/eth.1994.22.2.02a00020.

23. George E. Newman and Paul Bloom, "Physical Contact Influences How Much People Pay at Celebrity Auctions," *Proceedings of the National Academy of Sciences* 111, no. 10 (2014): 3705–8, doi:10.1073/pnas.1313637111.

24. Eva Krumhuber et al., "Facial Dynamics as Indicators of Trustworthiness and Cooperative Behavior," *Emotion* 7, no. 4 (November 2007): 730–35, doi:10.1037/1528-3542.7.4.730.

25. Francesca Gino, Maryam Kouchaki, and Adam D. Galinsky, "The Moral Virtue of Authenticity: How Inauthenticity Produces Feelings of Immorality and Impurity," *Psychological Science* 26, no. 7 (2015): 983–96, doi:10.1177/0956797615575277.

26. Michael Harkin, "Modernist Anthropology and Tourism of the Authentic," *Annals of Tourism Research* 22, no. 3 (1995): 650–70, doi.org/10.1016/0160-7383(95)00008-T; Robert L. Goldman and Stephen Papson, *Sign Wars: The Cluttered Landscape of Advertising* (New York: Guilford Press, 1996); George E. Newman and Ravi Dhar, "Authenticity Is Contagious: Brand Essence and the Original Source of Production," *Journal of Marketing Research* 51, no. 3 (June 2014): 371–86, doi.org/10.1509/jmr.11.0022.

27. George E. Newman and Paul Bloom, "Art and Authenticity: The Importance of Originals in Judgments of Value," *Journal of Experimental Psychology: General* 141, no. 3 (August 2012): 558–69, doi:10.1037/a0026035.

28. Joshua Hammer, "The Greatest Fake-Art Scam in History?" *Vanity Fair,* October 10, 2012, https://www.vanityfair.com/culture/2012/10/wolfgang-beltracchi-helene-art-scam.

29. Balázs Kovács, Glenn R. Carroll, and David W. Lehman, "Authenticity and Consumer Value Ratings: Empirical Tests from the Restaurant Domain," *Organization Science* 25, no. 2 (July 2013): 458–78, doi.org/10.1287/orsc.2013.0843.

30. M. Yeomans et al., "Making Sense of Recommendations," 2018, unpublished working paper.

31. Berkeley J. Dietvorst, Joseph P. Simmons, and Cade Massey, "Algorithm Aversion: People Erroneously Avoid Algorithms after Seeing Them Err," *Journal of Experimental Psychology: General* 144, no. 1 (2014): 114–26, doi.org/10.1037/xge0000033.

Chapter 3: The Morality of Humanity

1. Qianfan Zhang, *Human Dignity in Classical Chinese Philosophy: Confucianism, Mohism, and Daoism* (New York: Palgrave, 2016).
2. Immanuel Kant, *Grounding for the Metaphysics of Morals: On a Supposed Right to Lie Because of Philanthropic Concerns* (Indianapolis: Hackett Publishing, 1993), 36.
3. James Legge, *The Works of Mencius: The Chinese Classics* (Oxford: Clarendon Press, 1861), 471.
4. Lt. Col. Dave Grossman, *On Killing: The Psychological Cost of Learning to Kill in War and Society* (New York: Back Bay Books, 1995).
5. S. L. A. Marshall, *Men Against Fire: The Problem of Battle Command* (Norman: University of Oklahoma Press, 2000).
6. Molly J. Crockett et al., "Harm to Others Outweighs Harm to Self in Moral Decision Making," *Proceedings of the National Academy of Sciences* 111, no. 48 (December 2014): 17320–25, doi.org/10.1073/pnas.1408988111.
7. Lukas J. Volz et al., "Harm to Self Outweighs Benefit to Others in Moral Decision Making," *Proceedings of the National Academy of Sciences* 114, no. 30 (July 2017): 7963–68, doi.org/10.1073/pnas.1706693114.
8. Fiery Cushman et al., "Simulating Murder: The Aversion to Harmful Action," *Emotion* 12, no. 1 (February 2012): 2–7, doi:10.1037/a0025071.
9. Albert Bandura, Bill Underwood, and Michael E. Fromson, "Disinhibition of Aggression Through Diffusion of Responsibility and Dehumanization of Victims," *Journal of Research in Personality* 9, no. 4 (December 1975): 253–69, doi.org/10.1016/0092-6566(75)90001-X.
10. Michael J. Osofsky, Albert Bandura, and Philip G. Zimbardo, "The Role of Moral Disengagement in the Execution Process," *Law and Human Behavior* 29, no. 4 (August 2005): 371–93, doi:10.1007/s10979-005-4930-1.
11. Maria Andersson et al., "Patient Photographs—A Landmark for the ICU Staff: A Descriptive Study," *Intensive and Critical Care Nursing* 29, no. 4 (2013): 193–201.
12. Cecilia Neto, Tilda Shalof, and Judy Costello, "Critical Care Nurses' Responses to Patient Photographs Displayed at the Bedside," *Heart and Lung: The Journal of Acute and Critical Care* 35, no. 3 (2006): 198–204.
13. Mary Gatter et al., "Relationship Between Ultrasound Viewing and Proceeding to Abortion," *Obstetrics and Gynecology* 123, no. 1 (January 2014): 81–87, doi:10.1097/AOG.0000000000000053.
14. Ushma D. Upadhyay et al., "Evaluating the Impact of a Mandatory Pre-Abortion Ultrasound Viewing Law: A Mixed Methods Study," *PloS One* 12, no. 7 (2017): e0178871.
15. Emma Green, "Science Is Giving the Pro-Life Movement a Boost,"

The Atlantic, January 18, 2018, https://www.theatlantic.com/politics/archive/2018/01/pro-life-pro-science/549308/.

16. Kazumitsu Kushida et al., "Introduction of Honda ASV-3 (motorcycles)," *Honda R and D Technical Review* 18, no. 2 (2006): 13.

17. Jan Theeuwes and Stefan Van der Stigchel, "Faces Capture Attention: Evidence from Inhibition of Return," *Visual Cognition* 13, no. 6 (2006): 657–65, doi.org/10.1080/13506280500410949.

18. Thomas C. Schelling, "The Life You Save May Be Your Own," in *Choice and Consequence: Perspectives of an Errant Economist* (Cambridge, MA: Harvard University Press, 1984), 115–16, 126.

19. Deborah A. Small, George Loewenstein, and Paul Slovic, "Sympathy and Callousness: The Impact of Deliberative Thought on Donations to Identifiable and Statistical Victims," *Organizational Behavior and Human Decision Processes* 102, no. 2 (2007): 143–53, doi:10.1016/j.obhdp.2006.01.005.

20. Paul Slovic et al., "Iconic Photographs and the Ebb and Flow of Empathic Response to Humanitarian Disasters," *Proceedings of the National Academy of Sciences* 114, no. 4 (January 2017): 640–44, doi.org/10.1073/pnas.1613977114.

21. Alexander Genevsky et al., "Neural Underpinnings of the Identifiable Victim Effect: Affect Shifts Preferences for Giving," *Journal of Neuroscience* 33, no. 43 (October 2013): 17188–96, doi.org/10.1523/JNEUROSCI.2348-13.2013.

22. Cynthia Cryder and George Loewenstein, "The Critical Link between Tangibility and Generosity," in *The Science of Giving: Experimental Approaches to the Study of Charity*, ed. D. M. Oppenheimer and C. Y. Olivola (New York: Taylor and Francis, 2010), 237–51.

23. C. Daryl Cameron and B. Keith Payne, "Escaping Affect: How Motivated Emotion Regulation Creates Insensitivity to Mass Suffering," *Journal of Personality and Social Psychology* 100, no. 1 (January 2011): 1–15, doi:10.1037/a0021643.

24. Note that this quote was presented as is, in citation 138, but another version of this quote appears in the reference provided here, as, "I never look at the masses as my responsibility; I look at the individual. I can only love one person at a time—just one, one, one." Susan Conroy, *Mother Teresa's Lessons of Love and Secrets of Sanctity* (Huntington, IN: Our Sunday Visitor Publishing, 2003).

25. Adam Waytz and Liane Young, "The Group-Member Mind Trade-Off: Attributing Mind to Groups versus Group Members," *Psychological Science* 23, no. 1 (2012): 77–85.

26. David L. Hamilton and Steven J. Sherman, "Perceiving Persons and Groups," *Psychological Review* 103, no. 2 (April 1996): 336–55, http://dx.doi.org/10.1037/0033-295X.103.2.336.

27. Robert W. Smith, David Faro, and Katherine A. Burson, "More for the Many: The Influence of Entitativity on Charitable Giving." *Journal of Consumer Research* 39, no. 5 (2012): 961–76.

28. Daniel Västfjäll et al., "Compassion Fade: Affect and Charity Are Greatest for a Single Child in Need," *PloS One* 9, no. 6 (2014): e100115.

29. Francesca Gino, Lisa Shu, and Max H. Bazerman, "Nameless + Harmless = Blameless: When Seemingly Irrelevant Factors Influence Judgment of (Un) ethical Behavior," *Organizational Behavior and Human Decision Processes* 111, no. 2 (2010): 93–101, http://dx.doi.org/10.1016/j.obhdp.2009.11.001.

30. Adam Waytz, John Cacioppo, and Nicholas Epley, "Who Sees Human? The Stability and Importance of Individual Differences in Anthropomorphism," *Perspectives on Psychological Science* 5, no. 3 (2014): 219–32, doi:10.1177/1745691610369336.

31. Catherine Bertenshaw and Peter Rowlinson, "Exploring Stock Managers' Perceptions of the Human-Animal Relationship on Dairy Farms and an Association with Milk Production," *Anthrozoös* 22, no. 1 (2009): 59–69, https://doi.org/10.2752/175303708X390473.

32. Brock Bastian and Steve Loughnan, "Resolving the Meat-Paradox: A Motivational Account of Morally Troublesome Behavior and Its Maintenance," *Personality and Social Psychology Review* 21, no. 3 (May 2016): 278–99, https://doi.org/10.1177/1088868316647562.

33. Brock Bastian et al., "Don't Mind Meat? The Denial of Mind to Animals Used for Human Consumption," *Personality and Social Psychology Bulletin* 38, no. 2 (February 2012): 247–56, https://doi.org/10.1177/0146167211424291.

34. James A. Serpell "Anthropomorphism and Anthropomorphic Selection— Beyond the 'Cute Response,'" *Society and Animals* 10, no. 4 (2002): 437–54, doi:10.1163/156853002320936926.

35. Laura Entis, "Pets Are Basically People," *Fortune*, September 7, 2016, http://fortune.com/2016/09/07/pets-are-basically-people/.

36. Max E. Butterfield, Sarah E. Hill, and Charles G. Lord, "Mangy Mutt or Furry Friend? Anthropomorphism Promotes Animal Welfare," *Journal of Experimental Social Psychology* 48, no 4. (July 2012): 957–60, https://doi.org/10.1016/j.jesp.2012.02.010.

37. Personal communication, March 15, 2018.

38. Personal communication, March 30, 2018.

39. Jeff Mackey, "NYC: Drop Dead (Meat)," PETA, July 29, 2010, http://www.peta.org/blog/nyc-drop-dead-meat/.

40. S. Plous, "Psychological Mechanisms in the Human Use of Animals," *Journal of Social Issues* 49, no. 1 (1993): 11–52, https://doi.org/10.1111/j.1540-4560.1993.tb00907.x.

41. Stephen R. Kellert, *The Value of Life: Biological Diversity and Human Society* (Washington, DC: Island Press, 1996).

42. Gregg Mitman, "Pachyderm Personalities: The Media of Science, Politics, and Conservation," in *Thinking with Animals: New Perspectives on Anthro-*

pomorphism, ed. Lorraine Daston and Gregg Mitman (New York: Columbia University Press, 2005), 175–95.

43. Christopher Lehmann-Haupt, "Books of the Times; The Allure of Elephants; In Their Grace and Folly," *New York Times*, March 10, 1988, http://www.nytimes.com/1988/03/10/books/books-of-the-times-the-allure-of -elephants-in-their grace-and-folly.html.

44. Stacey K. Sowards, "Identification through Orangutans: Destabilizing the Nature/Culture Dualism," *Ethics and the Environment* 11, no. 2 (2006): 45–61, doi:10.1353/een.2007.0007.

45. "World Declaration on Great Primates," GAP Project, http://www.projetogap .org.br/en/world-declaration-on-great-primates/.

46. Nurit Bird-David and Danny Naveh, "Relational Epistemology, Immediacy, and Conservation: Or, What Do the Nayaka Try to Conserve?" *Journal for the Study of Religion, Nature and Culture* 2, no. 1 (2008): 55–73, doi:10.1558/jsrnc.v2i1.55.

47. Danny Naveh and Nurit Bird-David, "How Persons Become Things: Economic and Epistemological Changes Among Nayaka Hunter-Gatherers," *Journal of the Royal Anthropological Institute* 20, no. 1 (January 2014): 74–92, https://doi.org/10.1111/1467-9655.12080.

48. Ananya Bhattacharya, "India's Sacred Rivers Now Have Human Rights," *Quartz*, March 22, 2017, https://qz.com/938190/the-ganga-and-yamuna-rivers-in-india-were-given-human-rights-to-protect-them-from-pollution/.

49. Jesse Chandler and Norbert Schwarz, "Use Does Not Wear Ragged the Fabric of Friendship: Thinking of Objects as Alive Makes People Less Willing to Replace Them," *Journal of Consumer Psychology* 20, no. 2 (April 2010): 138–45, https://doi.org/10.1016/j.jcps.2009.12.008.

50. Peter H. Kahn Jr. et al., "'Robovie, You'll Have to Go into the Closet Now': Children's Social and Moral Relationships with a Humanoid Robot," *Developmental Psychology* 48, no. 2 (March 2012): 303–14, doi:10.1037/a0027033.

51. Jeroen Vaes et al., "Minimal Humanity Cues Induce Neural Empathic Reactions Towards Non-Human Entities," *Neuropsychologia* 89 (August 2016): 132–40, doi:10.1016/j.neuropsychologia.2016.06.004.

Chapter 4: Human Influence as the Engine of Action

1. Adam Waytz, "Do Cultural Critics Have Any Value Left?" *Pacific Standard*, July 11, 2013, https://psmag.com/social-justice/the-value-of-cultural-critics -books-movies-television-art-62131.

2. Matthew J. Salganik, Peter Sheridan Dodds, and Duncan J. Watts,

"Experimental Study of Inequality and Unpredictability in an Artificial Cultural Market," *Science* 311, no. 5762 (2006): 854–56, doi:10.1126/science.1121066.

3. Stanley Milgram, "Behavioral Study of Obedience," *Journal of Abnormal and Social Psychology* 67, no. 4 (1963): 371–78.

4. Stanley Milgram, "Some Conditions of Obedience and Disobedience to Authority," *Human Relations* 18, no. 1 (1975): 57–76, doi:10.1177/001872676501800105.

5. Robert M. Bond et al., "A 61-Million-Person Experiment in Social Influence and Political Mobilization," *Nature* 489 (September 2012): 295–98, doi:10.1038/nature11421.

6. Elizabeth Levy Paluck, "The Salience of Social Referents: A Field Experiment on Collective Norms and Harassment Behavior in a School Social Network," *Journal of Personality and Social Psychology* 103, no. 6 (December 2012): 899–915; Elizabeth Levy Paluck, Hana Shepherd, and Peter M. Aronow, "Changing Climates of Conflict: A Social Network Experiment in 56 Schools," *Proceedings of the National Academy of Sciences* 113, no. 3 (January 2016): 566–71, https://doi.org/10.1073/pnas.1514483113.

7. Cure Violence, "Scientific Evaluations," http://cureviolence.org/results/scientific-evaluations/.

8. Daniel W. Webster et al., "Effect of Baltimore's *Safe Streets* Program on Gun Violence: A Replication of Chicago's *CeaseFire* Program," *Journal of Urban Health* 90, no. 1 (June 2012): 27–40, doi:10.1007/s11524-012-9731-5.

9. Sheyla Delgado, Laila Alsabahi, and Jeffrey A. Butts, "Young Men in Neighborhoods with Cure Violence Programs Adopt Attitudes Less Supportive of Violence," John Jay College Research and Evaluation Center (JohnJayREC), March 16, 2017, https://johnjayrec.nyc/2017/03/16/databit201701/.

10. David Broockman and Joshua Kalla, "Durably Reducing Transphobia: A Field Experiment on Door-to-Door Canvassing," *Science* 352, no. 6282 (April 2016): 220–24, doi:10.1126/science.aad9713.

11. Christie Aschwanden and Maggie Koerth-Baker, "How Two Grad Students Uncovered an Apparent Fraud—And a Way to Change Opinions on Transgender Rights," *FiveThirtyEight*, April 7, 2016, https://fivethirtyeight.com/features/how-two-grad-students-uncovered-michael-lacour-fraud-and-a-way-to-change-opinions-on-transgender-rights/.

12. Lacey Rose, "Bill Simmons Breaks Free: His 'F-ing Shitty' ESPN Exit, Who Courted Him and Details of His HBO Show," *Hollywood Reporter*, June 8, 2016, http://www.hollywoodreporter.com/features/bill-simmons-espn-hbo-900291.

13. Jessica Contrera, "As 'the Fathers of Daughters,' They Were Offended by Harassment. But What Did That Really Mean?" *Washington Post*, October

13, 2017, https://www.washingtonpost.com/lifestyle/style/as-the-fathers
-of-daughters-they-were-offended-by-harassment-but-what-did-that-
really-mean/2017/10/13/c1991f70-aed7-11e7-9e58-e6288544af98_story
.html.

14. Henrik Cronqvist and Frank Yu, "Shaped by Their Daughters: Executives,
Female Socialization, and Corporate Social Responsibility," *Journal of
Financial Economics* (September 2017), working paper.

15. Paul A. Gompers and Sophie Q. Wang, "And the Children Shall Lead:
Gender Diversity and Performance in Venture Capital" (NBER working
paper no. 23454, The National Bureau of Economic Research, 2017).

16. Adam N. Glynn and Maya Sen, "Identifying Judicial Empathy: Does Having Daughters Cause Judges to Rule for Women's Issues?" *American Journal
of Political Science* 59, no. 1 (2014): 37–54, doi:10.1111/ajps.12118.

17. Jessica M. Nolan et al., "Normative Social Influence Is Underdetected,"
Personality and Social Psychology Bulletin 34, no. 7 (2008): 913–23, https://
doi.org/10.1177/0146167208316691.

18. Jessica M. Nolan, Jessica Kenefick, and P. Wesley Schultz, "Normative
Messages Promoting Energy Conservation Will Be Underestimated by
Experts . . . Unless You Show Them the Data," *Social Influence* 6, no. 3
(July 2011): 169–80, https://doi.org/10.1080/15534510.2011.584786.

19. Markus Barth, Philipp Jugert, and Immo Fritsche, "Still Underdetected—
Social Norms and Collective Efficacy Predict the Acceptance of Electric
Vehicles in Germany," *Transportation Research Part F Traffic Psychology and
Behavior* 37 (February 2016): 64–77, doi:10.1016/j.trf.2015.11.011.

20. Dan Glaun, "Michelle Carter Found Guilty by Judge in Text Message Suicide Case," Masslive.com, June 16, 2017, http://www.masslive.com/news/
index.ssf/2017/06/michelle_carter_found_guilty_i.html.

21. Alban Murtishi, "Michelle Carter Trial: Last Text Message Conrad Roy
Sent Carter Was 'Okay. I'm Almost There,'" Masslive.com, June 16, 2017,
http://www.masslive.com/news/index.ssf/2017/06/take_a_look_at_the_
text_messag.html.

22. Vanessa K. Bohns, "(Mis)Understanding Our Influence over Others: A
Review of the Underestimation-of-Compliance Effect," *Current Directions
in Psychological Science* 25, no. 2 (April 2016): 119–23, https://doi.org/10
.1177/0963721415628011.

23. Francis J. Flynn and Vanessa K. Lake, "If You Need Help, Just Ask: Underestimating Compliance with Direct Requests for Help," *Journal of Personality and Social Psychology* 95, no. 1 (2008): 128–43, http://digitalcommons
.ilr.cornell.edu/articles/1074.

24. Vanessa K. Bohns, M. Mahdi Roghanizad, and Amy Z. Xu, "Underestimating Our Influence Over Others' Unethical Behavior and Decisions,"

Personality and Social Psychology Bulletin 40, no. 3 (March 2014): 348–62, https://doi.org/10.1177/0146167213511825.

25. Mahdi Roghanizad and Vanessa Bohns, "Ask in Person: You're Less Persuasive Than You Think over Email," *Journal of Experimental Social Psychology* 66 (March 2017): 223–26, doi:10.1016/j.jesp.2016.10.002.

26. Jamil Zaki, Jessica Schirmer, and Jason P. Mitchell, "Social Influence Modulates the Neural Computation of Value," *Psychological Science* 22, no. 7 (July 2011): 894–900, doi:10.1177/0956797611411057.

27. Rita Mae Brown, *Venus Envy* (New York: Bantam, 1994), 88.

Chapter 5: Human-Centered Motivation

1. Adam M. Grant, "Does Intrinsic Motivation Fuel the Prosocial Fire? Motivational Synergy in Predicting Persistence, Performance, and Productivity," *Journal of Applied Psychology* 93, no. 1 (2008): 48–58, doi:10.1037/0021 -9010.93.1.48.

2. Adam M. Grant et al., "Impact and the Art of Motivation Maintenance: The Effects of Contact with Beneficiaries on Persistence Behavior," *Organizational Behavior and Human Decision Processes* 103, no. 1 (May 2007): 53–67, http://dx.doi.org/10.1016/j.obhdp.2006.05.004.

3. Adam M. Grant, "Employees without a Cause: The Motivational Effects of Prosocial Impact in Public Service," *International Public Management Journal* 11, no. 1 (March 2008): 48–66, https://doi.org/10 .1080/10967490801887905.

4. Sandra A. Waddock and Samuel B. Graves, "The Corporate Social Performance-Financial Performance Link," *Strategic Management Journal* 18, no. 4 (April 1997): 303–19, http://www.jstor.org/stable/3088143.

5. Heli Wang and Cuili Qian, "Corporate Philanthropy and Corporate Financial Performance: The Roles of Stakeholder Response and Political Access," *Academy of Management Journal* 54, no. 6 (December 2011): 1159–81, https://journals.aom.org/doi/10.5465/amj.2009.0548.

6. Vanessa C. Burbano, "Can Firms Pay Less and Get More . . . By Doing Good? The Effect of Corporate Social Responsibility on Employee Salary Requirements and Performance" (working paper, UCLA Anderson, 2014).

7. Mirco Tonin and Michael Vlassopoulos, "Corporate Philanthropy and Productivity: Evidence from an Online Real Effort Experiment," *Management Science* 61, no. 8 (April 2014): 1795–1811, https://doi.org/10.1287/mnsc .2014.1985.

8. Jim Ziolkowski, "Why I Gave Up a High-Paying Corporate Career to Start

a Charity," *Parade*, September 23, 2013, https://parade.com/155634/parade/why-i-gave-up-a-high-paying-corporate-career-to-start-a-charity/.

9. Yvonne Carter, "Why I Left My Career in Finance for a Nonprofit," *LearnVest—Financial Planning Services and Personal Finance News*, December 28, 2012, https://www.learnvest.com/2012/12/why-i-left-my-career-in-finance-for-a-nonprofit.

10. Christiane S. Bode and Jasjit Singh, "Taking a Hit to Save the World? Employee Participation in a Corporate Social Initiative" (INSEAD working paper No. 2017/56/STR, September 2017).

11. Christiane Bode, Jasjit Singh, and Michelle Rogan, "Corporate Social Initiatives and Employee Retention," *Organization Science* 26, no.6 (October 2015): 1702–20, https://doi.org/10.1287/orsc.2015.1006.

12. Ben Paynter, "Why IBM Pays Its Employees to Take Time Off to Tackle the World's Problems," *Fast Company*, July 26, 2017, https://www.fastcompany.com/40442966/why-ibm-pays-its-employees-to-take-time-off-to-tackle-the-worlds-problems.

13. Alex Imas, "Working for the 'Warm Glow': On the Benefits and Limits of Prosocial Incentives," *Journal of Public Economics* 114 (June 2014): 14–18, https://doi.org/10.1016/j.jpubeco.2013.11.006.

14. Patricia L. Lockwood et al., "Prosocial Apathy for Helping Others When Effort Is Required," *Nature Human Behavior* 1 (June 2017): 0131, doi:10.1038/s41562-017-0131.

15. Ayelet Gneezy et al., "Shared Social Responsibility: A Field Experiment in Pay-What-You-Want Pricing and Charitable Giving," *Science* 329, no. 5989 (July 2010): 325–27, doi:10.1126/science.1186744.

16. Greer K. Gosnell, John A. List, and Robert Metcalfe, "A New Approach to an Age-Old Problem: Solving Externalities by Incenting Workers Directly" (NBER working paper no. w22316, National Bureau of Economic Research, 2016).

17. Adam M. Grant and David A. Hofmann, "It's Not All about Me: Motivating Hand Hygiene among Health Care Professionals by Focusing on Patients," *Psychological Science* 22, no. 12 (November 2011): 1494–99, https://doi.org/10.1177/0956797611419172.

18. C. A. Umscheid et al., "Estimating the Proportion of Healthcare-Associated Infections That Are Reasonably Preventable and the Related Mortality and Costs," *Infection Control and Hospital Epidemiology* 32, no. 2 (February 2011): 101–14, doi:10.1086/657912.

19. Vicki Erasmus et al., "Systematic Review of Studies on Compliance with Hand Hygiene Guidelines in Hospital Care," *Infection Control and Hospital Epidemiology* 31, no. 3 (March 2010): 283–94, doi:10.1086/650451.

20. Lalin Anik et al., "Prosocial Bonuses Increase Employee Satisfaction and Team Performance," *PloS One* 89, no. 9 (September 2013): e75509, https://doi.org/10.1371/journal.pone.0075509.

21. Thoey Bou, "How Our Peer-to-Peer Bonus Program Delivered on Our Values," Poll Everywhere's Blog, February 10, 2017, https://blog.polleverywhere.com/peer-to-peer-bonus/.

22. Yuval Noah Harari, *Sapiens: A Brief History of Humankind* (London: Harvill Secker, 2014), 443, 42, 105.

23. Adam M. Grant and Sabine Sonnentag, "Doing Good Buffers against Feeling Bad: Prosocial Impact Compensates for Negative Task and Self-Evaluations," *Organizational Behavior and Human Decision Processes* 111, no. 1 (2010): 13–22, doi:10.1016/j.obhdp.2009.07.003.

Chapter 6: Humanizing Work in the Automation Age

1. Reverend Dr. Martin Luther King Jr, "Beyond Vietnam: A Time to Break Silence," speech, New York, April 4, 1967, American Rhetoric, http://www.americanrhetoric.com/speeches/mlkatimetobreaksilence.htm.

2. Simon Baron-Cohen, Rebecca C. Knickmeyer, and Matthew K. Belmonte, "Sex Differences in the Brain: Implications for Explaining Autism," *Science* 310, no. 5749 (2005): 819–23, doi:10.1126/science.1115455.

3. Hikaru Takeuchi et al., "Association Between Resting-State Functional Connectivity and Empathizing/Systemizing," *Neuroimage* 99 (October 2014): 312–22, doi:10.1016/j.neuroimage.2014.05.031.

4. Michael D. Fox et al., "The Human Brain Is Intrinsically Organized into Dynamic, Anticorrelated Functional Networks," *Proceedings of the National Academy of Sciences* 102, no. 27 (2005): 9673–78; Anthony I. Jack et al., "fMRI Reveals Reciprocal Inhibition between Social and Physical Cognitive Domains," *NeuroImage* 66 (2013): 385–401.

5. Carl Benedikt Frey and Michael A. Osborne, "The Future of Employment: How Susceptible Are Jobs to Computerization?" *Technological Forecasting and Social Change* 114 (2017): 254–80, doi:10.1016/j.techfore.2016.08.019.

6. Melanie Arntz, Terry Gregory, and Ulrich Zierahn, "Revisiting the Risk of Automation," *Economics Letters* 159 (October 2017): 157–60, doi.org/10.1016/j.econlet.2017.07.001.

7. Katja Grace et al., "When Will AI Exceed Human Performance? Evidence from AI Experts," 2017, arxiv.org/abs/1705.08807.

8. Daron Acemoglu and Pascual Restrepo, "Robots and Jobs: Evidence from US Labor Markets" (NBER working paper no. 23285, National Bureau of Economic Research, 2017).

9. Adam Waytz and Michael I. Norton, "Botsourcing and Outsourcing: Robot, British, Chinese, and German Workers Are for Thinking—Not Feeling—Jobs," *Emotion* 14, no. 2 (April 2014): 434–44, doi:10.1037/a0036054.

10. David J. Deming, "The Growing Importance of Social Skills in the Labor Market," *Quarterly Journal of Economics* 132, no. 4 (November 2017): 1593–640, doi.org/10.1093/qje/qjx022.

11. Nicole Torres, "Research: Technology Is Only Making Social Skills More Important," *Harvard Business Review,* August 26, 2015, https://hbr.org/2015/08/research-technology-is-only-making-social-skills-more-important.

12. Ryan Feit, "How to Stop Robots from Taking Your Job," *Fortune,* December 1, 2014, http://fortune.com/2014/12/01/how-to-stop-robots-from-taking-your-job/.

13. Personal communication, April 9, 2018.

14. John Hagel, "John Hagel: Rethinking Race Against the Machines—Video," Big Think, December 29, 2012, http://bigthink.com/videos/john-hagel-rethinking-race-against-the-machines.

15. Greg Satell, "If You Want to Avoid Being Replaced by a Robot, Here's What You Need to Know," *Forbes,* March 7, 2014, https://www.forbes.com/sites/gregsatell/2014/03/07/if-you-want-to-avoid-being-replaced-by-a-robot-heres-what-you-need-to-know/.

16. Personal communication, October 11, 2017.

17. Guido Matias Cortes, Nir Jaimovich, and Henry E. Siu, "Disappearing Routine Jobs: Who, How, and Why?" (NBER working paper no. 22918, National Bureau of Economic Research, 2016).

18. David Autor, "The Polarization of Job Opportunities in the US Labor Market: Implications for Employment and Earnings," Center for American Progress and the Hamilton Project, 2010, 2.

19. "What Employers Can Do to Encourage Their Workers to Retrain," *The Economist,* January 14, 2017, https://www.economist.com/news/special-report/21714171-companies-are-embracing-learning-core-skill-what-employers-can-do-encourage-their-workers-to-retrain.

20. Ibid.

21. Accenture, "Digital Disconnect in Customer Engagement," https://www.accenture.com/us-en/insight-digital-disconnect-customer-engagement; Elizabeth S. Mitchell, "Surprising Study: Millennials Prefer Human Interaction over Digital," *Adweek,* September 8, 2015, http://www.adweek.com/digital/surprising-study-millenials-prefer-human-interaction-over-digital/.

22. Aspect, "The End of Customer Service as We Know It: Aspect Software's Consumer Experience Index Survey Shows Self-Service, AI, Redefining How Consumers View Customer Service," February 7, 2018, https://www

.aspect.com/compny/news/press-releases/the-end-of-customer-service-as
-we-know-it-aspect-softwares-consumer-experience-index-survey-shows
-self-service-ai-redefining-how-consumers-view-customer-service

23. Belinda Palmer, "Corporate Empathy Is Not an Oxymoron," *Harvard Business Review,* January 8, 2015, https://hbr.org/2015/01/corporate-empathy-is -not-an-oxymoron.

24. Pauline I. Erera, "Empathy Training for Helping Professionals: Model and Evaluation," *Journal of Social Work Education* 33, no. 2 (1997): 245–60; Robert Paul Butters, *A Meta-Analysis of Empathy Training Programs for Client Populations* (Salt Lake City: University of Utah, 2010); Emily Teding van Berkhout and John M. Malouff, "The Efficacy of Empathy Training: A Meta-Analysis of Randomized Controlled Trials," *Journal of Counseling Psychology* 63, no. 1 (2016): 32–41.

25. William A. Gentry, Todd J. Weber, and Golnaz Sadri, "Empathy in the Workplace: A Tool for Effective Leadership," 2007. http://www.ccl.org/wp -content/uploads/2015/04/EmpathyInTheWorkplace.pdf.

26. Janine Prime and Elizabeth R. Salib, "Inclusive Leadership: The View from Six Countries," Catalyst, May 07, 2014, http://www.catalyst.org/knowledge/ inclusive-leadership-view-six-countries.

27. Personal communication, February 22, 2018.

28. Adam M. Grant, "How Customers Can Rally Your Troops," *Harvard Business Review* 89, no. 6 (2011): 96–103.

29. Lesley Latham et al., "Teaching Empathy to Undergraduate Medical Students Using a Temporary Tattoo Simulating Psoriasis," *Journal of the American Academy of Dermatology* 67, no. 1 (2012): 93–99, doi:10.1016/j .jaad.2011.07.023.

30. Aleksandra Kacperczyk, "Social Isolation in the Workplace: A Cross-National and Longitudinal Analysis," *SSRN Electronic Journal* (November 2011): doi:10.2139/ssrn.1961387.

31. Tom Rath and Jim Harther, "Your Friends and Your Social Well-Being," Gallup, August 19, 2010, http://www.gallup.com/businessjournal/127043/ friends-social-wellbeing.aspx.

32. Toni Vranjes, "Employers Embrace Peer-to-Peer Recognition," Society for Human Resource Management, October 23, 2014, https://www.shrm.org/ hr-today/news/hr-magazine/pages/1114-peer-recognition.aspx.

33. Ichiro Kawachi and Lisa F. Berkman. "Social Ties and Mental Health," *Journal of Urban Health* 78, no. 3 (2001): 458–67.

34. S. Leikas and V. J. Ilmarinen, "Happy Now, Tired Later? Extraverted and Conscientious Behaviors Are Related to Immediate Mood Gains, but to Later Fatigue," *Journal of Personality* 85, no. 5 (October 2017): 603–15, doi:10.1111/jopy.12264.

35. Bill Ervolino, "We're Exhausted: Stress and Social Media Are Taking Their Toll," Northjersey.com, October 9, 2017, https://www.northjersey.com/story/entertainment/2017/10/09/everybody-exhausted-stress-and-social-media-taking-their-toll/707329001/.

36. Laura F. Bright, Susan Bardi Kleiser, and Stacy Landreth Graub, "Too Much Facebook? An Exploratory Examination of Social Media Fatigue," *Computers in Human Behavior* 44 (March 2015): 148–55, https://doi.org/10.1016/j.chb.2014.11.048.

37. Susan Cain, *Quiet: The Power of Introverts in a World That Can't Stop Talking* (New York: Random House, 2013).

38. Leigh Weingus, "Surprise! You May Be an Ambivert," *HuffPost,* July 29, 2015, https://www.huffingtonpost.com/entry/you-might-be-an-ambivert_us_ 55b8ce95e4b0224d88347f63.

39. Charles R. Figley, "Compassion Fatigue: Toward a New Understanding of the Costs of Caring," in *Secondary Traumatic Stress: Self-Care Issues for Clinicians, Researchers, and Educators,* ed. B. Hudnall Stamm (Baltimore: The Sidran Press, 1995).

40. Liane Wardlow, "Individual Differences in Speakers' Perspective Taking: The Roles of Executive Control and Working Memory," *Psychonomic Bulletin and Review* 20, no. 4 (August 2013): 766–72, doi:10.3758/s13423-013-0396-1.

41. Tony Hsieh, "How I Did It: Zappos's CEO on Going to Extremes for Customers," *Harvard Business Review* (July/August 2010), https://hbr.org/2010/07/how-i-did-it-zapposs-ceo-on-going-to-extremes-for-customers.

42. Richard Hackman and Greg R. Oldham, "Development of the Job Diagnostic Survey," *Journal of Applied Psychology* 60, no. 2 (1975): 159–70.

43. Lauren A. Wegman et al., "Placing Job Characteristics in Context: Cross-Temporal Meta-Analysis of Changes in Job Characteristics Since 1975," *Journal of Management* 44, no. 1 (January 2018): 352–86, doi:10.1177/0149206316654545.

44. Stephen E. Humphrey, Jennifer D. Nahrgang, and Frederick P. Morgeson, "Integrating Motivational, Social, and Contextual Work Design Features: A Meta-analytic Summary and Theoretical Extension of the Work Design Literature," *Journal of Applied Psychology* 92, no. 5 (September 2007): 1332–56, doi:10.1037/0021-9010.92.5.1332.

45. Sara Zaniboni, Donald M. Truxillo, and Franco Fraccaroli, "Differential Effects of Task Variety and Skill Variety on Burnout and Turnover Intentions for Older and Younger Workers," *European Journal of Work and Organizational Psychology* 22, no. 3 (April 2013): 306–17, doi.org/10.1080/1359432X.2013.782288.

46. Bradley R. Staats and Francesca Gino, "Specialization and Variety in Repet-

itive Tasks: Evidence from a Japanese Bank," *Management Science* 58, no. 6 (March 2012): 1141–59, doi.org/10.1287/mnsc.1110.1482.

47. Jackson G. Lu, Modupe Akinola, and Malia F. Mason, "'Switching On' Creativity: Task Switching Can Increase Creativity by Reducing Cognitive Fixation," *Organizational Behavior and Human Decision Processes* 139 (March 2017): 63–75, doi:10.1016/j.obhdp.2017.01.005.

48. Bernd Beber and Alexandra Scacco, "The Devil Is in the Digits: Evidence That Iran's Election Was Rigged," *Washington Post*, June 20, 2009, http://www.washingtonpost.com/wp-dyn/content/article/2009/06/20/AR2009062000004.html.

49. Bernard Beber and Alexandra Scacco, "What the Numbers Say: A Digit-Based Test for Election Fraud," *Political Analysis* 20, no. 2 (2012): 211–34, doi.org/10.1093/pan/mps003.

50. Paul Bakan, "Response-Tendencies in Attempts to Generate Random Binary Series," *American Journal of Psychology* 73, no. 1 (1960): 127–31, http://www.jstor.org/stable/1419124.

51. Nicolas Gauvrit et al., "Human Behavioral Complexity Peaks at Age 25," *PLoS Computational Biology* 13, no. 4 (April 2017): e1005408, doi.org/10.1371/journal.pcbi.1005408.

52. Derek Dean and Caroline Webb, "Recovering from Information Overload," *McKinsey Quarterly* 1, no. 1 (January 2011): 80–88.

53. Arthur T. Jersild, "Mental Set and Shift," *Archives of Psychology* 89 (1927): 81.

54. Renata F. I. Meuter and Alan Allport, "Bilingual Language Switching in Naming: Asymmetrical Costs of Language Selection," *Journal of Memory and Language* 40, no. 1 (January 1999): 25–40, doi.org/10.1006/jmla.1998.2602.

55. Diwas Singh KC, "Does Multitasking Improve Performance? Evidence from the Emergency Department," *Manufacturing and Service Operations Management* 16, no. 2 (2013): 168–83.

56. Decio Coviello, Andrea Ichino, and Nicola Persico, "Time Allocation and Task Juggling," *American Economic Review* 104, no. 2 (February 2014): 609–23, doi:10.1257/aer.104.2.609.

57. Christopher K. Hsee, Adelle X. Yang, and Liangyan Wang, "Idleness Aversion and the Need for Justifiable Busyness," *Psychological Science* 21, no. 7 (June 2010): 926–30, doi.org/10.1177/0956797610374738.

58. Christopher K. Hsee et al., "Overearning," *Psychological Science* 24, no. 6 (April 2013): 852–59, doi.org/10.1177/0956797612464785.

59. Ed O'Brien and Ellen Roney, "Worth the Wait? Leisure Can Be Just as Enjoyable with Work Left Undone," *Psychological Science* 28, no. 7 (June 2017): 1000–1015, doi.org/10.1177/0956797617701749.

60. Project: Time Off, "Vacation's Impact on the Workplace," https://www
.projecttimeoff.com/research/vacation's-impact-workplace.

61. Alexander C. Kaufman, "Virgin's Unlimited Vacation Plan for Workers May
Not Be as Good as It Seems," *HuffPost,* September 23, 2014, http://www
.huffingtonpost.com/2014/09/23/virgin-unlimited-vacation_n_5869708
.html.

62. Glassdoor, "Glassdoor Survey Reveals Average American Employee Only
Takes Half of Earned Vacation/Paid Time Off; 61 Percent Report Working
While on Vacation," news release, April 3, 2014, Glassdoor.

63. Jena McGregor, "U.S. Workers—Especially Millennial Women—Aren't
Taking All Their Earned Vacation," *Los Angeles Times,* May 26, 2017, http://
www.latimes.com/business/la-fi-millennials-vacation-20170526-story.html.

64. Ron Friedman, "Dear Boss: Your Team Wants You to Go on Vacation,"
Harvard Business Review, June 18, 2015, https://hbr.org/2015/06/dear-boss
-your-team-wants-you-to-go-on-vacation.

65. Gwen Moran, "Should Companies Make Vacation Mandatory?" *Fast
Company,* June 9, 2017, https://www.fastcompany.com/40427648/should-
companies-make-vacation-mandatory.

66. Jeanne Sahadi, "Forget Unlimited Time Off. Vacation Is Mandatory at These
Companies," CNN, December 15, 2015, http://money.cnn.com/2015/12/15/
pf/mandatory-vacation/index.html.

67. Jillian D'Onfro, "The Truth About Google's Famous '20% Time' Policy,"
Business Insider, April 17, 2015, http://www.businessinsider.com/google-20
-percent-time-policy-2015-4.

68. Adam Waytz, "The Dangers of Mandatory Fun," *Harvard Business Review,*
October 4, 2017, https://hbr.org/2017/10/the-dangers-of-mandatory-fun.

69. Meredith Mealer et al., "Feasibility and Acceptability of a Resilience Training Program for Intensive Care Unit Nurses," *American Journal of Critical
Care* 23, no. 6 (November 2014): e97–e105, doi:10.4037/ajcc2014747.

70. Peter Dockrill, "This 4-Day Work Week Experiment Went So Well, the Company Is Keeping It," *Science Alert,* July 23, 2018, https://www.sciencealert
.com/this-4-day-work-week-experiment-went-so-well-company-keeping-it
-perpetual-guardian-engagement-balance.

Chapter 7: Building Human-Machine Partnerships

1. Bertram F. Malle et al., "Sacrifice One for the Good of Many?" *Proceedings
of the Tenth Annual ACM/IEEE International Conference on Human-Robot
Interaction—HRI 15* (2015): 117–24, doi:10.1145/2696454.2696458.

2. Jim A. Everett, David A. Pizarro, and Molly J. Crockett, "Inference of Trust-

worthiness from Intuitive Moral Judgments," *Journal of Experimental Psychology: General* (June 2016): 772, doi:10.2139/ssrn.2726330.

3. Yochanan E. Bigman and Kurt Gray, "People Are Averse to Machines Making Moral Decisions," *Cognition* 181, no. 1 (December 2018): 21–34.

4. Brian Uzzi, "How Human-Machine Learning Partnerships Can Reduce Unconscious Bias," *Entrepreneur,* July 31, 2016, https://www.entrepreneur.com/article/278214.

5. David Infold and Spencer Soper, "Amazon Doesn't Consider the Race of Its Customers. Should It?" *Bloomberg,* April 21, 2016, https://www.bloomberg.com/graphics/2016-amazon-same-day/.

6. Rafi Letzter, "Amazon Just Showed Us That 'Unbiased' Algorithms Can Be Inadvertently Racist," *Business Insider,* April 21, 2016, http://www.businessinsider.com/how-algorithms-can-be-racist-2016-4.

7. Safiya U. Noble, *Algorithms of Oppression: How Search Engines Reinforce Racism* (New York: New York University Press, 2018), 18.

8. Tom Simonite, "Photo Algorithms ID White Men Fine—Black Women, Not So Much," *Wired,* February 6, 2018, https://www.wired.com/story/photo-algorithms-id-white-men-fineblack-women-not-so-much/.

9. Aylin Caliskan, Joanna J. Bryson, and Arvind Narayanan, "Semantics Derived Automatically from Language Corpora Contain Human-Like Biases," *Science* 356, no. 6334 (April 2017): 183–86, doi:10.1126/science.aal4230.

10. Julia Angwin et al., "Machine Bias," Pro Publica, May 23, 2016, https://www.propublica.org/article/machine-bias-risk-assessments-in-criminal-sentencing.

11. Jon Kleinberg et al., "Human Decisions and Machine Predictions" (NBER working paper no. 23180, National Bureau of Economic Research, 2017).

12. Personal communication, October 11, 2017.

13. Tess Townsend, "Eric Schmidt Said ATMs Led to More Jobs for Bank Tellers. It's Not That Simple," *Recode,* May 8, 2017, https://www.recode.net/2017/5/8/15584268/eric-schmidt-alphabet-automation-atm-bank-teller.

14. Kalyan Veeramachaneni et al., "AI^2: Training a Big Data Machine to Defend," *2016 IEEE 2nd International Conference on Big Data Security on Cloud (BigDataSecurity), IEEE International Conference on High Performance and Smart Computing (HPSC), and IEEE International Conference on Intelligent Data and Security (IDS)* (April 2016): 49–54, doi:10.1109/bigdatasecurity-hpsc-ids.2016.79.

15. Corey Fedde, "How This AI-Human Partnership Takes Cybersecurity to a New Level," *Christian Science Monitor,* April 20, 2016, https://www.csmonitor.com/Technology/2016/0420/How-this-AI-human-partnership-takes-cybersecurity-to-a-new-level.

16. Cybersecurity Ventures, "Cybersecurity Jobs Report 2018–2021," https://cybersecurityventures.com/jobs/.

17. Steve Lohr, "A.I. Is Doing Legal Work. But It Won't Replace Lawyers, Yet," *New York Times,* March 19, 2017, https://www.nytimes.com/2017/03/19/technology/lawyers-artificial-intelligence.html.

18. Meeri Kim, "Let Robots Handle Your Emotional Burnout at Work—How We Get to Next," Medium, March 23, 2017, https://howwegettonext.com/let-robots-handle-your-emotional-burnout-at-work-e09babbe81e8.

19. H. James Wilson, Allan Alter, and Prashant Shukla, "Companies Are Reimagining Business Processes with Algorithms," *Harvard Business Review,* March 1, 2018, https://hbr.org/2016/02/companies-are-reimagining-business-processes-with-algorithms.

20. Selma Sabanovic et al., "PARO Robot Affects Diverse Interaction Modalities in Group Sensory Therapy for Older Adults with Dementia," *2013 IEEE 13th International Conference on Rehabilitation Robotics* (June 2013): 1–6, doi:10.1109/icorr.2013.6650427; Kazuyoshi Wada et al., "Psychological and Social Effects of Robot Assisted Activity to Elderly People Who Stay at a Health Service Facility for the Aged," *2003 IEEE International Conference on Robotics and Automation* (April 2005): 2785–90, doi:10.1109/robot.2003.1242211.

21. Personal communication, March 15, 2018.

22. Paula Cocozza, "No Hugging: Are We Living Through a Crisis of Touch?" *The Guardian,* March 7, 2018, https://www.theguardian.com/society/2018/mar/07/crisis-touch-hugging-mental-health-strokes-cuddles.

23. Adam Waytz, Joy Heafner, and Nicholas Epley, "The Mind in the Machine: Anthropomorphism Increases Trust in an Autonomous Vehicle," *Journal of Experimental Social Psychology* 52 (May 2014): 113–17, doi:10.1016/j.jesp.2014.01.005.

24. Masahiro Mori, "The Uncanny Valley," *Energy* 7, no. 4 (1970): 33–35.

25. Steven Levy, "Why Tom Hanks Is Less Than Human," *Newsweek,* November 21, 2004, 305–6.

26. "Hayao Miyazaki's Thoughts on an Artificial Intelligence," YouTube video, 2:19, posted by "Mahattan Project for a Nuclear-Free World," November 15, 2016, https://www.youtube.com/watch?v=ngZ0K3lWKRc.

27. Karl F. MacDorman, "Subjective Ratings of Robot Video Clips for Human Likeness, Familiarity, and Eeriness: An Exploration of the Uncanny Valley," *ICCS/CogSci-2006 Long Symposium: Toward Social Mechanisms of Android Science* (July 2006): 26–29, http://www.damiantgordon.com/Courses/CaseStudies/CaseStudy3c.pdf.

28. Nicholas Carr, "These Are Not the Robots We Were Promised," *New York*

Times, September 9, 2017, https://www.nytimes.com/2017/09/09/opinion/sunday/household-robots-alexa-homepod.html.

29. Clifford Nass and Scott Brave, *Wired for Speech: How Voice Activates and Advances the Human-Computer Relationship* (Cambridge, MA: MIT Press, 2005), 3–4.

30. Juliana Schroeder and Nicholas Epley, "The Sound of Intellect," *Psychological Science* 26, no. 6 (June 2015): 877–91, doi:10.1177/0956797615572906.

31. Juliana Schroeder and Nicholas Epley, "Mistaking Minds and Machines: How Speech Affects Dehumanization and Anthropomorphism," *Journal of Experimental Psychology: General* 145, no. 11 (November 2016): 1427–37, doi:10.1037/xge0000214.

32. Fumihide Tanaka, Aaron Cicourel, and Javier R. Movellan, "Socialization between Toddlers and Robots at an Early Childhood Education Center," *Proceedings of the National Academy of Sciences* 104, no. 46 (November 2007): 17954–58, doi:10.1073/pnas.0707769104.

33. Adam Waytz et al., "Making Sense by Making Sentient: Effectance Motivation Increases Anthropomorphism," *Journal of Personality and Social Psychology* 99, no. 3 (2010): 410–35, doi:10.1037/a0020240.

34. "Mimus," ATONATON, https://atonaton.com/mimus.

35. Personal communication, February 20, 2018.

36. Ellen J. Langer and Judith Rodin, "The Effects of Choice and Enhanced Personal Responsibility for the Aged: A Field Experiment in an Institutional Setting," *Journal of Personality and Social Psychology* 32, no. 2 (1976): 191–98, doi:10.1017/cbo9780511759048.031.

37. Alexander Reben et al., "The Implications of Artificial Intelligence" (lecture, Chicago Ideas, Chicago).

38. Adam Waytz and Michael I. Norton, "Botsourcing and Outsourcing: Robot, British, Chinese, and German Workers Are for Thinking—Not Feeling—Jobs," *Emotion* 14, no. 2 (April 2014): 434–44, doi:10.1037/a0036054.

39. Jennifer Goetz, Sara Kiesler, and Aaron Powers, "Matching Robot Appearance and Behavior to Tasks to Improve Human-Robot Cooperation," *The 12th IEEE International Workshop on Robot and Human Interactive Communication, 2003. Proceedings. ROMAN 2003,* doi:10.1109/roman.2003.1251796.

40. Gale M. Lucas et al., "It's Only a Computer: Virtual Humans Increase Willingness to Disclose," *Computers in Human Behavior* 37 (August 2014): 94–100, doi.org/10.1016/j.chb.2014.04.043.

41. Clifford Nass and Kwan Min Lee, "Does Computer-Synthesized Speech Manifest Personality? Experimental Tests of Recognition, Similarity-Attraction, and Consistency-Attraction," *Journal of Experimental Psychology: Applied* 7, no. 3 (2001): 171–81, doi:10.1037//1076-898X.7.3.171.

42. Ing-Marie Johnsson et al., "Matching In-Car Voice with Driver State: Impact on Attitude and Driving Performance," *Proceedings of the Third International Driving Symposium on Human Factors in Driver Assessment, Training and Vehicle Design*, (2005): 173–80, doi.org/10.17077/driving assessment.1158.

Chapter 8: Seeing Human amid Conflict

1. Muzafer Sherif and Carolyn W. Sherif, *Groups in Harmony and Tension: An Integration of Studies of Intergroup Relations* (New York: Harper Brothers, 1953).
2. Emanuele Castaño and Roger Giner-Sorolla, "Not Quite Human: Infrahumanization in Response to Collective Responsibility for Intergroup Killing," *Journal of Personality and Social Psychology* 90, no. 5 (2006): 804–18, doi:10.1037/0022-3514.90.5.804.
3. Adam Waytz, Juliana Schroeder, and Nicholas Epley, "The Lesser Minds Problem," *Humanness and Dehumanization* (2013): 49–67, doi:10.4324/9780203110539.
4. Emily Pronin and Matthew B. Kugler, "People Believe They Have More Free Will Than Others," *Proceedings of the National Academy of Sciences* 107, no. 52 (2010): 22469–74, doi.org/10.1073/pnas.1012046108.
5. Nicholas Epley, Kenneth Savitsky, and Thomas Gilovich, "Empathy Neglect: Reconciling the Spotlight Effect and the Correspondence Bias," *Journal of Personality and Social Psychology* 83, no. 2 (2002): 300–312, doi: 10.1037//0022-3514.83.2.300.
6. Emily Pronin, Daniel Y. Lin, and Lee Ross, "The Bias Blind Spot: Perceptions of Bias in Self Versus Others," *Personality and Social Psychology Bulletin* 28, no. 3 (2002): 369–81, doi.org/10.1177/0146167202286008.
7. Nicholas Haslam et al., "More Human Than You: Attributing Humanness to Self and Others," *Journal of Personality and Social Psychology* 89, no. 6 (December 2005): 937–50, doi:10.1037/0022-3514.89.6.937.
8. Peter Koval et al., "Our Flaws Are More Human Than Yours: Ingroup Bias in Humanizing Negative Characteristics," *Personality and Social Psychology Bulletin* 38, no. 3 (September 2011): 283–95, https://doi.org/10.1177/0146167211423777.
9. Peter Beaumont, "Netanyahu Plans Fence around Israel to Protect It from 'Wild Beasts'," *The Guardian*, February 10, 2016, https://www.theguardian.com/world/2016/feb/10/netanyahu-plans-fence-around-israel-to-protect-it-from-wild-beasts.
10. "Netanyahu: Muslims Are 'Dangerous Animals,'" PNN, November 19, 2015, http://english.pnn.ps/2015/11/19/netanyahu-muslims-are-dangerous-animals/.

11. Roberta Strauss Feuerlicht, *The Fate of the Jews: A People Torn Between Israeli Power and Jewish Ethics* (New York: Crown Publishing, 1983).

12. Ellen Barry and Suhasini Raj, "Firebrand Hindu Cleric Ascends India's Political Ladder," *New York Times,* July 12, 2017, https://www.nytimes.com/2017/07/12/world/asia/india-yogi-adityanath-bjp-modi.html.

13. Jeffrey Gettleman, "Rohingya Recount Atrocities: 'They Threw My Baby into a Fire,'" *New York Times,* October 11, 2017, https://www.nytimes.com/2017/10/11/world/asia/rohingya-myanmar-atrocities.html.

14. Nour Kteily et al., "The Ascent of Man: Theoretical and Empirical Evidence for Blatant Dehumanization," *Journal of Personality and Social Psychology* 109, no. 5 (2015), doi: 10.1037/pspp0000048; Nour Kteily and Emile Bruneau, "Backlash: The Politics and Real-World Consequences of Minority Group Dehumanization," *Personality and Social Psychology Bulletin* 43, no. 1 (2016): doi:10.1177/0146167216675334.

15. Paul Bain et al., "Attributing Human Uniqueness and Human Nature to Cultural Groups: Distinct Forms of Subtle Dehumanization," *Group Processes and Intergroup Relations* 12, no. 6 (October 2009): 789–805, https://doi.org/10.1177/1368430209340415.

16. Phillip A. Goff et al., "Not Yet Human: Implicit Knowledge, Historical Dehumanization, and Contemporary Consequences," *Journal of Personality and Social Psychology* 94, no. 2 (2008): 292–306, doi:10.1037/0022-3514.94.2.292.

17. Sophie Trawalter, Kelly M. Hoffman, and Adam Waytz, "Racial Bias in Perceptions of Others' Pain," *PloS One* 7, no. 11 (November 2012), https://doi.org/10.1371/journal.pone.0048546; Brian B. Drwecki, Colleen F. Moore, Sandra E. Ward, and Kenneth M. Prkachin, "Reducing Racial Disparities in Pain Treatment: The Role of Empathy and Perspective-Taking," *Pain* 152, no. 5 (2011): 1001–6; Kelly M. Hoffman, Sophie Trawalter, Jordan R. Axt, and M. Norman Oliver, "Racial Bias in Pain Assessment and Treatment Recommendations, and False Beliefs about Biological Differences between Blacks and Whites," *Proceedings of the National Academy of Sciences* 113, no. 16 (2016): 4296–301; Kimberley A. Kaseweter, Brian B. Drwecki, and Kenneth M. Prkachin, "Racial Differences in Pain Treatment and Empathy in a Canadian Sample," *Pain Research and Management* 17, no. 6 (2012): 381–84. Raymond C. Tait and John T. Chibnall, "Racial/Ethnic Disparities in the Assessment and Treatment of Pain: Psychosocial Perspectives," *American Psychologist* 69, no. 2 (2014): 131–41, doi:10.1037/a0035204.

18. R. Sean Morrison et al., "'We Don't Carry That'—Failure of Pharmacies in Predominantly Nonwhite Neighborhoods to Stock Opioid Analgesics," *New England Journal of Medicine* 342, no. 14 (April 2000): 1023–26, doi:10.1056/NEJM200004063421406.

19. Rob Haskell, "Serena Williams on Motherhood, Marriage, and Making Her Comeback," *Vogue,* January 10, 2018, https://www.vogue.com/article/serena-williams-vogue-cover-interview-february-2018.

20. Kelly M. Hoffman et al., "Racial Bias in Pain Assessment and Treatment Recommendations, and False Beliefs about Biological Differences between Blacks and Whites," *Proceedings of the National Academy of Sciences* 113, no. 16 (April 2016): 4296–4301, https://doi.org/10.1073/pnas.1516047113.

21. "Reproductive Health," Centers for Disease Control and Prevention, February 8, 2018, https://www.cdc.gov/reproductivehealth/maternalinfanthealth/pregnancy-relatedmortality.htm.

22. Adam Waytz, Kelly Marie Hoffman, and Sophie Trawalter, "A Superhumanization Bias in Whites' Perceptions of Blacks," *Social Psychological and Personality Science* 6, no. 3 (October 2014): 352–59, https://doi.org/10.1177/1948550614553642.

23. Toni Morrison et al., "Black Studies Center Public Dialogue Part 2" (panel, Portland State University, Portland, 1975).

24. Adam Waytz, Liane L. Young, and Jeremy Ginges, "Motive Attribution Asymmetry for Love vs. Hate Drives Intractable Conflict," *Proceedings of the National Academy of Sciences* 111, no. 44 (2014): 15687–92, doi:10.1073/pnas.1414146111.

25. From Gina Perry, *"The Lost Boys": Inside Muzafer Sherif's Robbers Cave Experiment* (Melbourne: Scribe Publications, 2018).

26. United with Israel, "Israeli and Palestinian Children Learn Peace through Soccer," May 27, 2013, https://unitedwithisrael.org/israeli-and-palestinian-children-learn-peace-through-soccer/.

27. Sharon Udasin, "Israelis, Palestinians Build Start-Ups Together at Brandeis Incubator," *Jerusalem Post,* June 11, 2017, http://www.jpost.com/International/Israelis-Palestinians-build-start-ups-together-at-Brandeis-incubator-496324.

28. Jonathan Haidt, "How Common Threats Can Make (Political) Ground" (address, TEDSalon NY2012, New York City).

29. Ting Zhang, Francesca Gino, and Michael I. Norton, "The Surprising Effectiveness of Hostile Mediators," *Management Science* 63, no. 6 (May 2016): 1972–92, https://doi.org/10.1287/mnsc.2016.2431.

30. Jennifer K. Bosson et al., "Interpersonal Chemistry through Negativity: Bonding by Sharing Negative Attitudes about Others," *Personal Relationships* 13, no. 2 (2006): 135–50, https://doi.org/10.1111/j.1475-6811.2006.00109.x.

31. Mark Levine et al., "Identity and Emergency Intervention: How Social Group Membership and Inclusiveness of Group Boundaries Shape Helping Behavior," *Personality and Social Psychology Bulletin* 31, no. 4 (April 2005): 443–53, https://doi.org/10.1177/0146167204271651.

32. Samuel L. Gaertner et al., "The Common Ingroup Identity Model: Recategorization and the Reduction of Intergroup Bias," *European Review of Social Psychology* 4, no. 1 (March 2011): 1–26, https://doi.org/10.1080/14792779343000004.

33. Jason A. Nier et al., "Changing Interracial Evaluations and Behavior: The Effects of a Common Group Identity," *Group Processes and Intergroup Relations* 4, no. 4 (October 2001): 299–316, https://doi.org/10.1177/1368430201004004001.

34. Samuel L. Gaertner, Mary C. Rust, and John F. Dovidio, "The Contact Hypothesis: The Role of a Common Ingroup Identity on Reducing Intergroup Bias," *Small Group Research* 25, no. 2 (May 1994): 224–49, https://doi.org/10.1177/1046496494252005.

35. Britni de la Cretaz, "Georgia Tech Dancer Raianna Brown Shares Why She Kneels," *Teen Vogue,* September 26, 2017, https://www.teenvogue.com/story/georgia-tech-dancer-viral-photo-shares-why-she-kneels.

36. Phillip L. Hammack, "Identity, Conflict, and Coexistence: Life Stories of Israeli and Palestinian Adolescents," *Journal of Adolescent Research* 21, no. 4 (July 2006): 323–69, https:// doi.org/10.1177/0743558406289745.

37. Cara C. MacInnis and Elizabeth Page-Gould, "How Can Intergroup Interaction Be Bad If Intergroup Contact Is Good? Exploring and Reconciling an Apparent Paradox in the Science of Intergroup Relations," *Perspectives on Psychological Science* 10, no. 3 (2015): 307–27.

38. Ryan D. Enos, "Causal Effect of Intergroup Contact on Exclusionary Attitudes," *Proceedings of the National Academy of Sciences* 111, no. 10 (2014): 3699–3704, https://doi.org/10.1073/pnas.1317670111.

39. Arie Nadler and Ido Liviatan, "Intergroup Reconciliation: Effects of Adversary's Expressions of Empathy, Responsibility, and Recipients' Trust," *Personality and Social Psychology Bulletin* 32, no. 4 (April 2006): 459–70, https://doi.org/10.1177/0146167205276431.

40. John F. Dovidio, Samuel L. Gaertner, and Tamar Saguy, "Commonality and the Complexity of "We": Social Attitudes and Social Change," *Personality and Social Psychology Review* 13, no. 1 (February 2009): 3–20, https://doi.org/10.1177/1088868308326751.

41. W. E. B. Du Bois, *The Souls of Black Folks*, ed. Manning Marable (London: Routledge, 2015), 2.

42. Tasnim Ahmed, "The Melting Pot That Never Was," *Harvard Crimson*, March 5, 2014, https://www.thecrimson.com/article/2014/3/5/harvard-not-melting-pot/.

43. Jan Pieter Van Oudenhoven, Karin S. Prins, and Bram P. Buunk, "Attitudes of Minority and Majority Members Towards Adaptation of Immigrants," *European Journal of Social Psychology* 28, no. 6 (1998): 995–1013, https://doi.org/10.1002/(SICI)1099-0992(1998110)28:6<995::AID-EJSP908>3.0.CO;2-8.

44. "A Call for Unity," *Birmingham News*, April 12, 1963.

45. Elana Zak, "How NFL Owners Responded to Trump," *CNN*, September 25, 2017, https://money.cnn.com/2017/09/24/media/nfl-owners-trump-unity/index.html.

46. Chimamanda Ngozi Adichie, "Now Is the Time to Talk about What We Are Actually Talking About," *The New Yorker*, December 2, 2016, http://www.newyorker.com/culture/cultural-comment/now-is-the-time-to-talk-about-what-we-are-actually-talking-about.

47. Nour Kteily et al., "Negotiating Power: Agenda Ordering and the Willingness to Negotiate in Asymmetric Intergroup Conflicts," *Journal of Personality and Social Psychology* 105, no. 6 (2013): 978, doi:10.1037/a0034095.

48. Tamar Saguy, John F. Dovidio, and Felicia Pratto, "Beyond Contact: Intergroup Contact in the Context of Power Relations," *Personality and Social Psychology Bulletin* 34, no. 3 (March 2008): 432–45, doi:10.1177/0146167207311200.

49. Emile G. Bruneau and Rebecca Saxe, "The Power of Being Heard: The Benefits of 'Perspective-Giving' in the Context of Intergroup Conflict," *Journal of Experimental Social Psychology* 48, no. 4 (July 2012): 855–66, https://doi.org/10.1016/j.jesp.2012.02.017.

50. Juan E. Ugarriza and Enzo Nussio, "The Effect of Perspective-Giving on Postconflict Reconciliation. An Experimental Approach," *Political Psychology* 38, no. 1 (February 2017): 3–19, https://doi.org/10.1111/pops.12324.

51. Vincent Bevins, "Brazilian Police Drag Out Students Occupying Schools to Protest Lunch Money Scandal," *Los Angeles Times,* May 6, 2016, http://www.latimes.com/world/mexico-americas/la-fg-brazil-student-protests-20160506-story.html.

52. Vijhay Vick, "We Just Wanted to Be Heard," *Malay Mail,* November 21, 2013, https://www.malaymail.com/s/566505/we-just-wanted-to-be-heard.

53. Darcie Moran, "Students Protest Racism, Building Name on University of Michigan Campus," *Michigan Live,* September 25, 2017, http://www.mlive.com/news/ann-arbor/index.ssf/2017/09/protesters_block_bus_terminal.html.

54. Personal communication, May 4, 2018.

55. Hilary B. Bergsieker, J. Nicole Shelton, and Jennifer A. Richeson, "To Be Liked versus Respected: Divergent Goals in Interracial Interactions," *Journal of Personality and Social Psychology* 99, no. 2 (2010): 248.

56. N. Shnabel and A. Nadler, "A Needs-Based Model of Reconciliation: Satisfying the Differential Emotional Needs of Victim and Perpetrator as a Key to Promoting Reconciliation," *Journal of Personality and Social Psychology* 94, no. 1 (2008): 116–32, doi:10.1037/0022-3514.94.1.116.

57. Eran Halperin et al., "Promoting the Middle East Peace Process by Changing Beliefs about Group Malleability," *Science* 333, no. 6050 (September 2011): 1767–69, doi:10.1126/science.1202925.

58. Matthew Feinberg and Robb Willer, "From Gulf to Bridge: When Do Moral Arguments Facilitate Political Influence?" *Personality and Social Psychology Bulletin* 41, no. 12 (2015): 1665–81, https://doi.org/10.1177/0146167215607842.

59. Jonathan Haidt, *The Righteous Mind: Why Good People Are Divided by Politics and Religion* (New York: Vintage Books, 2012).

60. Matthew Feinberg and Robb Willer, "The Moral Roots of Environmental Attitudes," *Psychological Science* 24, no. 1 (2013): 56–62, https://doi.org/10.1177/0956797612449177.

61. Audre Lorde, "Age, Race, Class, and Sex: Women Redefining Difference," in *Women in Culture: An Intersectional Anthology for Gender and Women's Studies*, ed. Bonnie Kime Scott (Hoboken: Wiley Blackwell, 1980), 16–23.

Chapter 9: Humanizing Close Relationships through Critical Distance

1. C. Daniel Batson, Jim Fultz, and Patricia A. Schoenrade, "Distress and Empathy: Two Qualitatively Distinct Vicarious Emotions with Different Motivational Consequences," *Journal of Personality* 55, no. 1 (1987): 19–39, doi:10.1111/j.1467-6494.1987.tb00426.x.

2. Meghan L. Meyer et al., "Empathy for the Social Suffering of Friends and Strangers Recruits Distinct Patterns of Brain Activation," *Social Cognitive and Affective Neuroscience* 8, no. 4 (2012), doi:10.1093/scan/nss019.

3. Octavia E. Butler, *Parable of the Sower* (New York: Grand Central, 1993), 11.

4. Laura Müller-Pinzler et al., "When Your Friends Make You Cringe: Social Closeness Modulates Vicarious Embarrassment-Related Neural Activity," *Social Cognitive and Affective Neuroscience* 11, no. 3 (2015): 466–75, doi:10.1093/scan/nsv130.

5. Constantine Sedikides et al., "The Self-Serving Bias in Relational Context," *Journal of Personality and Social Psychology* 74, no. 2 (1998): 378.

6. Kenneth Savitsky et al., "The Closeness-Communication Bias: Increased Egocentrism among Friends versus Strangers," *Journal of Experimental Social Psychology* 47, no. 1 (2011): 269–73, doi:10.1016/j.jesp.2010.09.005.

7. Victor Bockris, *Transformer: The Lou Reed Story* (New York: Simon & Schuster, 1997), 42.

8. Sandra L. Murray et al., "Kindred Spirits? The Benefits of Egocentrism in Close Relationships," *Journal of Personality and Social Psychology* 82, no. 4 (2002): 563–81, doi:10.1037//0022-3514.82.4.563.

9. Eli J. Finkel, *The All-or-Nothing Marriage: How the Best Marriages Work* (New York: Dutton, 2017), 95.

10. "R/Ask Men—Have You Ever Dated Someone Who Was Too Similar to You?" Reddit, https://www.reddit.com/r/AskMen/comments/2ck4bb/have_you_ever_dated_someone_who_was_too_similar/.

11. John Gottman, "Debunking 12 Myths about Relationships," Gottman Institute, March 13, 2016, https://www.gottman.com/blog/debunking-12-myths-about-relationships/.

12. Abraham Tesser, "Toward a Self-Evaluation Maintenance Model of Social Behavior," *Advances in Experimental Social Psychology* 21 (1988): 181–227, doi:10.1016/s0065-2601(08)60227-0.

13. Steven R. H. Beach and Abraham Tesser, "Decision Making Power and Marital Satisfaction: A Self-Evaluation Maintenance Perspective," *Journal of Social and Clinical Psychology* 12, no. 4 (1993): 471–94, doi:10.1521/jscp.1993.12.4.471.

14. Jacquie D. Vorauer and Tamara A. Sucharyna, "Potential Negative Effects of Perspective-Taking Efforts in the Context of Close Relationships: Increased Bias and Reduced Satisfaction," *Journal of Personality and Social Psychology* 104, no. 1 (2013): 70–86, doi:10.1037/a0030184.

15. Eli J. Finkel et al., "A Brief Intervention to Promote Conflict Reappraisal Preserves Marital Quality over Time," *Psychological Science* 24, no. 8 (2013): 1595–1601.

16. Jacquie D. Vorauer and Matthew Quesnel, "You Don't Really Love Me, Do You? Negative Effects of Imagine-Other Perspective-Taking on Lower Self-Esteem Individuals' Relationship Well-Being," *Personality and Social Psychology Bulletin* 39, no. 11 (2013): 1428–40, doi:10.1177/0146167213495282.

17. "Detachment with Love Gains New Meaning," How to Help an Addict by Detaching with Love | Hazelden Betty Ford Foundation, July 22, 2015, http://www.hazeldenbettyford.org/articles/detachment-with-love-gains-new-meaning.

18. Larissa MacFarquhar, *Strangers Drowning: Impossible Idealism, Drastic Choices, and the Urge to Help* (New York: Penguin Books, 2016), 163.

19. Paul Bloom, *Against Empathy: The Case for Rational Compassion* (New York: Harper Collins, 2017), 50.

20. Matthew R. Jordan, Dorsa Amir, and Paul Bloom, "Are Empathy and Concern Psychologically Distinct?" *Emotion* 16, no. 8 (December 2016): 1107–16, http://psycnet.apa.org/buy/2016-46141-001.

21. Elaine N. Aron and Arthur Aron, "Love and Expansion of the Self: The State of the Model," *Personal Relationships* 3, no. 1 (1996): 45–58, doi:10.1111/j.1475-6811.1996.tb00103.x.

Epilogue: Time, Connection, and Mattering

1. Leslie A. Perlow, "The Time Famine: Toward a Sociology of Work Time," *Administrative Science Quarterly* 44, no. 1 (1999): 57–81, doi:10.2307/2667031.
2. Julianne Holt-Lunstad, Timothy B. Smith, and J. Bradley Layton, "Social Relationships and Mortality Risk: A Meta-Analytic Review," *PLoS Medicine* 7, no. 7 (2010): e1000316.
3. Julianne Holt-Lunstad et al., "Loneliness and Social Isolation as Risk Factors for Mortality: A Meta-Analytic Review," *Perspectives on Psychological Science* 10, no. 2 (2015): 227–37.
4. James S. House, Karl R. Landis, and Debra Umberson, "Social Relationships and Health," *Science* 241, no. 4865 (1988): 540–45.
5. John T. Cacioppo and William Patrick, *Loneliness: Human Nature and the Need for Social Connection* (New York: W. W. Norton, 2009).
6. Daniel Kahneman and Angus Deaton, "High Income Improves Evaluation of Life but Not Emotional Well-Being," *Proceedings of the National Academy of Sciences* 107, no. 38 (2010): 16489–93.
7. Scott Atran, *Talking to the Enemy: Faith, Brotherhood, and the (Un)Making of Terrorists* (New York: Harper Collins, 2010); Johann Hari, *Chasing the Scream: The First and Last Days of the War on Drugs* (London: Bloomsbury, 2015).
8. Brock Bastian and Nick Haslam, "Excluded from Humanity: The Dehumanizing Effects of Social Ostracism," *Journal of Experimental Social Psychology* 46, no. 1 (2010): 107–13.

Index